2015
THE BEST
TEN-MINUTE PLAYS

2015
THE BEST
TEN-MINUTE PLAYS

Edited by
Lawrence Harbison

SMITH AND KRAUS PUBLISHERS   2016

TABLE OF CONTENTS

In this volume, you will find fifty terrific new ten-minute plays, culled from the several hundred I read last year, all successfully produced during the 2014-2015 theatrical season. They are written in a variety of styles. Some are realistic plays; some are not. Some are comic (laughs); some are dramatic (no laughs). The ten-minute play form lends itself well to experimentation in style. A playwright can have fun with a device which couldn't be sustained as well in a longer play. Many of these plays employ such devices. I have also included a comprehensive list of theatres which do ten-minute plays.

In years past, playwrights who were just starting out wrote one-act plays of thirty to forty minutes in duration. One thinks of writers such as A. R. Gurney, Lanford Wilson, John Guare and several others. Now, new playwrights tend to work in the ten-minute play genre, largely because there are so many production opportunities. Twenty-five or so years ago, there were none. I was Senior Editor for Samuel French at that time, and it occurred to me that there might be a market for these very short plays. Actors Theatre of Louisville had been commissioning them for several years, for use by their Apprentice Company, and they assisted me in compiling an anthology of these plays, which did so well that Samuel French has published several more anthologies of ten-minute plays from ATL. For the first time, ten-minute plays were now published and widely available, and they started getting produced. There are now many ten-minute play festivals every year, not only in the U.S. but all over the world.

What makes a good ten-minute play? Well, first and foremost I have to like it. Isn't that what we mean when we call a play, a film, a novel "good?" We mean that it effectively portrays the world *as I see it*, written in a style which interests *me*. Aside from this, a good ten-minute play has to have the same elements that *any* good play must have: a strong conflict, interesting, well-drawn characters and compelling subject matter. It also has to have a clear beginning, middle and end. In other words, it's a full length play which runs about ten minutes. Many of the plays which are submitted to me each year are scenes, not complete plays; well-written scenes in many case, but scenes nonetheless. They leave me wanting more. I chose plays which are complete in and of themselves, which I believe will excite those of you who produce ten-minute plays; because if a play isn't produced, it's the proverbial sound of a tree falling in the forest far away. In the Rights & Permissions section at the back of this book you will find information on whom to contact when you decide which plays you want to produce, in order to acquire performance rights.

There are a few plays in this book by playwrights who are fairly well-known, such as Don Nigro, Bruce Graham, Sherry Kramer, Darrah Cloud, Craig Pospisil and Jenny Lyn Bader but most are by exciting new playwrights you've probably never heard of who I have no doubt will become far better known when their full-length plays start getting produced by major theatres, playwrights such as Rod Mc-Fadden, Carey Crim, Rachel Bonds, Dave Hanson, David Strauss, Nicole Pandolfo and Erin Moughon—and you read their work first here!

Lawrence Harbison
Brooklyn, New York

2 ACTORS

ORIGINAL PRODUCTION:

> Annabel Lee was first produced by the Apothecary Theatre Company at St. Mazie's in Brooklyn, New York.

> Directed by Melissa Firlit

> CAST:
> ANNABEL: Caitlin Rigney
> REYNOLDS MICHAEL: Thomas Walker

Thanks to Tom Pelphrey

CHARACTERS:
> ANNABEL: Early twenties.
> REYNOLDS: Late forties.

Setting: Reynolds' office in the English department of a small college in New England. A desk. Books. A chair. A sofa.

> *And neither the angels in Heaven above,*
> *Nor the demons down under the sea,*
> *Can ever dissever my soul from the soul*
> *Of the beautiful Annabel Lee.*
> > —Edgar Allan Poe,
> > "Annabel Lee"

Night. The office of Reynolds, in the English department of a small college in New England. A desk. A chair. A sofa. Books scattered about. Some disorder. It's near midnight on a cold, windy night. Reynolds sits at the desk, drinking from a flask. His desk lamp makes a circle of light. Around him, not quite darkness. Annabel enters.

ANNABEL: Professor Reynolds?

REYNOLDS: We're closed. Come back next week.

ANNABEL: I saw your light.

REYNOLDS: I'm not here. It's an optical illusion.

ANNABEL: I just wanted to talk to you about my paper.

REYNOLDS: Come back tomorrow.

ANNABEL: I was hoping I could get some work done tonight. I just wanted to run it by you.

REYNOLDS: It's fine.

ANNABEL: You haven't heard my idea yet.

REYNOLDS: Whatever it is, it's fine.

ANNABEL: I want to write about "Annabel Lee."

REYNOLDS: Fine.

ANNABEL: I have a couple of ideas about it.

REYNOLDS: One is usually enough.

ANNABEL: I've always been attracted to that poem, because

my parents named me after it. I think they were really high and they were reading poems and the book opened to that page and they thought it was a sign, like Edgar Allan Poe sending them a revelation or something. I used to get teased a lot, but I always loved my name. And ever since I was a little girl I've always thought that somehow that poem was about me. Kind of a private message to me, you know what I mean?

REYNOLDS: It's not.

ANNABEL: Well, that's not for you to say, is it? I mean, if it's a private message to me, it's really nobody else's business.

REYNOLDS: Then why do you want to write about it?

ANNABEL: Because it speaks to me.

REYNOLDS: Fine. Go home and let it speak to you there. It's late.

ANNABEL: I know. You're here late all the time. I always see the light in your window at night when I'm walking home from the library. The rest of the building is all dark. Everybody else has gone home. It's really kind of spooky in this big old building, coming up the steps in the dark. Are you staying late to work on a new book of poems or something?

REYNOLDS: Something.

ANNABEL: I've read your poems. They're really beautiful.

REYNOLDS: I don't do that any more.

ANNABEL: Although the more recent ones are really dark. Very, very dark.

REYNOLDS: They were written at night. It's dark at night. Go home.

ANNABEL: Did you know this poem was a big inspiration for Nabokov when he wrote *Lolita*?
It wasn't actually going to be called *Lolita*. He was going to call it *Kingdom By The Sea*. But he changed his mind. Good move, I think.

REYNOLDS: I'm really kind of busy here.

ANNABEL: You don't look busy. You look like a horse ran over you. Look, I don't want to keep you. I'll just be a minute. See, the connection with *Lolita* is that they're both about a man who loves a child. Of course, in the poem, they were both children when the man was in love with her. It's actually not clear whether they were really children or whether it's a metaphor, whether he's talking about how innocent their love was, like the love of children, although I'm not sure a child's love is all that innocent, in my experience, anyway. But the guy in the poem is older now, because he says it was "many and many a year ago," so she's been dead a while, whereas in Lolita, he's a grown man and she's a child, although he talks about his first love, whose name was Annabel Leigh, spelled different, but sounds the same, when they were both about Lolita's age. As if he's trying to recapture it with her. But he can't, quite. Because every time we love, it's like we're actually loving a person we miss, who came before, and we're trying to recapture that feeling, or make it work out right this time, with this substitute person we've projected our feelings upon, but it doesn't usually work. Especially if you're some sort of pervert. I don't know if Nabokov was actually a pervert or not but he's always struck me as kind of creepy, like a big creepy insect. Cold, you know? I mean, who likes sticking pins in butterflies? That's not a good sign. And of course, Poe is probably talking about his dead wife, who was a child when he married her, and was his cousin and sort of like his sister and sort of like his daughter. I don't know if they had sex or not. Do you think they had sex?

REYNOLDS: I'm forty-seven years old. I have no idea who has sex.

ANNABEL: And the angels are jealous. Because their love is so great, and so pure. So they kill her. The angels kill her. This is a poem with homicidal angels. How weird is that? Maybe the reason the angels are so jealous is because they're incapable of love, I mean, human love. Romantic love. Physical love. Which would mean, then, I suppose, that they did have sex, I mean, Poe and his wife, or the narrator and Annabel, because of course we can't presume that the narrator of the poem is identical to the poet, I know that, but still—

REYNOLDS: Don't get bogged down in a lot of biographical horse shit about the author. Just deal with the poem.

ANNABEL: I agree, it's possible to make too much out of the author's biographical references, but still, poems come from some place, and certainly in the case of Poe, you've got to admit—

REYNOLDS: I don't have to admit anything. It's damned near midnight. The raven is about to croak, and so am I.

ANNABEL: She dies at night. Annabel does. On a cold night like tonight. She dies of a cold wind. She dies of coldness. Maybe his coldness. I'm thinking maybe one reason he can't let go of this memory is that he feels guilty. Like maybe he loved her too much to touch her. And she died of lack of warmth. And then they steal her away from him. Her highborn kinsmen. They come and take her away. As if he was never good enough for her in the first place.

REYNOLDS: Miss—what's your name again? I'm sorry. My brain hasn't been working too well in the cold.

ANNABEL: Annabel.

REYNOLDS: Annabel, I honestly couldn't care less. It's almost midnight, and I'm very tired, and, frankly, at this moment, anyway, I really don't give a shit what you write your paper about.

ANNABEL: I thought maybe this poem would mean a lot to you. I mean, given your situation.

REYNOLDS: My situation? What situation?

ANNABEL: You know. I mean, with your daughter being dead and all. And your wife leaving you. I'm sorry. I don't mean to get personal. We don't really know each other that well.

REYNOLDS: We don't know each other at all.

ANNABEL: It's just, sometimes I feel so bad for you. In class. I sit there and watch you every day and I can't seem to look away. It's like passing some sort of horrible accident. You seem so sad. Your eyes are so sad. Then sometimes you get caught up in some poem or something, like when you were reading this poem out loud to us, and your eyes come alive, and there's this incredible intensity in you, it's really stunning, like you're alive again, for a minute, like the poem has brought you back from the dead, but then, when the poem is over, your eyes go all dead again. And that's what a poem should be, like this moment of really intensely observed and felt life. Don't you think? I'm really sorry about your daughter. And your wife leaving. You must be very lonely.

REYNOLDS: What I am or am not is none of your concern, and is in any case totally irrelevant to any conversation regarding the contents of your paper. Now go away and leave me alone.

ANNABEL: The thing is, I don't trust this guy.

REYNOLDS: What guy?

ANNABEL: Poe. The narrator. I know, I know they're not the same person, except I think they are. He keeps insisting too much, he goes on and on about how much he loved her and how pure his love was and how much he misses her, and it just seems really suspicious to me.

REYNOLDS: Why is it suspicious?

ANNABEL: Well, I mean, it's been a long time, he says so himself, but he just can't let go of it. That's the part I thought maybe you could relate to. I mean, because of your daughter dying and all—

REYNOLDS: How the hell do you know anything about my daughter?

ANNABEL: Everybody knows. About your daughter and the drug overdose and all that. And they all know your wife left you. This is a small college. Everybody knows everything.

REYNOLDS: You don't know anything. And you've got no business coming up here bothering me at midnight on the coldest night of the year, making incredibly offensive and totally inappropriate comments about my personal life. You don't know a damned thing about me.

ANNABEL: I know you stay up here every night drinking.

REYNOLDS: You don't know I'm drinking.

ANNABEL: You're drinking now. It smells like a distillery in here. And your hands are shaking. You're a mess. Look, I don't want to disturb you, but I'm really kind of excited about this subject, and I thought, correct me if I'm wrong, I thought maybe it was your job to encourage that sort of thing. All I'm saying is I think we might have an unreliable narrator here. I mean, why is he trying so hard to convince us how much he loved her? People who are always telling you how much they love you, those are the ones you've got to watch out for, in my experience.

REYNOLDS: And you've had a lot of experience, have you?

ANNABEL: I've had some experience.

REYNOLDS: So what does your experience tell you this particular unreliable narrator is trying to hide?

ANNABEL: I don't know. Maybe the angels didn't kill her. Maybe he did. Or maybe he feels like he did. I mean, look, he worships her. Like a person worships God. And what do we do to God? We kill him. We crucify him. And then we eat him. Body and blood. And maybe that's why after all this time this poor guy is still so hung up on this girl that he goes into her sepulchre by the sea every night and lays down beside her. He's devouring her. Well, maybe not literally devouring her. I don't think he's necessarily gnawing on her clavicle or anything. Symbolically he's devouring her. He's swallowing her. He's taking her inside himself so he can possess her entirely. Because I think that's what all this is about. He's feeling really guilty about her dying and he wants to possess her, to completely envelop her. So he can save her. But he can't save her. Because she's gone. And he can't get her back. Like your wife.

REYNOLDS: Will you shut up about my wife? You know nothing about my wife.

ANNABEL: I know she's been fucking some guy in the phys ed department.

REYNOLDS: Get out of here.

ANNABEL: I'm just saying, I think you can relate to this

---

poem in more ways than you want to admit to yourself, and that's why you're so touchy about it.

REYNOLDS: I'm not touchy about it. I just don't want to sit here in the middle of the night and talk to some girl I don't know about my wife's sexual behavior.

ANNABEL: He could be fucking the corpse.

REYNOLDS: I don't care what he's doing to the corpse. I just want you to go away and leave me alone.

ANNABEL: I don't think so.

REYNOLDS: You don't think so?

ANNABEL: No. I think you're really lonely. And I've seen the way you look at me in class.

REYNOLDS: I don't look at you in class.

ANNABEL: You mentally undress me in class.

REYNOLDS: I don't mentally undress you anywhere.

ANNABEL: You're mentally undressing me now.

REYNOLDS: I'm not undressing anybody.

ANNABEL: And that's why you're so lonely. Like Poe.

REYNOLDS: I'm not like Poe.

ANNABEL: He was a drunk who wrote poetry and everybody he loved either died or betrayed him or went away, and he drank himself to death. He was just like you. Except he had a mustache.

REYNOLDS: He was nothing like me.

ANNABEL: And he died in a drunken stupor, raving about how he was looking for somebody named Reynolds, and nobody has ever been able to figure out who this mysterious Reynolds person was. But I've figured it out. It was you.

REYNOLDS: It was me?

ANNABEL: Your name is Reynolds.

REYNOLDS: A lot of people are named Reynolds.

ANNABEL: But they don't write poems and teach Poe. He was really talking to you. He was trying to tell you something.

REYNOLDS: I wasn't even born then.

ANNABEL: It doesn't matter. Time is an illusion. All of Poe's work is about the human desire to transcend time.

Which is what writing poems is really about. And there at the end of his life he almost succeeded. Just before he died, he saw you, he connected to you, he could feel how much you were hurting, and he sent you this message.

REYNOLDS: What message?

ANNABEL: The message in the poem, that love transcends time. That love transcends space. That it transcends death. That love is stronger than anything. That no matter what horrible things happen, as long as love is possible, even if the person you love is dead or gone or doesn't love you back, it doesn't matter, not death or betrayal or anything else, because love is stronger than all of that. Love endures no matter what. That's what he was trying to tell you.

(Pause.)

REYNOLDS: Miss—

ANNABEL: Annabel.

REYNOLDS: Annabel. Are you on some sort of medication?

ANNABEL: No. Well, I was, but I stopped taking it. It was dulling my edge.

REYNOLDS: I think you need to get back on it.

ANNABEL: No I don't.

REYNOLDS: Well, you need something.

ANNABEL: You need something.

REYNOLDS: What I need is not relevant here.

ANNABEL: But it is. That's the whole point.

REYNOLDS: What point? There is no point.

ANNABEL: I knew your daughter. I went to high school with her. She wrote beautiful poems. Did you ever read any of her poems?

REYNOLDS: Please.

ANNABEL: Because they're all about you. She really loved you.

REYNOLDS: Please.

ANNABEL: So I really feel like I know you.

REYNOLDS: You don't know me.

ANNABEL: And I can understand how, after she died, you just kind of closed up in a ball. Which is what people do sometimes. Which is what I did when my father died. And how your wife was so unhappy she started sleeping with somebody else. Somebody who wasn't as smart as you or as nice as you but who she didn't have to think about anything when she was with him. You need to forgive her for that. I forgave my father for dying. And for cheating on my mother with an airline stewardess. And for a number of other crimes and misdemeanors which perhaps we can discuss on some later occasion. Because that's what love is. We forgive the people we love. Even for not loving us any more. Even for dying. And we keep loving them. But we also go on with our lives, and we learn to love somebody else, too. Which is what you need to do now.

REYNOLDS: *(Sitting down on the sofa with his head in his hands.)* It doesn't work like that.

ANNABEL: Yes it does.

REYNOLDS: No it doesn't.

ANNABEL: How does it work?

REYNOLDS: I don't know. But it's not like that.

ANNABEL: What is it like? Come on. You're the teacher. Tell me what it's like.

REYNOLDS: It's just—it's just death. It's just a very cold place to lie down by the sea. Nobody is alive there. Everything there is cold and dead.

ANNABEL: And there's demons. Under the sea. In the poem. There's angels in Heaven, who kill the people you love, so what's left for the demons to do? If the angels kill the people you love, what do the demons down under the sea do?

REYNOLDS: They don't let you forget. They make it impossible for you to forget.

ANNABEL: You don't need to forget. You need what I need.

REYNOLDS: What do you need?

ANNABEL: *(Sitting down beside him.)*
Just company. On a very cold night. Just the illusion of contact.
(She puts her hand on his.)

REYNOLDS: You shouldn't touch me.

ANNABEL: Why not?

REYNOLDS: Because if you get too close to me, the angels
   will kill you.
ANNABEL: Well, maybe. But until then—
REYNOLDS: Until then what?
ANNABEL: Until then is a poem.
   *(She rests her head on his shoulder, holding his hand.
   The light fades on them and goes out. Just the sound
   of the wind in the darkness.)*

BANG FOR THE BUCK

Shari D. Frost

ORIGINAL PRODUCTION

Boston Playwrights' Theatre as part of the Boston Theatre Marathon on May 11, 2014 at the Calderwood Pavilion at the Boston Center for the Arts

Directed by Bridget Kathleen O'Leary

CAST
JOE: Dale Place
BOB: Steve Barkhimer

CHARACTERS:

> BOB: Manager, dressed in a cowboy hat, fifties, pudgy.
> JOE: Vice President, dressed in a suit, fifties.

PLACE:

> A Hostess Brands office in the west.

TIME:

> Fall, 2012.

At rise JOE, mid-50s, fit and professional, sits behind a desk that, along with two chairs, indicates an office. A photo rests on the desk. Western gunfight music plays. BOB, pudgy and wearing a cowboy hat, swaggers in.

BOB: You wanted to see me, boss?

JOE: Yeah, Bob, come in.

> *(BOB and JOE eye each other up and down, each waiting for the other to make a move. BOB stands feet apart, shooting arm at the ready. HE reaches . . . and draws . . . a small golden cake. HE rips open the packaging, takes a bite, then holds the bitten end up for Joe to see.)*

BOB: Look at that. My boys done good. That is perfection, right there that is. You want one? I thought we might . . . break bread. Together. You and me. Like ol' times. Friday nights. Those were happy times. Am I right Joe? Huh? Am I right?

> *(JOE indicates a chair. BOB sits.)*

JOE: Haven't had one of those in years. Okay, so, there's no nice way to say this. It's a good package. Six months severance—

> *(BOB, still munching, picks up the photo.)*

BOB:—You got any plans for the holidays?

JOE: Not this year.

BOB: They always come up so fast. Don't the holidays come up fast?

JOE: Yeah. I guess so.

BOB: Why'd we stop spending the holidays together? Getting the families together? Those were happy times, huh? Am I right? Huh? Like when little Emma and Billy built that giant golden Christmas tree out of these.
(indicating his golden cake.)

JOE: I don't remember Emma building any golden Christmas tree.

BOB: (*looking at photo*) Yeah. Billy helped her. They were like, what, three years old? She starting to think about college, Emma? I bet she's starting to think about—

JOE: —Not really. Not yet. So, okay, six months severance—

BOB: —Cause Billy, he's thinking about college. Getting catalogues. Have you seen what they're getting for a semester these days?

JOE: It's a bit daunting, I know.

BOB: And room and board. Billy wants to go to school in New York. Can you believe that?

JOE: Bob, you've got to let me say this. I know you don't want to hear it.—

BOB: —What are you gonna do in New York, I asked him. You won't be able to carry one of these babies out in the open like this, I told him.
(BOB opens his suit jacket to reveal a holstered gun.)

JOE: If you don't mind . . .
(BOB releases his suit jacket and conceals his gun with a conciliatory gesture. HE takes another bite.)

BOB: Go ahead. Say it.

JOE: Nah.

BOB: Yeah. Say it. You know you want to.

JOE: Nah.

BOB: Come on.

JOE: Yeah?

BOB: Yeah!

JOE: It's a lot harder to get shot—

BOB: —when there isn't a gun around to shoot. Jeez Louise! Cracks me up every time.

JOE: Life's dangerous enough already.

BOB: You got that much right. Hell, sometimes I think it's the *wild fucking west* out there.

JOE: Look, Bob, I got another appointment after you.—

BOB: —See, so really, it's a lot harder to get shot, when you're the one with the gun. Huh? Am I right? The one with the gun? You know I'm right!

JOE: You know the company's struggling. Talking about shutting down.

BOB: The one with the gun. Then people know exactly who they're dealing with.

JOE: This isn't personal. In fact, I'm probably doing you a big favor.

(BOB fondles his gun through his jacket.)

BOB: I like being the one with the gun.

JOE: Are you . . . is that a threat? Is that what you're doing?

BOB: Now how could you say that? After all we've been through. You and me. Started at this company, on the line, together, how many years ago?

JOE: I don't know. Thirty?

BOB: Thirty *two*. Thirty two years ago you and me started going to happy hour every Friday night. Every Friday. Those were good times. Huh? Am I right? Whatever happened to happy hour? Do you ever wonder? Happy hour, I am sorry to say, is just not what it used to be. The camaraderie, the bonding, it is just not there no more, you know?

JOE: Bob, it's full pay, the package. Full pay—

BOB: —Camaraderie, that's important. It's . . . it's team building—

JOE: —Health benefits—

BOB: —It's "I got your back."

JOE: —The works.

BOB: —These days we need more "happy hour." More "I got your back."

JOE: This isn't my decision. You know if it were up to me—

BOB: —I know it was up to you when they passed me up for promotion. Again. And again.

JOE: That was not my fault. The company has an image to

uphold.

BOB: (*patting his pudgy belly*) Right. Cause eatin' these makes a guy lean an' mean.

JOE: I wrote a nice recommendation for you.

BOB: Well I am by far the best on that dang line.

JOE: You are.

BOB: My stats, if I remember right, were always higher than yours. Output per day an' such.

JOE: Fastest arm in the west. Can't argue that. No one can stuff'em like you.

(Beat.)

BOB: You mean fill'em, right? Fill'em, not stuff'em. Or was that supposed to be funny? (*again indicating his paunch*) Funny, like ha ha, some of my other stats were higher than yours too? That kind of funny? Cause I think I find that kind of humor a little inappropriate for a business conversation. Is it wrong that I believe in my product? Am I gettin' fired—

JOE: —laid off—

BOB: —for believin' in my product? When, after all, according to company policy, we are invited to snack, here and there.

JOE: No one's saying anything about—

BOB: —But you, you never did. Huh? Am I right? Huh? And now, now you're all skin an' bones on that side of the desk trying to make sure I am no longer on any side of any desk.

JOE: Look, it's out of my hands. You think I like doing this? I don't do my job, I get laid off!

BOB: I'm asking nicely. For old time's sake. I love this place. And I have worked hard. Been loyal. I got a mortgage. A family. A teen-age boy eatin' me out of house and home.

JOE: You'll find another job. Things are picking up. Just not around here.

BOB: You kiddin'? I'm fifty-four years old. You know damn well what's going on out there. There just ain't no demand for what I do no more.

JOE: You're a manager—

BOB: —Of guys who squirt creamy filling into spongy golden cakes! (*beat*) I mean, don't get me wrong, I love that creamy filling. It's what I know. What I do. I believe, in my heart of hearts

BOB (*cont'd.*): that, me and my guys, why we bring a passion, an artistry, to a delicacy more American than apple pie. To a delicacy that used to be beloved by all, might I add. It was important work. But now . . . now . . . wouldn't you know, I met me a kid the other day who never even tasted one of these before. Never even tasted one! Just about broke my heart, it did. To think what he'd been missing. A simple right o' passage. A simple part of what binds us all as . . . Americans. (*holding up golden cake*) Jeez Louise Joe, I give my heart and soul day in and day out. But all they see today is . . . is "saturated fat," and . . . and "sodium stearoyl lactylate" and "cellulose gum." All these years, Joe. Is this how it ends? What was it all for? Who am I?

JOE: You're my friend.

BOB: Am I? Am I Joe? Cause, thing is, it don't really feel like that. I been giving it a lot of thought. What it all means. Loyalty. Camaraderie. It's just not there no more. But I think you and me, we can get it back. Am I right? Huh? Don't you think we can get it all back?

(*BOB rises, then sits on the desk. HE opens his jacket to reveal his holstered gun once more, and fondles it.*)

JOE: What the fuck Bob? Huh? You think you can walk into my office—

BOB: —Now, you called me in—

JOE: —And whip out your gun—

BOB: —To fire me, might I add—

JOE: —To lay you off. It's layoffs!

BOB: (*looking inside his golden cake*)
And I wish you wouldn't say "whip" out. That's just . . . well that's just disrespectful to all that truly is "whipped."

JOE: Threaten me—

BOB: —Now, see, there, right there, I'm sorry but I'd have to disagree with you again. If you feel threatened, well that's just your take on the situation. Me, I say we're chatting. Two old friends.

BOB *(cont'd.)*: Catching up. *(indicating golden cake)* Like, for example, you're a V.P. and you haven't had one of these in years? See, I didn't even know that about you. And me, well, you ain't even asked, but see, the wife, she still ain't found herself a new job. So that mortgage I was mentioning. We're a bit behind. She's been so worried. Has all this time on her hands. All this nervous energy. So, you know what I did? I took her to the range. I did. *(BOB withdraws his gun from the holster.)*

BOB *(cont'd)*: Showed her how to aim. Real steady. *(BOB demonstrates, aiming his gun at JOE.)*

JOE: You know what? You're right. We are just chatting. Just "shooting the shit." No pun intended. Well, maybe just a little . . . intended. *JOE rises slowly, draws a gun of his own.*

BOB: Well howdy do! Look at you!

JOE: I hate that I have to own one of these. But you are not the only one I'm firing today—

BOB: —You mean laying off?—

JOE: —who's come in here carrying. Just what kind of a stupid fuck do you think I am? Everyone I've laid off so far has pulled this shit. It has been one helluva day! *(BOB starts slowly circling around the desk toward JOE, gun still aimed. JOE circles as well.) (Only one tense half circle should be completed as the two slowly swap places.)*

JOE *(cont'd)*: Put the gun down. Please. Before someone gets hurt.

BOB: Not someone, Joe. You.

JOE: You think a life sentence is the answer to all your problems?

BOB: Let's see here . . . three meals a day, a free "gym membership," all the TV a guy could watch and the time to watch it, a "free ride" to college for Billy, what with his dad in prison and his mom bankrupt and all. Yeah. That kind of *LIFE* might be just what I need. I been job

---

hunting. You think I didn't see this day coming? What kind of a stupid fuck do you think I am?!

JOE: Put the gun down.

BOB: Or what?

JOE: Or . . .

JOE "cocks" his gun.

BOB: Yeah?

BOB "cocks" his gun. Beat.

JOE: It was a Nativity scene. A golden manger. Emma and Billy built a Nativity scene!

BOB: Yeah . . . yeah, you're right.

JOE: And we ate the whole thing, every last cake. You and me.

BOB: Every last cake.

JOE: Those were good times.

BOB: (*seeing the past for what it truly was*)Puked all night.

JOE: Every last cake. How the hell did those two guys become the two guys standing here? It is a shame about happy hour. You put that gun away, I will take you out for a drink on Friday. And next Friday. And any Friday you want. I mean it. Let's put these away. For old times' sake!

BOB: For old times' sake? Truth is, you shoot me, you'd be throwing away your whole future. Am I right? Huh? (*THEY complete the 1/2 circle. BOB is behind the desk for the first time.*)

JOE: What future?—

BOB: —I have to say—

JOE: —No one eats this shit any more!—

BOB: (*fondling the desk*) —I do like it back here.—

JOE: —Do your kids eat those?

BOB: Not good for their health, I'm told.

JOE: (*indicating gun*) But they carry around one of these.

BOB: (*shrugging*) Kids. They read the papers too.

JOE: So what headline is Emma going to read tomorrow?

BOB: "Sugar kills. Disgruntled employee opens fire on co-worker."

JOE: Then we better figure out who's the disgruntled employee, and who's the co-worker.

BOB: Please, Joe. I'm only askin' for what's mine. Fair an'

square. It's real artistry I done brought to this place.

JOE: It is. I agree. It is.

BOB: So? Whaddaya say?

JOE: I say let's put these away. For Emma and Billy. It's a lot harder to get shot—

BOB: —When there isn't a . . . yeah, maybe you're right.
(Western gunfight music plays again. BOB and JOE'S eyes lock. BOB re-holsters his gun. JOE follows suit.)

BOB *(cont'd):* So? Whaddaya say?

JOE: I wish I could. The American dream, huh?

BOB: More like a wake-up call, if you ask me.
(BOB and JOE both draw. Bang! BOB drops over the desk, golden cake in hand.)

JOE: Bob? Bob!
JOE checks BOB out, then, desperate, places the cake to BOB's lips.

JOE *(cont'd):* Here! Take a bite! Bob?
(BOB does not respond, and a despondent JOE unconsciously takes a bite of the golden cake in his hand. Mmm! It's delicious! HE looks at it, then takes another ravenous bite, momentarily forgetting about BOB. BOB groans, then musters enough energy to fire off one last shot. A stunned JOE drops over the desk. BOB appears to want to see if JOE is okay, but instead grabs the cake and takes a bite, before expiring himself.)

END OF PLAY

ORIGINAL PRODUCTION

Fine Arts Association 18th Annual One Act Festival-
Hot From the Oven Smorgasbord, Willoughby, Ohio,
March 28-April 12 2014, Corning Auditorium

Directed by Ann Hedger

CAST:
WILL: Don Knepper
JUDY: Evie Koh

CONTACT: ahedger@fineartsassociation.org

MOST RECENT PRODUCTION

Theatre Odyssey, Sarasota, Florida   Asolo Rep
Theatre (Cook Theatre) May 1,2,3,4 2014 Awarded
"Best Play"

CHARACTERS:

WILL: thirties to sixties, alcoholic. Came from a wealthy family and blames his condition and short-comings on his father. Likeable, but not dependable.
JUDY: thirties to sixties, alcoholic, divorced, mother of two. Sarcastic. Blames herself for her condition-loathes herself.

SETTING:

A room with no doors somewhere in the Universe or beyond. Center of stage is a small table with a large bottle of vodka on it. Stage right is a chair and stage left is a chair. NOTE: The sound effect of an electrifying zapping sound is necessary so that every time Will and Judy touch the invisible shield, they get zapped.

TIME:

Present.

AT RISE: As lights come up we hear the sound of a car crash then a pause. Then we hear the sound of an ambulance. We see Will, seemingly, thrown on stage right.Looking confused, he walks around try-ing to figure out where his is. He spots the bottle of vodka, smiles, and approaches it. He looks around to see if anyone is watching and reaches for the bottle but his hand is stopped by some invisible shield. He walks to the other side and tries again but is blocked from getting the vodka. He sits in chair stage right and puts his head in hands.
He then laughs out loud. Stage left a woman is seemingly thrown onto stage and she stumbles in her high heels to gain her balance. She walks around confused, and Will stands and takes a couple of steps.

JUDY: Stop right there. *(She takes one of her high heels as a weapon.)* Don't come any closer or I'll scream!

WILL: Scream away. *(He sits again.)*

JUDY: Where am I? *(Hiccups)* Is this some kind of joke?

WILL: Yeah, it's real funny. An empty room with no doors and a bottle of vodka.

JUDY: I must be hallucinating again. *(She slaps herself.)* I'm awake. Are you going to tell me where I am?

WILL: Look lady, I just got here myself.

JUDY: You did?

WILL: Yep.

JUDY: *(Walks to bottle of vodka.)* Grey Goose? Nice brand. I'm impressed. I'm used to Absolute, if I'm lucky. This situation calls for a drink.

WILL: Good luck with that.

JUDY: *(She reaches for the bottle but her hand is stopped by invisible shield.)* What the hell!

WILL: Now you're getting close.

JUDY: What? You think this is hell? *(She walks with one shoe on and one off.)*

WILL: Where else?

JUDY: Well I was just in the hospital, that . . . terrible accident. Three people were around me doing the defibrillator thing with the paddles and saying "clear" and all that. They must have zapped me three or four times. Only I was looking down from above . . . I guess an out of body experience. I kept thinking, jeez, my roots look bad. I really need a dye job. But I wasn't wearing these shoes on that bed. Strange.

WILL: So did you see a bright light or something? Walk down a tunnel, see loved ones?

JUDY: No, *(Hiccups)* not at all.

WILL: Me either, that's why I think this is hell.

JUDY: I'm looking down at myself, from above, and all of a sudden I'm hit by something big . . . like maybe a baseball bat and here I am.

WILL: Last I remember was the crash . . . that loud crash and the feel of glass going through my body, then, wham! I'm here, in my own personal hell.

JUDY: Could I really be dead? I mean I know I shouldn't

---

have been driving but I never had an accident like that before. Was it the same crash?

WILL: Maybe. I was driving on state road 54 going east. How about you?

JUDY: I was going west.

JUDY AND WILL: HEAD-ON!

WILL: You dozed off and came into my lane, didn't you?

JUDY: No, I mean I don't remember that.

WILL: But you were drunk weren't you?

JUDY: Why would you say that?

WILL: Because it all makes sense. Two alcoholics are drunk, hit head on, they croak, and their hell is this!

JUDY: No. I can't believe God would be that cruel . . . I mean I didn't mean to hurt anybody. *(Seems to be sobering up now.)* Oh my God, did we hit anyone else?

WILL: I don't know, but I don't remember another car around so probably not.

JUDY: Whew! Least I didn't take somebody's child with me. This must just be a weigh station or something, you know, like in the movie HEAVEN CAN WAIT.

WILL: Think what you want. My name is Will. We might be here together for eternity so it might be helpful for us to be on a first name basis.

JUDY: Judy.

WILL: Judy, I'd rather have met you in my earthly life, but hi. *(Will offers his hand and they shake.)*

JUDY: I'm really getting scared now because I'm starting to believe you. *(Tries unsuccessfully to get to the bottle again.)* How can we get this bottle open? Help me will you?

WILL: I will repeat once more, this is our hell; we'll never be able to drink that vodka! We'll go through the DT's, everything, and be here for eternity.

JUDY: *(Sarcastically)* Hey, don't try to gloss it over for me or anything here. I don't deserve this. *(Sits, pause.)* Yes I do!

WILL: You couldn't have been as bad as me, really. I am such a low life.

JUDY: I'm a drunk. Is that what you want to hear? Is this a test maybe, trying to get me to repent.

(Rises, looks around and yells.)

I repent, do you hear me, I repent!

WILL: Who are you yelling at?

JUDY: I don't know . . . God, Satan, anyone who can get me out of here. I need to get home and . . . and . . . dye my hair.

WILL: Have no one to go home to, do you?

JUDY: Not really. My cat even left me. Found someone who'd feed her regularly I guess.

WILL: Let me say this. No matter how bad you think you are, you can't begin to compare to me.

JUDY: Oh yes I can. *(Sits and starts to cry as she speaks.)* I am so bad my children won't even speak to me. Even if my X let me see them, they wouldn't want to see me.

WILL: *(Walking over to her to give comfort.)* Judy, you don't strike me as being a bad person. Alcoholism is a disease you know. Don't be so hard on yourself. I've blown every opportunity for recovery . . . all because my dear old Dad. I got this from him, being a drunk I mean. It's genetic you know. We can't help it.

JUDY: I could help it. Doesn't run in my family at all . . . my brother's as sober as they come and my Mom and Dad never had a problem with booze. It's me . . . I'm just a worthless human being . . . one with a very bad hangover *(Grabs her head.)* Couldn't God or Satan or whoever have had pity and left some aspirin around?

WILL: I don't deserve pity. I used to hide bottles in my desk at work.

(They try to outdo one another with their confessions.)

JUDY: Well, I hid them in my linen closet. I changed sheets a lot.

WILL: I always had one in the garbage can, except on Thursdays-that was garbage day.

JUDY: No one in my family liked tomato juice so I'd just put vodka in there and drank it when I wanted . . . they never knew!

WILL: Had it under the seat in my car.

JUDY: I had this pair of pants with an elastic waistband. Put the bottle there like it was a pouch on a frickin kangaroo.

WILL: You know those carpenter pants? The bottom pocket.

JUDY: I'd empty out little bottles of shampoo and put it in there. They're great to have in your purse. Once I blew bubbles after a swig.

WILL: I didn't need a purse. I'd use little mouthwash bottles and keep them in my pocket. Everyone thought I had the freshest breath!

JUDY: Well, I went through AA three times.

WILL: Four for me.

JUDY: Step 9.

WILL: Make amends?

JUDY: That's all the farther I get . . . to 9. All three times I've tried to make amends with my daughter, and she won't talk to me. Never made it to 10. And the last time . . . I really thought I could get her to forgive me . . . I don't even remember what step 10 is.

WILL: Oh I've made it through the steps all right. I even go early to meetings twice a week to make the coffee. On the way I stop at this fish place out in the country. Believe it or not, they still have a phone booth outside. I wouldn't exactly call it a booth but I act like I'm on the phone . . . while I'm drinking my vodka. I'm skunked at the AA meeting-now that's pathetic.

JUDY: That is bad, but I've gotten two DUI's.

WILL: Three for me.

(They are really trying to outdo one another now.)

JUDY: I once picked my kids and my neighbor's kids up from Bible school, toasted!

WILL: I slept in a park and was beaten and mugged!

JUDY: I stole from my daughter's piggybank and from a passed out homeless man!

WILL: I was a passed out homeless man! Was that you?

(Judy shrugs her shoulders.)

JUDY: I sent my kids to school with no lunch money . . . just some crackers!

WILL: I lied to my sponsor a gazillion times!

JUDY: I left my sponsor at a Starbucks and she thought I

just went to pee!

WILL: I lost my license for 6 months!

JUDY: I still don't have my license back!

WILL: I've drunk mouthwash!

JUDY: I taught Sunday school with a buzz on!

WILL: I let my nephew walk out on thin ice!

JUDY: *(Yelling, slowly, and emphatically.)* I got plastered at my niece's wedding and slept with my husband's brother!

WILL: *(His demeanor has changed now and he's not trying to outdo her anymore. Very serious.)* I was too afraid to have kids.

JUDY: *(Also very serious.)* I lost mine.

WILL: *(Going to Judy.)* Seems to me as if we have a lot in common. Like you might be able to understand me because you've been there.

JUDY: I feel like I know you better than people I've spent years with. Are you married?

WILL: Are you kidding? Who could live with me?

JUDY: Will, will you hold me for a minute?

WILL: Sure. *(Holding her.)*

JUDY: Thanks.

(Will kisses her and she responds favorably. There's obviously a physical attraction.)

WILL: Whew! I haven't felt like that in a long time.

JUDY: I haven't felt anything for so long.

WILL: *(In thought, walking to stage right, leaving Judy stage left.)* You know, maybe I was all wrong . . . maybe this is not hell.

JUDY: Maybe this is our heaven?

WILL: Yes, someone to be with who totally understands me.

JUDY: Someone who can hold me and comfort me.

WILL: Someone I can make mad passionate love to!

(They walk towards each other, about to touch, when an invisible shield center stage blocks them from touching.)

JUDY: Will?

WILL: Judy?
> *(They move up and down stage center trying to touch but are still blocked from each other and the vodka.)*

Lights fade.

END OF PLAY

The New York premiere of CASEY229 was produced, performed and directed by the Collective—NY as part of "Collective: 10" in 2014, with the following cast and director:

PAM: Karen Chamberlain
KEN: John Norwell
Director: Margaret Champagne

The Alliance of Los Angeles Playwrights produced CASEY229 in 2014 at the Hollywood Fringe Festival, as part of "Sex, Lies and Social Media." It opened June 9, 2014 and ran for five performances, withthe following cast:

PAM: Elin Hampton
KEN: David Fury
Director: David Fury

"A dream you dream alone is only a dream. A dream you dream together is reality."

—John Lennon

"People who need people are the luckiest people in the world."

—Bob Merrill

CHARACTERS:
> PAM: An attractive well-dressed woman, slightly past child-bearing age.
> CASEY: An overweight, middle-aged, balding man. He wears a T-shirt and sweatpants.

TIME: Lunchtime.

PLACE: A few miles from a better neighborhood

Two garden chairs sit on the front porch of what charitably would be called a "humble house." Casey, an out-of-shape schlump, sits on one of them. He wears a t-shirt from a previous weight, sweats, slippers, tiny sun shades, and ear buds. He listens to his I-Pod. Pam, an impeccable well-dressed woman in business attire, approaches him. She checks out the neighborhood with judgment, and looks at her phone, making sure the address is

PAM: Hello? Is this 1017 South Andover?
> *He jumps.*
CASEY: I didn't expect you 'til tomorrow.
PAM: What?
CASEY: But everything's ready to go. Lemme put some shoes on. I can help you to the car. The wheelchair's kinda cumberishsome.
PAM: No, I'm not here for a wheelchair.

CASEY: Oh, just her clothes. Sure. I'm an idiot. Goodwill wouldn't send a lady. A lady in heels to get her equipment. Mom was seventy pounds at the end. Her stuff weighs about three times that.

PAM: Omigod. No, I'm not here to pick up—I'm really sorry for your loss. Mr . . . .

CASEY: Chester. Ken. Thanks. It was a long time coming. But you're never really prepared.

PAM: I imagine that's true. Um, I'm actually looking for someone. Your daughter, maybe?

CASEY: My daughter?

PAM: Or, I don't know, sister? A young woman. I know she lives here.

CASEY: There's no young woman here.

PAM: I know for a fact there is. The detective I hired tracked down her IP address.

CASEY: Detective? What the hell—

PAM: I regret the timing, I do, with your mom and all, but ever since I found out, I've been sick. Literally. Lost five pounds in two days. Shit, that was insensitive! You just told me about your mother withering away, and here I am blabbering about five pounds.

CASEY: You look fi—

PAM: But I was completely blind-sided by this. I thought I was a smart person, but the truth is, I didn't have a clue.

CASEY: Who ARE you?

PAM: Pam, look, I'm not here to cause a scene, I just want this to stop. So tell the whore who's living here to leave Frank alone!

CASEY: Who's Frank?

PAM: My husband. Frank, or MeUnderscoreButch . . . whatever the hell he's calling himself these days.

She opens her I-Pad to reveal a photo of a young woman.

PAM *(CONT'D)*: He left his laptop opened with this picture of her. Casey229 Any psychiatrist would tell you . . . he wanted me to find out.

Casey shakes his head.

CASEY: Wait. You're Butch's wife?

PAM: Frank's wife. Now where is this "Casey," if that's her real name?

CASEY: I'm Casey.

PAM: Right. You said your name was Ken.

CASEY: Kenton Chester. When I was a kid they called me KC. Eventually, it just became "Casey."

PAM: I get it. You're protecting her.

CASEY: There's no her! I'm Casey. Casey229. Leap Day. My shitty birthday.

PAM: Then, *(Re: I-Pad)* who's she?

CASEY: I don't know. I got her picture off Christian Mingle. com

PAM: So, let me get this straight. You're my husband's mistress?!

CASEY: It's not like that. Please don't trivialize it. Like it's something sordid and cheap. Casey229 and MeUnder-scoreButch are in—

PAM: What? Are you telling me my husband's gay?!

CASEY: You'd know better than me. Butch and me . . . we've never met face to face.

PAM: So you're gay, and—

CASEY: No! I'm straight. First time we chatted, I assumed MeUnderscoreButch was a lesbian. I like lesbians. Really, what guy would call himself Butch? Now, I think it's kinda cute. I saw what he was going for. I was just looking for someone to talk to . . . a friend. I don't expect you to understand.

PAM: You got that right.

CASEY: Hey. You're not the only one who's hurting here, Pamela.

PAM: Pam. Just, Pam.

CASEY: It's a lonely life taking care of an invalid mother, day after day. After the amputation, she needed full-time help. Now you're probably thinking, "Why didn't he hire someone?"

PAM: I wasn't actually—

CASEY: I did. The first nurse just watched those so-called

"reality" shows all day. The next one was nuts. She stole my mother's prosthetic leg and pawned it. I was an only child. Mom wasn't perfect, but I owed her. She gave me life. If I didn't take care of her, who would?

PAM: Still not understanding—

CASEY: It's not so easy to have a great social life when you spend most of your adult years housebound with your mother. Her disability check was enough for the two of us to get by, but there wasn't a whole lot left over to wine and dine the ladies, if you get my drift.

PAM: Okay. But where did Frank come in?

CASEY: I'm getting to it. Here I am, pretty much in the dark about, you know, taking care of my eighty-seven-year-old-one- legged-mother. Not as easy as you'd think. So, I sign up for an on-line course to teach me the basics of home nursing care. Boy, when you sign up for anything on the Internet, suddenly you're on the list for like everything else out there. So this one day, I'm eating lunch. Onion soup au gratin and right at that instant, some school sends me a link about learning French. I wasn't looking to take a French class, but it's like when you go grocery shopping and you're about to leave and then you see a candy bar in the checkout line and you just can't pass it up.

PAM: Impulse buying.

CASEY: Right. That's what it was. So, I signed up. Did you know "au gratin" means with cheese?

PAM: Yes.

CASEY: Well I didn't. But, I do now. Then, coupla months later, I joined French Chat, y'know, to practice speaking all the words with other people. That's where we met.

PAM: You met Frank in a French chat room.

CASEY: MeUnderscoreButch. She definitely impressed me. I mean, "he."

PAM: He's originally from Quebec. Frank used to try to teach me French, but I didn't have the ear for it. I had no idea the language was that important to him.

CASEY: Oh yeah. It's a big part of our relationship. So Butch and me start talking and by the time I realize he's a guy and he thinks I'm a girl, we're already, I don't know, connected. Really connected. A first for me. Never had that with anyone, not unless you count my mother, who sometimes put her arms around my neck, probably for support, but I kept telling myself it was a hug.

PAM: O-oh.

CASEY: I know. Pathetic, right? I'm telling you, if it hadn't been for Butch, there woulda been days I couldn't gotten outta bed. He's the one that kept me going.

Pam is moved. She touches his arm.

PAM: That's so sweet.

CASEY: After about a year, he proposed . . . and I said "yes."
     Pam pulls her hand back.

PAM: You're married?!

CASEY: Going on two wonderful years.

PAM: This is insane.

CASEY: Love is insane, Pam.

PAM: Love? It's not love. It's pretend. Frank and I live in the real world! Our marriage may not be perfect, but it's REAL.

CASEY: Oh, ours is real. And I'm not going to lie to you, Pam, it hasn't been without its ups and downs either. Online marriage counseling really helped. We thought it was important for the kids to see us as a strong unit.

PAM: Kids?!

CASEY: Oh, yeah. I can see where that would come as a shock. When Casey and Butch met, I was single mom.

PAM: Oh, Jesus.

CASEY: I know. I know. I got carried away. SassyKira's six now, but she thinks she's an adult.

PAM: She is an adult. She's you!

CASEY: Butch is amazing with her. I wouldn't have married him if he wasn't. He's such a good father.

PAM: No, he's not! We don't have any children.

CASEY: Oh, I'm sorry.

PAM: It's okay. He couldn't . . . and it was a blessing in disguise. I'm really busy at work. Believe me, it's better this way.

CASEY: If you say so. Actually, we talked about having a kid of our own, but after my hysterectomy . . .

PAM: O-mi-god.

CASEY: So we adopted. Montego RV.

PAM: Montego.

CASEY: RV. An Ethiopian special needs child.

PAM: Sounds adorable.

CASEY: He will be. Just as soon as he gets the surgery for his cleft palette.

PAM: Okay.

CASEY: Whatever he needs. We're his parents and we love him.

PAM: Nice.

CASEY: The surgery isn't cheap, and insurance might not cover it, but Butch always provides for us, even if he has to work seven days a week to make ends meet. Thank God everyone needs a plumber!

PAM: Frank's not a plumber. He went to Princeton. He was at the top of our class. That's where we met.

CASEY: Wow. Princeton. Now, that's impressive. What does Frank do?

PAM: He works for me. At my law firm.

CASEY: He's a lawyer!

PAM: No, he's a paralegal. A degree in philosophy and romance languages doesn't prepare one for much of a career.

CASEY: Huh.

PAM: I'm so confused. It's like I'm married to a stranger. I really thought he was happy, Ken.

CASEY: I'm sure he is. Look at you . . . you got it all.

PAM: Right? I thought we did. We have a beautiful apartment with a doorman and a view, we eat in restaurants, we make charitable contributions, we take vacations. Spontaneously!

CASEY: So, no complaints.

PAM: Well, everyone has complaints. It's just that it doesn't sound like your life with Butch is an improvement over what Frank has with me. Am I missing something? It seems as though you two have made-up a life riddled with problems.

CASEY: Challenges. We call 'em challenges. It's all the way you look at it, I guess. I think Butch was happy to have our family to take care of, and I sure liked being taken care of. (Then) At any rate, I didn't know about you or think that I was hurting anybody. But now that I know, I'm gonna break it off. It's what's right.

PAM: Yes. Good.

She starts to leave, then stops and turns around.

PAM: No, don't. Don't break it off. Frank/Butch needs this. He needs Casey229.

CASEY: Yeah. Yeah. I think he does.

PAM: What you two have is beautiful.

CASEY: You sure?

PAM: Maybe we can co-exist. I just want him to be happy.

CASEY: Yeah, me too.

Pam hugs Casey. He awkwardly accepts it.

This is a hug, right?

PAM: Yeah.

CASEY: Adieu.

She leaves. Casey watches her go.

Huh.

FADE TO BLACK.

END OF PLAY.

THE CRAFT
Andrew Biss

Produced by MadLab Theatre as part of Theatre Roulette 2014, May 8-24, 2014.

Directed by Jim Azelvandre

CAST:
ACTOR 1: Travis Horseman
ACTOR 2: Erin Prosser

PLAYWRIGHT'S NOTE: This play contains very little 'actual' stage direction, as almost all of it is revealed by the actors themselves within their inner dialogues. It should also be noted that since the dialogue in this play consists entirely of the actors' inner dialogues, neither of them at any time is actually hearing what the audience hears. Furthermore, both actors should—as far as possible—attempt to match their expressions and body language to what is being experienced by the characters in the play-within-the-play, rather than reflecting the emotions of the actors' inner dialogues.

ACTOR 1: A cocky, bravura exterior masks the frustrated, insecure actor within. Male. Twenties to thirties.

ACTOR 2: Centered, professional, committed to her work, with an aversion to suffering fools. Female. Twenties to thirties.

SETTING:

A stage.

TIME:

The present.

At rise: There is a small table placed downstage center, with a chair to the right of it, and a small bench seat to the left. ACTOR 1 enters.

ACTOR 1: Act Two, Scene Three. I enter from stage right . . . nervous but in character, cross to the chair placed downstage center, next to the small table, and sit. I look up, seemingly forlorn, and begin my brief soliloquy that speaks of the turmoil and heartache inside of me that was all-too-obviously telegraphed in the previous scene. *(beat)*
I direct it to the fourth wall, as if speaking to anyone and no one, *and yet* . . . some woman in the third or fourth row is wearing a blouse of a color so loud and garish that I find my peripheral vision is being constantly distracted by it, thus diminishing the gravitas of what I'm attempting to impart to the audience at large. God I hate her—she's really screwing this up for me.
(beat)
I'm ignoring her as best I can and concentrate on the words. Okay, I'm done. God, I hate her—she really threw me off.
(beat)
I think my expression at the end really got them, though . . . despite the distraction of Coco the Clown in row C

or D or wherever the hell she is.

(beat)

All right then, darling, let's be having you . . . make your entrance please . . . *now.*

(beat)

Christ, where is she? Come on, come on!

(beat)

All right, don't panic. Try to look deep in thought, as if there's a very important inner dialogue raging inside of you—then maybe the audience will think it's all deliberate.

(beat)

God, I could strangle her right now! *Where the hell is she?*

(ACTOR 2 enters from stage left.)

ACTOR 2: I enter hurriedly from stage left.

ACTOR 1: *At last!*

ACTOR 2: I run across the stage, desperately seeking the whereabouts of my one true love . . . even though I can see him sitting right there and would have to be half blind not to have spotted him immediately . . . *but* . . . this is theatre, so on I search, hoping, hoping, until . . . oh yes, there he is . . . my heart's desire . . . in the form of one of the most obnoxious and egotistical jerks I've ever had the misfortune of working with. I smile sweetly.

ACTOR 1: I suddenly become aware of her presence . . . and of the very dark circles under her eyes, which no amount of make-up was able to disguise, apparently. Out on the town with the director again last night, I'm assuming. My, what a far cry from the delicate little flower she's attempting to fob off on the audience right now. Drunken old slattern. I turn away, hurt.

ACTOR 2: I drop to my knees and beseech him. If he only knew why I had to rebuff him in the library in the previous scene. If he only knew of the deep dark secret I've been forced to keep hidden from him. If he only . . . if he only . . . if he'd only look me in the eye for just a second! I mean, come on, we're supposed to be doing

---

this thing together. It's called acting. It's reacting as well as speaking, you know? I need something to work with here. Hello? Hello?

ACTOR 1: I wonder if there's any agents in the audience tonight. I invited six but none of them responded. Wait a second . . . that guy back there with the glasses looks like he might be.

(beat)

On second thoughts, no . . . too hip. Useless bastards. I expect they were all "too busy." Yeah, too busy propping up some bar, getting wasted after a hard day's skimming cash off the backs of their clients' hard work. Parasites. They should be sat out there doing their job . . . scouting for talent . . . witnessing art.

(beat)

Oh, look out—her big speech is about to end. And not before time. She milks that thing like a Jersey cow.

(beat)

I look up at her with a mixture of pity and confusion, and demand that she tells me her deep dark secret so that I can feign shock and surprise for yet another evening.

ACTOR 2: Oh look, it does have eyes after all. Good evening and thank you for joining me. It's so nice to have company. So . . . you want to know my terrible secret, do you? All right, I'll tell you. It's an almost uncontrollable desire to see you stripped naked and strung up by your balls from the light rigging, with a large prop of my choosing rammed up that vain, self-important and utterly talentless asshole of yours. But . . . since that's unlikely to transpire and not actually in the text, I suppose I'd better stick with the scripted version.

(beat)

She covers her face with her hands, dreading his reaction to what she is about to disclose.

ACTOR 1: Yes, cover it up, dear—it's hard staring into those dark, puffy eyes for too long. I feel like I'm sharing a scene with a panda bear.

(beat)

And if there are any agents out there tonight, I hope they're taking note, because *this* is acting. Not only am I having to navigate this scene alone with Ling-Ling here, but I mean, really—she had an abortion two years ago after a brief romp in the rhododendrons with the former gardener? I mean, who writes this crap? I'm supposed to be shocked and appalled by this revelation? It's hardly the stuff of Gran Guigonol. Now, if she'd been raped by her father and given birth to a hideously deformed, inbred monstrosity that she kept chained to a post behind the summerhouse, *then . . . then* we'd have a revelation *. . . then* we'd have something to work with. But no, it's just your average, plain vanilla abortion saga, in response to which—and to great effect, using every skill at my disposal—I fix her with a steely gaze that betrays neither outrage nor compassion.

ACTOR 2: I pause briefly, looking into his eyes to see if my words have been met with pity or loathing.
(beat)
As it turns out, it's neither. It's that same vacant, idiotic expression he wears every time the director gives him a note—he tries to pretend he's understood, but in truth just looks lobotomized. And his parents, with the benefit of hindsight, would probably agree with me now that that might have been the best option.
(beat)
I express lots of guilt, etcetera, and explain how my father forced me into it.

ACTOR 1: An abortion? I'll tell you what an abortion is—this script. Hard to believe it got a first production, let alone a revival. I should be doing Mamet or Pinter or Shepard, not this potboiling drivel.
(Pause.)

ACTOR 2: Oh Christ, he's forgotten his lines—and *always* at the same spot.

ACTOR 1: If I had an agent I wouldn't have to do crap like this. I'd get the roles I deserve . . . meaty ones . . . in juicy scripts . . . not this crap.

ACTOR 2: He has—he's forgotten his lines again!

ACTOR 1: God, I hate agents.

ACTOR 2: God, you idiot!

ACTOR 1: Useless bastards.

ACTOR 2: Think, you idiot, think!

ACTOR 1: Wait a second—where are we? Oh shit, it's my line!

ACTOR 2: Think!

ACTOR 1: Um . . . um, um, um, um . . . oh yeah—the very sudden, very clunky, not to mention plot-convenient change of heart, where I quickly forgive all and reaffirm my undying love. Urgh!

ACTOR 2: At last! I could slap you sometimes, I really could.

ACTOR 1: As if anyone could ever love that . . . apart from another panda, I suppose.

ACTOR 2: Amateur!

ACTOR 1: Oh, and the director, of course . . . after he's had a few.

ACTOR 2: Tears of joy fill my eyes, as I cross stage left to the window and look out, as if to symbolize the new life and new beginning that now lay ahead. Hackneyed and cheesy, yes, but that's what's in the script, so that's what I must do.

ACTOR 1: I cross to her and grab her by the throat.
(beat)
Heh, heh, heh—just kidding. I tap her gently on the shoulder.

ACTOR 2: I turn around, my heart overflowing, to face my dear true love. My dear, true, lobotomized-looking love.

ACTOR 1: I get down on one knee, and from my pocket I produce a small box.

ACTOR 2: My eyes light up. Could it be . . . could it truly be . . .

ACTOR 1: Empty?

ACTOR 2: Oh shit!

ACTOR 1: Oh no!

ACTOR 2: You complete moron!

ACTOR 1: I swear it was there earlier. I swear it was. I

checked . . . I think.

ACTOR 2: All right, don't panic, you idiot, just mime it.

ACTOR 1: Maybe it fell out. Maybe it's in my pocket. Perhaps I should check. No, I can't—the audience would know for sure then—it'd be obvious.

ACTOR 2: Just mime it.

ACTOR 1: What am I gonna put on her finger?

ACTOR 2: Mime it!

ACTOR 1: I'll just mime it.

ACTOR 2: He slips the engagement ring onto her finger, which she then lovingly admires—whilst deftly using her other hand to block its view from the audience—and proceeds to tell him how her heart is full of . . . well, actually, a death wish at this point.

ACTOR 1: That was quick thinking. The audience didn't suspect a thing. See, I don't panic in a crisis. That's the mark of a professional. You're learning from the best here, Ling-Ling.

ACTOR 2: Which now brings us to the sadly inevitable—the moment in the play that tortures my mind and churns my stomach eight times a week . . . the kiss. She turns her head to one side, coquettishly.

ACTOR 1: All right, Olivier, eat your heart out. I hope you're watching, wherever you are, because this, my friend, is the highest mountain an actor has ever had to climb. This is what separates the men from the boys, the hams from the Hamlets, for this is the moment where—after summoning every last ounce of strength and courage—I am called upon to . . . lock lips with bamboo breath.

ACTOR 2: Make it convincing, but make it quick.

ACTOR 1: I am fearless. I am an actor. I can do anything. Even this. He grabs the furry beast by its shoulders, making his intentions unmistakable.

ACTOR 2: She appears coy and vulnerable, her lower lip quivering slightly in anticipation of what she knows is to come. Her stomach, on the other hand, is gripped by nausea and revulsion . . . her head by a duty to the craft.

ACTOR 1: All right, Ling-Ling, here I come. And there'd

---

better not be any director residue left on those lips—from his mouth or otherwise.

ACTOR 2: Bracing herself, she doggedly repeats her mantra: It's Jude Law, it's Jude Law, it's Jude law, it's Jude–

(They kiss for several moments, before ACTOR 1 releases ACTOR 2 from his embrace.)

ACTOR 2: . . . Law.

ACTOR 1: Done! He emerges unscathed, and yet another night's meager wages are earned in full. They should give medals to some actors, not awards.

(beat)

He stands before her with a look of pride . . . as well he should after that feat.

ACTOR 2: She strokes his cheek affectionately . . . while resisting the overwhelming urge to wipe her mouth with the back of her hand, and imagining the poor creatures that have had to endure that revolting experience in real life . . . assuming there's actually been any.

ACTOR 1: He takes her hand and leads her stage right to the bench seat.

ACTOR 2: Why is he going so damned fast? The director's told him about this so many times! I'll trip and break my neck one of these days.

ACTOR 1: He gestures for her to sit.

ACTOR 2: She sits.

ACTOR 1: He sits and places his arm around her . . . and proceeds with the cloying speech about his plans for their future together, and how happy they'll be, and of the children she'll bear him . . . literally, in this case—half-man, half-bear.

ACTOR 2: She leans her head tenderly against his shoulder . . . and contemplates the true meaning of paying ones dues, knowing that one day . . . one day, when she's a sought after actress of fame and repute, all of this—every last unctuous, frustrating, degrading moment she's ever had to endure—will all have been worth it.

ACTOR 1: He holds her close to him . . . and waits impatiently for the lights to come down.

(beat)

Wait a second . . . did I turn my lights off when I pulled in here tonight? Oh no . . . I don't think I did. Oh shit . . . shit! Hurry the hell up with those damn lights, will you? I've gotta get out of here now! Come on, come on!

ACTOR 2: Thank God he gets murdered by my father in the next scene. She smiles contentedly . . . as the lights fade down . . . to black.

END OF PLAY

CROOKED FORK
Jonathan Yukich

Crooked Fork was first produced at the Salem Theatre Company's 2014 Moments of Play Festival in Salem, Massachusetts. The production was directed by Anna Stenberg and the cast was as follows:

CAST:
MAYOR BUTTONS: Jeffrey Phillips
CHET: Mark Davis

CHARACTERS:

MAYOR BUTTONS: the middle-aged, bumbling mayor of Crooked Fork.

CHET: the mayor's dedicated aide, younger than his superior.

SETTING:

The mayor's office. A desk and a couple of chairs will do.

TIME:

The present.

(MAYOR BUTTONS with CHET, his trusty advisor, in the mayor's office. MAYOR BUTTONS is holding a wrapped sandwich, aggravated.)

CHET: I'm sorry, Mr. Mayor.

MAYOR BUTTONS: You call this a sandwich!

CHET: It's from the vending machine.

MAYOR BUTTONS: Lunch from a vending machine! What is this—City Hall or a Stuckey's?

CHET: It's all I could find.

MAYOR BUTTONS: I sent you to the butcher's for lunch!

CHET: Yes, but I'm afraid Mr. Buchwald is unwell.

MAYOR BUTTONS:
(Concerned.)
Bucky? Unwell?

CHET: He's dead.

MAYOR BUTTONS: No—

CHET: Yes.

MAYOR BUTTONS: When?

CHET: This morning.

MAYOR BUTTONS: By god – Bucky the Butcher?

CHET: Yep.

MAYOR BUTTONS: Dead?

CHET: Yep.

MAYOR BUTTONS: But he was always so—

CHET: Alive?

MAYOR BUTTONS: No—

CHET: Conceited?

MAYOR BUTTONS: Yes. Bucky was an asshole. But he knew his meat.

CHET: Undeniably.

MAYOR BUTTONS: How did he—?

CHET: Electrocution.

MAYOR BUTTONS: Christ.

CHET: In his sleep.

MAYOR BUTTONS: How is that even possible?

CHET: Electric blanket.

MAYOR BUTTONS: Jesus.

CHET: Faulty wiring.

MAYOR BUTTONS: At least he went peacefully.

CHET: Probably not.

MAYOR BUTTONS: How's Maggie taking it?

CHET: You haven't heard?

MAYOR BUTTONS: Maggie too?

CHET: You haven't heard.

MAYOR BUTTONS: Christ.

CHET: Stepped on her cat.

MAYOR BUTTONS: That killed her?

CHET: Killed her cat. She fell down the stairs.

MAYOR BUTTONS: By god—there's no end.

CHET: There was for Maggie.

MAYOR BUTTONS: Who'll run the library—now that she's gone?

CHET: Libraries are dying.

MAYOR BUTTONS: Everything's dying.

(Pause. Distraught.)

That's the entire Buchwald family.

CHET: Including their cat.

MAYOR BUTTONS: As mayor, I feel accountable.

CHET: There's nothing you could do, sir.

MAYOR BUTTONS: I wonder if it's happening in other towns?

CHET: If what's happening?

MAYOR BUTTONS: People dying.

CHET: Well yes, people die in every town.

MAYOR BUTTONS: But not like this. People dying suddenly, and all of them by—by accident. It's a plague of accidents.

CHET: Perhaps it's just a run of bad luck.

MAYOR BUTTONS: It's more than that. Bad luck is a tornado or wildfire. These are isolated incidents. A steady stream of fatal misfortunes.

CHET: First there was Fred Trotter—

MAYOR BUTTONS: Drowned in his hot tub.

CHET: Then Pearl Butts—

MAYOR BUTTONS: A bad can of tuna.

CHET: They passed within days of each other.

MAYOR BUTTONS: Under such peculiar circumstances.

CHET: Coincidence, I thought.

MAYOR BUTTONS: It's what we all thought.

CHET: But then it really started.

MAYOR BUTTONS: Roger Mud—

CHET: Chainsaw mishap.

MAYOR BUTTONS: The Soot family—

CHET: Swallowed by a sinkhole.

MAYOR BUTTONS: The Peck twins—

CHET: Tandem bike crash.

MAYOR BUTTONS: Reverend Flum—

CHET: Rabid possum bite.

MAYOR BUTTONS: Sheriff Niblets—

CHET: Congenital syphilis.

MAYOR BUTTONS: And that's only the beginning. The list goes on!

CHET: Most of the town has succumbed. By my last count, sir, after Bucky's death, we may be the last left.

MAYOR BUTTONS: The last?

CHET: Yes sir.

MAYOR BUTTONS: The two of us?

CHET: If my numbers are correct—and they usually are.

MAYOR BUTTONS: What if the rest of the world has also perished by some quirk of fate? What if we're the only humans left on the face of the earth?

CHET: That would be quite a whimper.

MAYOR BUTTONS: It's time we enter crisis mode.

CHET: Crisis mode? What do we do in crisis mode?

MAYOR BUTTONS:

(First thing that comes to mind.)

We go into lockdown! Chet, lock my office door!

CHET: It's already locked.

MAYOR BUTTONS: Good, great! I feel better already!

CHET: What's next in crisis mode?

MAYOR BUTTONS: We pray.

CHET: Do you think it'll help?

MAYOR BUTTONS: It can't hurt.

CHET: But I'm an atheist.

MAYOR BUTTONS: Use your imagination.

CHET: Maybe, first, it would be best if we alert outside authorities.

MAYOR BUTTONS: Excellent, Chet! It's ideas like this that could make you mayor one day!

CHET: Big shoes to fill, sir.

MAYOR BUTTONS: I'll write a letter asking the neighboring town for help—assuming they're still there.

CHET: Why not just phone or email them? It would be much faster.

MAYOR BUTTONS: The internet's been down for days, and the cell reception is terrible in here.

CHET: We could go to my office.

MAYOR BUTTONS: We're in lockdown, Chet. No one comes, no one goes. It'll have to be a letter.
(Searching his desk.)
Pen, pen . . . where's a pen? I need a pen, Chet.

CHET: Here, use my pencil.

(MAYOR BUTTONS takes a pencil from CHET. He begins to compose a letter. As he contemplates the next phrase to write, he habitually sucks on the tip of the pencil.)

MAYOR BUTTONS: Fine, fine. How should I start?

CHET: A salutation.

MAYOR BUTTONS: Grand.

(Writes.)

"Dear Sirs and Madams"

CHET: That'll hook them. Now ease your way into the crisis. We don't want it to seem like we're only writing them out of desperation.

MAYOR BUTTONS: Yes, yes.

(Writes.)

"What beautiful foliage we're having this fall season."

CHET: Nice touch.

MAYOR BUTTONS: "Regrettably, like the leaves, our citizens are also popping off."

CHET: Very tactful, sir.

MAYOR BUTTONS: "It seems our entire population is very nearly extinct. Emoticon: frowny face. We're clueless as to why. Perhaps the drinking water, a voodoo hex, or mere arbitrary happenings. Regardless, send help – and fresh sandwiches. Cordially, Mayor Buttons and the dwindling city of Crooked Fork." There.

CHET: Stirring rhetoric, sir.

MAYOR BUTTONS: We'll just put this with the outgoing mail and wait for the troops to arrive.

CHET: There is no outgoing mail. Howie the Postman was cut in half by his John Deere last week.

MAYOR BUTTONS: I take it he did not survive?

CHET: No sir he did not.

MAYOR BUTTONS: By god—I'm out of ideas. What's the point of being mayor if there's no one left to vote for you?

CHET: It's their loss, sir.

MAYOR BUTTONS: I suppose it does take some pressure off. Governing is no cakewalk. People want things! But now I'm free to do as little as I'd like! Budgets smudgets, I say! Still, it's a hollow feeling overseeing a town done in by happenstance. It seems, by some cosmic glitch, all the world's flukes have befallen us at once. Will any be spared? It's events like this that make us reflect on our mortality, our transience, and whether we're all just pawns surfing the flighty whims of destiny.

CHET: Beautifully said, sir.

MAYOR BUTTONS: Budgets smudgets?

CHET: The latter part.

MAYOR BUTTONS: You're right. I should work it into the letter. Let's see here . . . Ah, it's refreshing to put pencil to paper. It's a dead art, letter writing.

CHET: That it is, sir.

MAYOR BUTTONS: Now what was it I said?

CHET: "It's events like this that make us reflect on our mortality, our transience, and whether we're all just pawns surfing the flighty whims of destiny."

MAYOR BUTTONS: Chet, I feel sickly.

CHET: Perhaps it is a bit wordy.

MAYOR BUTTONS: No no, physically. My mouth has gone numb. I've become dizzy. The pencil! I think I may have lead poisoning from sucking the pencil tip! Get a doctor immediately!

CHET: The doctor's dead, sir.

MAYOR BUTTONS: By god!

(MAYOR BUTTONS dies, head slamming to the desk.)

CHET: Mayor Buttons? Sir?

(Cautiously, CHET pokes him a few times. It's apparent MAYOR BUTTONS has expired. CHET begins to laugh nervously.)

CHET (CONT'D): Can it be? Sir? Oh happy day!

(CHET'S laughter gradually becomes ecstatic as he revels deliriously at his boss's death.)

CHET (CONT'D): The twit is dead! He's really dead! Now I'm in charge! The city is mine! All mine! At last we'll see what a real mayor does! Out of my chair, jelly brain! *(Removes MAYOR BUTTONS from his office chair, letting him thump to the floor. CHET sits behind the desk, liking it very much.)*

CHET *(CONT'D): (Settling in, getting comfortable, perhaps hugging the desk.)* Oh baby. Oh yeah. Oh, you feel good to papa. Oh yeah, papa could get used to this. Sweet, corrupting power—papa likes how you taste. Which reminds me: lunch!

(CHET takes the wrapped sandwich from earlier. Unwraps and begins to eat, mocking MAYOR BUTTONS as he does, chuckling and enjoying himself.)

CHET *(cont'd)*: "You call this a sandwich! Lunch from a vending machine! What is this – City Hall or a Stuckey's!" Ha ha! What a dip shit!

(CHET begins to choke on the sandwich. He coughs and clutches in a brief frenzy, finally surrendering to the inevitable.)

CHET *(cont'd)*: Am I the only one that didn't see this coming?

(CHET dies, head slamming to the desk.)

(Blackout.)

END OF PLAY

Dream Lover
Michael Weems

Dream Lover premiered at Playwrights Roundtable of Orlando – Summer Shorts 2014. Performed July 25 - August 3rd, 2014 at the Rita Lowndes Orlando Shakespeare Center's Santos Dantin Studio.

Produced by: Charles Dent

JULIA: Christi Griffith
RYAN: Laura Dewey
Directed by: Kristen Dewey

JULIA: Thirties. Insecure and on edge.
RYAN: Thirties. Comforting and worried about Julia.

SETTING: A bed room. Early morning.
PROPERTIES: Mobile phone. Pill bottle.

(Julia is in bed and getting ready to sleep. She has on glasses and is reading a book. Slowly she falls asleep. Ryan enters. He sits at the end of the bed and smiles)

RYAN: What's it going to be tonight?
(Julia stretches and looks up. Sleepy, she smiles)
JULIA: Ryan. Hello. Gosh, I don't know. So many options.
RYAN: Pirate and damsel on the high seas?
JULIA: Good, but a little complicated.
RYAN: Strangers on a business trip?
JULIA: I like that one too. I don't know—
RYAN: Did something go wrong today?
JULIA: Same old. Job sucks. Car's broken down. Took forever to fall asleep tonight, as usual.
RYAN: It's fine. Now you're asleep and I'm here.
JULIA: Why can't you happen in real life?
RYAN: Give it time.
JULIA: What if all this waiting is for nothing?
RYAN: It never is.
JULIA: Sure. Sure. Let's play.
RYAN: Where would you like to go tonight?
JULIA: A country wedding. The whole family is staying in one of those big plantation houses. One of those huge, elaborate week long weddings full with plans and brunches and revelry.
RYAN: The groom?
JULIA: Of course, silly.
RYAN: Of course.
JULIA: You'd look so handsome in just a suit. No tux.
RYAN: And you?
JULIA: A nice, elegant, non poofy dress.

RYAN: Sure.

JULIA: Well?

RYAN: We can play . . . it's just—

JULIA: What?

RYAN: This is different. Usually your dreams are a little more . . . risqué. Intimate. Adventurous.

JULIA: Sometimes a girl wants stability. Okay? For some, that's a fantasy. A dream.

RYAN: Did you see your doctor today?

JULIA: We've already talked about my day. Enough.

RYAN: Of course.

JULIA: *(Hesitant)* Yes, I saw Dr. Green today.

RYAN: And?

JULIA: I got the lecture.

RYAN: I'm sorry.

JULIA: Drink too much, smoke too much. And then I let slip about the sleeping pills.

RYAN: What?

JULIA: You too? Really?

RYAN: You've never had trouble sleeping.

JULIA: I know.

RYAN: You can't mess around with those.

JULIA: I just want to sleep longer. Every day. Don't you want to be with me?

RYAN: Of course.

JULIA: Problem solved. Where were we?

RYAN: A lovely, country wedding.

JULIA: I'm going to have five bridesmaids. No, four. Erin's a bitch.

RYAN: Then, I'll have four groomsmen. Even is good, right?

JULIA: Perfect. Would you like your own cake?

RYAN: Sure.

JULIA: What kind?

RYAN: Julia—

JULIA: Maybe I should just wake up tonight, hmm?

RYAN: I do enjoy our time together.

JULIA: Me too. Me too.

RYAN: Tomorrow, then?

JULIA: Sure.

(Julia lies back down and closes her eyes. Ryan lingers nearby.)

I'm having trouble waking up.

RYAN: Slowly.

JULIA: My eyes feel like they're glued shut.

RYAN: Have you tried sitting up?

JULIA: A lead weight on my chest.

RYAN: Oh well. Might as well stay the night.

JULIA: Don't sound disappointed.

RYAN: Did you set your alarm?

JULIA: Does it matter?

RYAN: No. You sleep through it every time. Your boss?

JULIA: Pissed as always. I'm on 'probation'. I have to be on time every day for a month or I get fired.

RYAN: That's ridiculous? No written warning? No chance to defend yourself?

JULIA: I burned through all of those last month.

RYAN: Right.

JULIA: It's okay. Like I said, job sucks. Always another one around the bend.

RYAN: Sure, Julia. Want to try this again?

JULIA: *(Unemotional)* Wedding, we kiss, we dance, we barely eat our food, we consummate, we wake up and it's another day.

RYAN: Maybe another time, huh?

JULIA: Yeah. Thanks for trying.

RYAN: It's getting bright out.

JULIA: Damn.

RYAN: How many of those did you take?

JULIA: Just one.

RYAN: Really?

JULIA: Geez, yes. I'll be careful, ok?

Ryan: Otherwise, we wouldn't get to see each other anymore.

JULIA: No way.

RYAN: That's a fact.

JULIA: This is the only thing that feels right. You. Why can't you be here with me all the time?

RYAN: I'd like that too.

JULIA: What if I just quit my job and nap all day?

RYAN: I'll be there.

JULIA: How am I going to get through this day?

RYAN: You can do this. Just get there on time, punch the clock, smile and nod—make sure you eat.

JULIA: And then?

RYAN: Drive home, no sleeping pills, close your eyes . . . .

JULIA: Where are we going tomorrow, Ryan?

RYAN: A tropical cruise. So many islands to explore.

JULIA: Lovely. When does this get easier?

RYAN: Soon, Julia. Soon.

(An alarm starts to sound)

You're being beckoned.

JULIA: Please, no. I want to stay here with you.

RYAN: I've got to go. Open your eyes, love.

JULIA: No, please?

(Ryan exits. Julia lays back. She closes her eyes. A moment later she sits up and opens them. The alarm is blaring and she's surrounded by noise. She hits the alarm hard, breaking it and silencing it. From her bedside, she pulls out a pill bottle. She unscrews the cap and takes one. She dials into her phone)

Voicemail, yes. *(She affects a sick voice)* This is Julia, sorry. Woke up sick. Don't want to contaminate everyone. Bye.

(She hangs up the phone. She takes a pill. She lays back and closes her eyes)

Ryan? (Long beat) Ryan . . . . where are you?

(Lights out)

End of Play

DRINKS BEFORE FLIGHT
Lisa Kenner Grissom

ORIGINAL PRODUCTION
Drinks Before Flight was originally produced by
Boston Playwrights' Theatre in association with
Theatre On Fire as part of the Boston Theatre Mara-
thon. Stanford Calderwood Pavilion, Boston, MA.
May11, 2014

Producer: Boston Playwrights' Theatre
Artistic Director, Kate Snodgrass
ksnodgra@bu.edu

CAST
Ellen: Susan Lombardi-Verticelli
Lucas: Bill Mootos
Directed by Linda M. Sutherland

ELLEN: mid-thirties/arty executive attire, any ethnicity. A successful landscape architect. She lives in
a city like New York or Chicago.

LUCAS: mid-thirties/ business suit, any ethnicity.
A political operative type, a lawyer. Lives in L.A.

SETTING:

This is Lucas' home city and Ellen is passing through.
The play takes place at LAX in one of the terminals
at a bar/restaurant; past security and apart from the
gates, but within earshot of PA announcements.

*The play takes place at LAX, but this could be any airport,
in any major city. If the production wishes to change the
location of the airport or the home cities of either of the
characters, the professions and references would need
to be changed to reflect the chosen city.*

AUTHOR'S NOTES:

A slash mark (/) indicates overlapping dialogue.
A dash (—) indicates interrupted dialogue.
Underlined (__) dialogue indicates simultaneous
dialogue.

*The actor playing Ellen is encouraged to find organic
places to check the time and can use her watch or her
phone, whichever is preferable. DRINKS BEFORE
FLIGHT*

*A bar/restaurant at Los Angeles International (LAX).
Ambient sounds of departure and gate announcements.
ELLEN and LUCAS sit across from each other with
drinks and a small bowl of nuts.*

ELLEN: Weird huh. A drink at the airport in your own town.
LUCAS: I'm in and outta here so much these days, it's practically my office.

ELLEN: I rarely get out this way so I figured what the hell/
LUCAS: Caution to the wind.
ELLEN: Something like that. Anyway, I'm glad I caught you.
She checks her watch or phone.
ELLEN (CONT'D): We don't have much time so I've come up with three questions.
LUCAS: Incredible. How about we have our drinks first.
ELLEN: To out-of-the-blue calls—I mean emails—from old friends.
They clink and drink. A beat, then
ELLEN (CONT'D): Are you happy?
LUCAS: Seriously. First question?
ELLEN: We only have about twenty minutes and—
He glances at her ticket.
LUCAS: You got plenty of time.
ELLEN: I like to get to the gate early and—
LUCAS: Right I remember. Gossip mags, check. Double latte, check.
ELLEN: I'm off coffee and I'm into podcasts now.
LUCAS: Gossipy podcasts?
(She gives him a look.)
Yes, gossipy podcasts.
ELLEN: We haven't seen each other in what . . .
(calculating)
LUCAS: Fourteen.
ELLEN: No—
LUCAS: Summer after college. I was headed to law school and you were—
ELLEN: Confused. I was confused for a while. Until I figured it out.
LUCAS: Now you're some kind of rockstar architect.
ELLEN: Landscape architect. Google me lately?
LUCAS: I know your firm. Innovative stuff. Sustainability, all that. Trying to get more of that going here.
ELLEN: You read about landscape architecture.
LUCAS: I'm well-rounded. And you're revamping the LACMA garden space for god's sake. How could I not know about that. Taking work away from LA firms.

ELLEN: We won the contract! Oh right. I forgot about the politics of real estate here.

LUCAS: Everywhere. But yes, especially here.

ELLEN: Your drought is killing my projects. I mean, I like designing with natives but even they're thirsty/
He looks at her quizzically.

ELLEN *(CONT'D)*: Plants, Lucas. I thought you were well-rounded. Well, I hear about you and your mayor all the time.

LUCAS: Since when are you up on politics/

ELLEN: Then all of a sudden I see you outta nowhere on Meet The Press/

LUCAS: You watch that? Party stuff. I hate doing those things.

ELLEN: You look good on TV.

LUCAS: On TV.
Awkward laugh. They drink.

LUCAS: Fourteen years.

ELLEN: That's just crazy/

LUCAS: Crazy. *(beat)* You look the same, but older.

ELLEN: Thanks.

LUCAS: I mean it in a good way. Your whole face sort of . . . contorts when you smile just like I remember. It's very/

ELLEN: Embarrassing/

LUCAS: Reassuring. That some things stay the same.

ELLEN: You didn't answer the question.

LUCAS: I'm avoiding it.

ELLEN: Clearly.

LUCAS: You're still blunt.

ELLEN: Blunt is underrated. I'm still . . . me. Aren't you?

LUCAS: I guess.

ELLEN: Did we know each other—really know each other?

LUCAS: We were twenty-one. We didn't know who we were—even to ourselves. Especially to ourselves.

ELLEN: But we were like . . . best friends.

LUCAS: The key word is "like."

ELLEN: We were more than best friends.

LUCAS: But not quite lovers.

ELLEN: That in-between place.

LUCAS: I would refer to it as that frustrating gray area of maddening confusion.

They laugh a little. She checks her watch/phone.

ELLEN: You might not want to admit this Lucas but there's a part of you that only I understand, and there's a part of me that only you understand. Before those parts got hidden by careers and magazine articles and all that . . . stuff. I know you know what I mean.

LUCAS: Maybe.

ELLEN: And I know it's still there. That part. I miss that part.

LUCAS: I don't suppose we have time for another drink/

ELLEN: I'll start since you won't. 'Are you happy Ellen?' 'Well Lucas . . . I would say that I am . . . modestly happy.'

LUCAS: What does that mean?

ELLEN: That means I am happy. For the most part.

LUCAS: I sense a but.

ELLEN: I'm leaving room for improvement.

LUCAS: Ah there it is/

ELLEN: I'm happily married but our relationship could be . . . more adventurous. The kids don't hate me yet. Work has plateaued but I've made it pretty far. So I'm modestly happy but I'd like to be more happy/

LUCAS: Happier.

ELLEN: Who wouldn't.

LUCAS: My work is . . . never boring.

ELLEN: That's an endorsement. Speaking of, you gonna run your own campaign one of these days? That was your big dream.

LUCAS: One day is getting further and further away so it's doubtful. *(beat)* I didn't want to have kids but we have them.

ELLEN: Lucas, that's a horrible thing to say. What if your wife heard you?

LUCAS: I love them and I couldn't imagine my life without them—

ELLEN: What's her name? I always/forget

LUCAS: What I mean is, I don't know if I'm the best father.

ELLEN: What are you talking about—you're amazing.

LUCAS: You don't know me Ellen. Now.

ELLEN: Ok, I don't know you. I know we could go from debating political theories to analyzing the hidden messages in Radiohead lyrics in a single conversation. I know you drove me to my first interview—which was two hours from campus by the way—because I had a flat tire. I got my first real job because of that. I know you invited me to the senior party . . . dance . . . whatever and then disinvited me/

LUCAS: Uninvited. And I didn't.

ELLEN: You did because in my picture I'm with some other guy whose name I don't remember. And I distinctly remember saying yes to you.

LUCAS: You've been looking through pictures.

ELLEN: Now and then.

LUCAS: You told me you wanted to date other people and . . . 'be free.' I didn't want that. I wanted you. *(beat)* That's why I asked someone else.

ELLEN: I didn't know that.

LUCAS: We were college seniors. Mixed signals abound at that age.

ELLEN: Abounded?

LUCAS: Abound.

ELLEN: Whatever.

LUCAS: What are you mad about? You're the one who asked me here.

ELLEN: You're right. Let's not squander the time.

LUCAS: Good usage.

ELLEN: What is your wife's name? It's driving me crazy.

LUCAS: Ellen.

ELLEN: You're kidding me right?

LUCAS: Nope.
    She drinks.

ELLEN: I was devastated when you broke up with me.
    He drinks.

LUCAS: That's funny. As I remember it, you broke up with

me.

She glances at her watch/phone.

ELLEN: Second question. If you could go back and change one thing, what would it be?

LUCAS: I would have done more drugs.

ELLEN: Seriously?

LUCAS: Seriously. I was too career-oriented. And I should have traveled more.

ELLEN: You travel all the time.

LUCAS: I mean—drive across the country on a motorcycle. That's probably out now. And I shouldn't have gotten married so young.

ELLEN: That's three things.

LUCAS: And . . .

ELLEN: What?

LUCAS: And we should have spent that night together. I shouldn't have let you go. Huh. I didn't expect to say that today. But you thought you could do better.

ELLEN: I never said—

LUCAS: You didn't have to. *(beat)* So did you? Do better?

ELLEN: I am not going to answer that.

LUCAS: Why do you get to ask all the questions? Say whatever you want. We probably won't see each other for another—

ELLEN: Don't say that.

LUCAS: That night came and went. And here we are.

ELLEN: That night might have changed our lives.

LUCAS: But it did.

ELLEN: Could today change our lives?

LUCAS: Are you suggesting a tryst in the first-class lounge? One-way tickets to, I dunno, Australia? Disappear?

ELLEN: Europe. Like . . . Brussels or Amsterdam or—

LUCAS: I could say yes. And then you could change your mind, like before. And where would that leave me? *(beat)* Besides, I might still run for office.

ELLEN: I just wanted to know that you think about it. About us.

LUCAS: I try not to.

It's an awkward moment. One of those moments when it

---

becomes clear they don't know each other as adults.

ELLEN: Rest of your week busy?

LUCAS: Packed. Yours?

ELLEN: Same.

A voice over the PA announces the boarding of her flight. Flustered, she collects her things.

ELLEN (CONT'D): It's time for me to go.

LUCAS: I thought you had three questions.

ELLEN: That's okay. Two was enough.

LUCAS: Go ahead. Shoot.

ELLEN: Did you love me, Lucas?

LUCAS: I did. This stings.

Ellen gets up to go. Then,

LUCAS (CONT'D): I do.

ELLEN: I do. Too.

They look at each other before she hurriedly walks away. He sits alone as lights dim. The PA announces final boarding

END OF PLAY

"Geniuses" was originally produced by the Underground Railway Theater on May 11, 2014, as part of the 16th annual Boston Theater Marathon. Directed by Emily Ranii, the play starred Eliza Rose Fichter as Polly and David Keohane as Wilfred.

Produced by Debra Wise
Artistic Director, Underground Railway Theater
dwise@undergroundrailwaytheater.org

CHARACTERS:

POLLY: a ten-year-old with a penchant for scientific observation.

WILFRED: her long-suffering twin brother with a penchant for setting things on fire.

The twins should not be played by actual ten-year-olds, but by teens or young adult actors.
The setting is a bedroom; the time is anytime in the 20th century.

(AT RISE. POLLY and WILFRED lie in separate beds. WILFRED turns to POLLY.)

WILFRED: I'm really sorry about what happened.
(POLLY does not answer. She reaches for a notebook and pen and begins to write.)

POLLY: 'Sunday, eighty-forty-five p.m. Wilfred issues an apology. Uninspired. Insincere.'

WILFRED: Hey, stop that! It was not insincere!

POLLY: Do you even know what 'insincere' means?

WILFRED: Do so. Lacking earnesty. Honestness. I mean... It was one of our Reading Words last week.

POLLY: I see.

WILFRED: Look, I'm sorry.

POLLY: *(writing)* 'Eight forty-seven. Wilfred attempts repeat apology. Truncated.'

WILFRED: Stop logging me.

POLLY: 'Wilfred projects displaced hostility upon the log.'

WILFRED: I give up. (Silence between the twins. Then . . .)

POLLY: A substantial apology, Wilfred, must fulfill a number of basic requirements.

POLLY (Cont.): For one thing, you should enumerate your offenses, rather than vaguely alluding to 'what happened.' The word 'sorry' ought to be voiced in an emphatic tone. And at the very least you should be on your feet.
(Pause. WILFRED sighs, then shuffles to his feet and stands before POLLY.)

WILFRED: Polly. I am very SORRY that I did not prepare

a project for the science competition, because I was extremely busy the whole week, as George and I were trying to catch a possum, which turned out to be a cat—and I am deeply APOLOGETIC that in order to find an entry to the science competition at the last minute I dug up Old Lady Spencer's rare chrysanthemum, then placed it in the tank where you were keeping your project—and I am extremely full of REMORSE that the chrysanthemum was loaded with pesticides and poisons that killed all the insects in the tank, thus forcing the salamanders to resort to cannibalism. I'm sorry.

(Very long pause as POLLY regards WILFRED.)

POLLY: *(clapping)* That was very good!

(POLLY retrieves a gold star sticker and affixes it to WILFRED'S forehead.)

WILFRED: Hey . . . !

POLLY: *(writing in log* 'Sunday, Eight-fifty-four. Following explicit and careful instruction, Wilfred demonstrates mastery of fundamental apologetic techniques.' Just one thing, though—*newts.*

WILFRED: What?

POLLY: Newts, Wilfred. My science experiment had to do with the habits of newts, not salamanders. They are quite similar, but they are ultimately not the same.

WILFRED: Oh. Sorry.

POLLY: All right, now, no need to go overboard on the sorries. One might start to suspect you're getting greedy for gold stars!

(WILFRED seethes. POLLY scribbles happily in log.)

WILFRED: Well. There may be one or two other things I haven't gotten round to apologizing over.

POLLY: *(still writing, distracted)* To be expected.

WILFRED: For example, I'm sorry I told Aunt Linda you were the one who shaved her dog's ears.

POLLY: Fascinating.

WILFRED: I'm also . . . distraught . . . that I used your red wagon to haul manure and didn't clean it up afterwards.

POLLY: 'Distraught'?

WILFRED: Reading word.

POLLY: Ah.

WILFRED: I'm sorry I used your toothbrush to scrub the toilet.

POLLY: Wilfred!

WILFRED: Do you think you can ever forgive me for telling Brian Fletchley that you've written twelve sonnets on the subject of his eyebrows?

POLLY: How dare you!

WILFRED: I'm also so, so, sorry that I poured maple syrup all over your favorite microscope.

POLLY: You haven't done that.

WILFRED: I plan to. Sorry!

POLLY: *(writing)* '9 o'clock p.m. Wilfred devolving rapidly. Abhorrent, filthy, repugnant child.'

WILFRED: I'll show you who's an Ab Hornet!
(WILFRED snatches log from POLLY, shoves her aside. Punctuates rant by tearing pages from log.)

WILFRED: Now, yesterday, a million years from now and forever, Polly is an annoying, stuck-up, bullying brainiac who deserves to have all her toothbrushes used as toilet scrubs!

POLLY: No!
(POLLY lunges at WILFRED to save her log, but WILFRED kicks her away and leaps triumphant on the bed, where he completes the destruction of the log.)

WILFRED: I . . . always . . . *hated* . . . those gold stars!

POLLY: You rotten fool! You've ruined everything. That was my science project!
(POLLY grabs one of the torn sheets and begins to sob.)

WILFRED: What are you talking about? That's just your stupid log.

POLLY: Idiot. The log was my entry into the competition! *You* were the subject.

WILFRED: No . . . I thought it was that fat salamander that ate all the others . . .

POLLY: Well it wasn't, it was you! I spent hours observing and monitoring and recording . . . And now it's all destroyed . . . My academic reputation in shambles . . . And he wasn't a salamander, he was a newt!

(Renewed sobs.)

WILFRED: What do you mean, I'm a science experiment?

POLLY: Isn't it obvious? The mediocre, thoroughly undistinguished twin sibling of a genius.

WILFRED: Thanks a lot.

POLLY: How can it be we shared a womb, but not a mind? How can we be so similar in so many ways, and yet so fundamentally different? How does the unimpressive sibling cope with the daily challenge of interacting with a superior mind?

WILFRED: It copes fine!

POLLY: I was so careful, so detailed . . . My report was going to break new ground in the scholarship of the merely normal!

(POLLY collapses in sobs. WILFRED sulks.)

WILFRED: Polly . . . Polly, stop.

(POLLY continues to sob.)

WILFRED: Polly . . .

POLLY: Y—yes?

WILFRED: Does this mean I can use the fat salamander?

POLLY: *(rising)* He . . . was . . . a . . . *NEWT!*

(POLLY and WILFRED face off, close in on each other menacingly with each shout.)

WILFRED: Salamander!

POLLY: Newt!

WILFRED: Salamander!

POLLY: Newt!

(WILFRED shouts "Salamander, Salamander, Salamander!" as POLLY begins an equally annoying rant of "Newt Newt Newt!" It builds to an unbearable peak until a loud thumping— as if someone is banging on a wall or the ceiling below—is heard. The twins freeze. A pause.)

WILFRED / POLLY: Sorry mother!

(The following is carried out in strained whispers.)

POLLY: Now look what you've done!

WILFRED: Me! This is your fault, for being such an Ab Hornet!

POLLY: Classic Wilfredian blunder—just the kind of thing that always makes our parents take irrational pity on you.

WILFRED: Believe me, they'll pity you plenty after I'm through.

POLLY: Are you threatening violence? Well—they'll hear!

WILFRED: Not if I rip all your hairs out. Very. Quietly.

POLLY: Don't forget, brother dear, that I happen to know shortcuts to all your essential arteries.
(seizes up pen)
You won't have time to scream!

WILFRED: *(raising hands to strangling position)* Neither will you if I'm choking you!

POLLY: I always knew it would come to this!
(They are poised to attack. Another thump.)

POLLY / WILFRED: WE'RE BEING QUIET!
(Thump.)

WILFRED: *(an epiphany)* Polly!

POLLY: What?

WILFRED: I just had a thought.

POLLY: For the first time, I presume?

WILFRED: Do you think our parents... could be doing an experiment on us?
(POLLY scoffs, but is begrudgingly intrigued. Lowers pen.)

POLLY: Elaborate.

WILFRED: I mean . . . Newts, salamanders, siblings . . . Do you think they've shut us in this room together and are just waiting to see how long it takes us to resort to cannibalism?

POLLY: That's complete and utter . . .

WILFRED: Fine, laugh . . .

POLLY: Genius!

WILFRED: Wait.

POLLY: Wilfred! That's brilliant! Why else would they force

two such fundamentally alien individuals into close, hostile contact with few outlets for respite if not to monitor our responses to the extremities of these conditions?

WILFRED: . . . Exactly!

POLLY: The shared room, the inequitable distribution of household labor—they hope to profit scholastically from our suffering. It all makes sense!

WILFRED: We're lab rats.

POLLY: They must have shelves of logs.

WILFRED: And beakers, and chemicals!

POLLY: It's the only plausible hypothesis.

WILFRED: They could be spying on us right now . . .

POLLY: Oh, Wilfred, you genius, you genius! Now we can take a leaf from your log, and ruin their whole experiment.

WILFRED: With fire!

POLLY: No, Wilfred, not with fire—with subterfuge. We mustn't give dear mother and father what they want.

WILFRED: Never.

POLLY: We won't resort to cannibalism!

WILFRED: We'll act like we like each other!

POLLY: Be helpful, encouraging . . .

WILFRED: Play fair . . .

POLLY: *(taking WILFRED'S hand)* Hold hands! Oh foolish parents, you'll rue the day you tried to trick us!

WILFRED: Yeah! You will so rue! . . . But let's not hold hands.

POLLY: Agreed. Wilfred. We'll have to commit. Until we find those logs, we've got to be the most loving and congenial pair of twins that ever was.

WILFRED: Anything it takes to get back at them. And then we'll find those papers . . .

POLLY: Yes!

WILFRED: And set them on fire!

POLLY: No!

WILFRED: Aw. I'm really good at fire.

POLLY: We have to make a copy first. Then we can set them on fire.

WILFRED: A copy . . . for blackmail!

POLLY: Precisely!

WILFRED: Genius.

POLLY: But we must make sure to hide the copies in a place where they'll never, ever be found.

WILFRED: In a salamander tank?

POLLY: Newt—oh, it doesn't matter. They're a little different, but…

WILFRED: Ultimately the same.

(WILFRED and POLLY embrace. The End.)

Glamping was originally produced by City Theatre and Island City Stage as part of Shorts Gone Wild 2 at Empire Stage in Ft. Lauderdale, Florida. It opened August 7, 2014.

Directed by Teddy Harrell

CAST
Myles: Craig Moody
Kate: Gladys Ramirez

CHARACTERS:

> MYLES: A guy, thirties. A New York. Likes his creature comforts.
>
> KATE: A girl, thirties. Also a New Yorker. Pretty decent camper.

SETTING:

> A campsite. Present Day. Afternoon.

There is a tent that has yet to be assembled as well as a backpack and a duffle bag on the ground. Kate and Myles are crouched down looking at something.

MYLES: I think we should kill it.

KATE: No way! We're the ones intruding on it's space.

MYLES: We're also way higher up on the food chain. This is where we're *sleeping* Kate. It could crawl into our mouths and—

That's an urban myth.

MYLES: It happened to my cousin Charlie. A spider crawled into his mouth and he swallowed it. Never even woke up. Just swallowed it in his sleep.

KATE: Then how does he know he swallowed it? He woke up with the taste of spider in his mouth? Urban myth. We're not killing Charlotte.

MYLES: Okay, A, don't name the spider. And B. . . I forgot what B is. *(Looking at tent)* Are we supposed to put this up ourselves?

KATE: They said camping. What did you expect?

MYLES: It's their wedding weekend and Lisa's father is loaded. I expected *glamping*.

KATE: What the hell is glamping? They start to unpack their stuff.

MYLES: There was an article about it in the travel section last week. It's camping but totally upscale. *Huge* tents, solar panels for electricity, people to cook for you, carry your stuff . . .

KATE: That hardly sounds like camping.

MYLES: Exactly. I'll bet the honeymoon tent is totally tricked out. Turkish rugs and lanterns and-KATE: I highly doubt it. Alex goes camping every year. Really remote spots too. Last year was Botswana. Just because *your* idea of roughing it is when the doormen go on strike . . .

Myles checks his phone. He holds it way up high trying to get a signal.

MYLES: I don't have a signal. Do you have a signal.

KATE: We said no phones this weekend.

Shit.

MYLES: *(Caught)*

KATE: I knew you couldn't stick to it.

MYLES: No. I just—My phone has a compass app. I thought we might need to, I don't know, *navigate* somewhere.

KATE: We'll use the stars.

MYLES: It's noon, Lewis and Clark. What stars?

KATE: Well, navigate *where*?

MYLES: The bathrooms for starters.

KATE: There are no bathrooms.

MYLES: The Port-a-potty, whatever they are.

Kate shakes her head, no.

MYLES: What? No way. I'm not doing that.

KATE: Oh come on, you've peed on 9th avenue more times than that schnauzer in 2A.

Once. I peed on 9th avenue once.

(Off her look)

Okay, twice. *(Beat.)* I've peed on 9th avenue three times. And in my defense, I was drunk all three times. And I'll *pee* outside. No problem. I'm talking about . . . the other thing. I'm not doing that.   I'll wait til we get home.

KATE: We're here for four days.

MYLES: Are you telling me you're going to shit in the woods Grizzly Adams? When did you become all Kum bah yah?

KATE: I think it's important to try new experiences.

MYLES: Some of us have already tried more than our share.

KATE: What is *that* supposed to mean?

MYLES: Where's the Off?

KATE: In my backpack. Seriously, what did you mean by that?
  Myles gets the bug spray and covers himself in it. Kate
  watches him.

MYLES: Nothing. You want some?

KATE: NO

MYLES: You should.   West Nile is no joke.

KATE: Mosquitoes never bite me. We need to hurry up. The
  rehearsal dinner is by some crazy beautiful waterfall but
  we have to hike there.

MYLES: What are we having?   Trail mix?

KATE: Alex is a gourmet chef. I'm sure it will be amazing.

MYLES: Yes yes. The ever amazing Alex. How could I forget?

KATE: What is your—
  Myles makes a loud and completely gross nasal sound.

MYLES: Where's the nasal spray?

KATE: In the duffle.

He gets it and sprays a few shots into each nostril.

KATE: You use too much of that stuff.

MYLES: I can't breathe.

KATE: You're not supposed to use it for more than three days.
  It has a rebound effect.   You'll actually end up *more*
  congested.

MYLES: Yes, but for a moment—Relief.
    (He sprays again)

KATE: You're addicted.

MYLES: It's Afrin, Kate, not heroine.

KATE: Can we just set this thing up.

MYLES: Fine.

KATE: GOOD
    *(They kneel down together and stare at the pile of sticks
    and canvas)*

MYLES: Okay, Pocahontas, Any ideas?

KATE: Oh my god, can you just be the guy for once?
  What is *that* supposed to mean?
    It's like dating Woody Allen.

MYLES: I thought you liked Woody Allen?

KATE: Not to date.

MYLES: Wow. Okay.

KATE: That's not what I- I didn't mean that I don't want to be with you, I just . . .

MYLES: Want me to be more manly. Like Alex.

KATE: *No.* I just want you to stop complaining about every little thing and—

MYLES: Just have fun at your ex's wedding?

KATE: *Ex* being the operative word. Not to mention *wedding.* *Ex's wedding.* And that was a shitty thing to say.

MYLES: What?

KATE: That Alex was manly.

MYLES: She would take that as a compliment and you know it.

KATE: No she wouldn't. Is this why you're being so pissy? You're threatened?

MYLES: By Alex? No. Yes. I don't know. *(Beat.)* It wasn't like you just experimented with a girl in college. You lived together.

KATE: And you lived with three different people before we met. At least they were all *women.*

KATE: So we have that in common.

MYLES: Yeah, well, not really the thing I ever thought I'd have in common with my *girl*friend so . . .

KATE: When we first started dating, you thought it was hot.

MYLES: Yes. In a sexist, girl on girl, let's make a Myles sandwich kind of way, I thought it was hot.

KATE: So now you suddenly have a problem with my past?

MYLES: No. I have a problem with your *present.*   You've been acting funky ever since we got the invitation. You've been criticizing everything I do. You're restless—

KATE: I'm always restless.

MYLES: This is different. It's like you're second guessing your whole life.

KATE: Isn't that kind of normal when an ex gets married?

MYLES: Probably. But, when your ex is a woman, and your current partner *isn't,* it's hard not to think that you might be questioning *everything.* Not just me but *men* in general.

KATE: I love *you,* Myles. Not men in general. And once upon a time, I loved Alex. In both cases, I fell in love with the person, not the gender.

MYLES: Because I know how to compete with a guy. I know my strengths and I'm pretty clear on my weaknesses. I may suck at camping but I'm relatively handsome, I'm well-read, I can name all the members of the supreme court and I make a killer chicken curry. And I also happen to be pretty good at- at- at . . . *you* know.

KATE: Yes, I do. And yes, you are. Better than most guys because I took the time to *learn*, to figure it all out down there. I *studied*. But no matter how good I am . . . there's no *way* I can be as good as another woman at it because . . . well she didn't have to figure it out. You'd be surprised.

MYLES: Really?

KATE: You'd be surprised.

MYLES: You really don't want to get back together with Alex?

KATE: I really don't.

MYLES: Then what is it?

KATE: She didn't want to marry *me*.

MYLES: I knew it!

KATE: I don't want to get back together with her, Myles. I just don't understand . . . why she didn't ask me? What's wrong with me?

MYLES: Nothing is wrong with you. I mean, you're a little neurotic and there is *always hair* and some sort of weird soap scum in your sink but . . . Look . . . She couldn't have asked you because it wasn't even legal when you two were together.

KATE: We could've had a ceremony. Symbolic.

MYLES: But you just said you didn't want to get back together with her.

KATE: She told me she didn't want to do it because it was too bourgeois. She said we were better than that. *More* than that. That we didn't have to fit into anyone else's box idea of what love was. She was obviously lying. Because here she is . . . Marrying a woman who isn't me. It was ten years ago, Kate. People change. Look at us.

KATE: It's not just her. I've been in more than one long-term relationship. Why hasn't anybody asked?

MYLES: You to marry them?

KATE: Yes.

MYLES: Wait. What conversation are we having right now?

KATE: I don't know.

MYLES: Well, because suddenly I feel like I'm supposed to do something here that I'm not sure I—

KATE: No.

MYLES: You're sure?

KATE: I'm sure Myles.

MYLES: Okay.

KATE: Okay. Unless . . . I mean, do you want to?

MYLES: Do you want me to want to?

KATE: Forget it. No! I don't know why I even—No.
    (Beat.)

MYLES: You could have asked *her* just as easily as—

KATE: I know.

MYLES: Why didn't you?

KATE: I couldn't see forever with her.

MYLES: Have you seen forever with anyone?

KATE: No.

MYLES: Probably good that no one has asked you then.

KATE: Almost. One time. I almost saw forever one time.

MYLES: With who.

She turns to him.

MYLES: Really?

KATE: The first time you spent the night at my apartment. It wasn't just the sex. Though that didn't suck. It was the morning after the sex. We were out on the fire escape, drinking our coffee, reading the Times . . . There was no epiphany or anything . . . I just had this flash of . . . forever. Like in some alternative universe, we already had. And then it was gone.

MYLES: And now I'm just this Nasal spray addicted, arachnid killing, Woody Allen.

KATE: Exactly.

MYLES: I'm not going to ask you to marry me this weekend, we should be clear on that.

KATE: Good because I'm not asking you either.

MYLES: Good. *(Beat.)* But if I *were* to ask you, say on

or around this time next year . . . is there a chance in hell you'd say yes?

KATE: There's a chance.

KATE: It's a date, then. Hell, we can even go camping.

KATE: It's a date. But no camping.

MYLES: Why not?

KATE: Because I fucking hate spiders. She tackles him. They start kissing. He stops and looks at her.
What?

MYLES: Flash.

KATE: Really?

MYLES: I'm still not asking you this weekend.

They continue kissing as the lights fade.

END OF PLAY

THE HAPPY F&*#@!G BLIND GUY
Bruce Graham

ORIGINAL PRODUCTION
Produced by Theater Breaking Through Barriers at
the Clurman Theatre—Theatre Row, June 12-29,
2014.

Directed by Russell Treyz

CAST
LARRY: Nicholas Viselli
TIM: David Rosar Stearns

(A grocery check out and a manager's office. Neither are overly realistic. When Tim is working he is miming.)

LIGHTS RISE on Tim, 30's, a pleasant looking man who happens to be blind. He's a bagger in a grocery store and the best damn bagger you ever saw. He deftly feels each purchase and knows instinctively how to bag it.
He's also the happiest sonuvabitch you ever met. Although we don't see the CUSTOMERS he speaks to we get the feeling they really like Tim. A lot.

Tim: Hi, Mrs. Kachinsky, how are you today? Oh, I'm fine. Got up this morning and my feet found the floor. Can't ask for more than that. I'm double bagging your chicken. *(LIGHTS RISE on LARRY, the store manager, who observes Tim from a distance. He will occasionally take notes.)*

TIM: Haven't seen you in a while. Ha—just kidding, I've never seen you.

Larry: That bastard . . .

TIM: Lighter bag today. Husband travelling again?
(Larry pulls out his watch, timing Tim.)

TIM: Oh, I'll travel someday. Lots of countries I'd love to smell.
(lowering his voice slightly but still a big smile)
How long is he gone this time?

LARRY: *(mumbling)* Happy sonuvabitch . . .

TIM: Have a nice day. Hi, Walt.
(Larry writes down the time in his notebook and exits, still muttering to himself.)

TIM: Wow, bacon and sausage today. Hey, none of my business but you were worried about your cholesterol last week. Have you ever tried that turkey bacon?
(Over the LOUDSPEAKER we HEAR Larry.)

LARRY: Tim to the manager's office. Tim to the manager's office.

TIM: Sorry, Walt. You have to finish yourself. Try the turkey

bacon. It's good, you'll see.
(laughing)
Which is more than I will.
(LIGHTS RISE on Larry's office. Larry paces, thinks a moment, pops a TUMS, then moves a chair to the far side of the room. Tim enters.)
LARRY: Hey, Tim—have a seat.
(Tim goes to sit, then stops as if he senses the chair is not there. He waves his cane, finds it, and wheels it back into position.)
TIM: How are you, Larry?
LARRY: Lousy. Wanta' Tums?
TIM: No thanks.
LARRY: I'll cut to the chase here, Tim. I'm getting some complaints about you.
TIM: Me?
LARRY: Yes. Any idea how long it takes you to fill a bag and get it in the cart?
TIM: No.
LARRY: No idea.
TIM: None.
LARRY: Four seconds. The average bagger here does it in twelve.
TIM: *(unsure where this is going)* Okay.
LARRY: And . . .
(an accusation)
You do it right. Eggs on top. Meat separately. Some of these idiots . . . chicken right in with the produce. Orange juice on top of the eggs. But not you. Everything's perfect.
TIM: Okay . . .
LARRY: *Annnnd* . . . you're so . . . happy while you're doing it.
(no reaction)
Well? What do you have to say?
TIM: Customers are complaining about this?
LARRY: No. It's the employees. You make them look bad.
TIM: I don't mean to.
LARRY: There's a lot of resentment. You're going to be Employee of the Month again in August. That's eleven

times in four years.

TIM: Name someone else. I don't mind. It's an honor but it doesn't mean anymore money.

LARRY: You get your picture in front of the store - big as life.

TIM: I'll take your word for it.

LARRY: Okay, this is awkward. And I have to be very careful how I phrase this but . . . well, part of the problem is - there's a rumor going around that you're not really blind. *(Larry moves closer, waving his hand back and forth in front of Tim's face.)*

TIM: Excuse me?

LARRY: Are-you-really-blind?

TIM: Since birth.

(Larry suddenly LEAPS forward to try and make Tim flinch. Nothing.)

TIM: Why would people think that I wasn't blind?

LARRY: How do you do it? How do you just—

(mime quick bagging)

Bang, bang, bang—everything in, everything right.

TIM: Practice.

LARRY: Noooo . . . it's more than that.

TIM: I guess it's because I have extremely sensitive tactile abilities. I can touch something and—for instance, a box of cereal. If you shake it slightly you can tell the difference between Rice Krispies and Cheerios. Cheerios are much more solid. Now with the produce—

LARRY: So you can just touch a product and tell me exactly what it is?

TIM: Canned soup is tough. Campbell's doesn't have braille labels. But most of the time, yes.

LARRY: Sensitive tactile abilities . . .

TIM: Sure. Blind people tend to overdevelop their other senses—

LARRY: Okay—the customers. How the hell do you know who they are?

TIM: I don't know all of them.

LARRY: Last Friday in a one hour span you recognized 74% of the people in line.

(Silence.)

TIM: You counted?

LARRY: It's my job to be on top of things around here, Tim.

TIM: You know there's a lot of stealing going on back on the loading dock. I don't want to tell you your job but maybe you ought to be—

(The PHONE RINGS. Larry grabs it.)

LARRY: Hello . . . what do you want? . . . I thought we weren't talking—it all goes through the lawyers . . . yeah, well, send me an e-mail 'cause I don't want to hear your fucking voice!

(SLAMS down the phone)

My wife. Where were we?

TIM: Seventy-four percent.

LARRY: *(picking up a stapler)* Seventy-four percent! Care to explain that?

TIM: Most of them say hello. "Hello, Tim." And I recognize their voices. Not tough, Larry. I have very sensitive hearing.

(Larry quickly THROWS the stapler at Tim, purposely missing but trying to get him to react. The stapler hits the floor.)

TIM: For instance, I can tell that was a stapler you just threw at me for some reason.

LARRY: And the ones that don't? The ones that don't come up gushing hello to everyone's favorite . . . bag guy. What about them?

TIM: Well, Rhonda Peters wears bracelets that always clank the same way. Walt Gunderson—he was just here— smells like an ashtray with a little beer spilled in it. Ellen Alberts wears this strong—I mean strong—perfume. Joe—don't know his last name —drags one foot. Think he had a stroke. Mrs. Azeem always—

LARRY: Okay, okay, I get it.

(the PHONE RINGS; he grabs it)

What? Jesus Christ, tell Andy to take care of it - what do you mean? I saw him here this morning - why'd he go home this time? Jeeezus, okay, get Diane, get somebody.

We can't have that stuff in the aisle.

(hangs up)

Okay, Tim. I believe you. You're blind.

TIM:

(rising)

Okay. Is that all you need?

LARRY: No . . . not quite.

(Tim sits back down. Larry doesn't speak at first, as if unsure how to proceed.)

LARRY: Okay . . . you want to know what the real problem is here, Tim? The realll reason your co-workers are annoyed. The realllll reason people thought you weren't—look, is "blind" okay? Do you have a preference? Handicapped? No, not handicapped —Christ, sorry. What is it now? Differently . . . challenged?

TIM: Blind is fine.

LARRY: Thanks. The reallll reason people thought you weren't blind? Or . . . you know, that blind.

TIM: Why?

LARRY: Well, it's a lot of things. One of them is . . . you make them all look bad.

TIM: How?

LARRY: How? You're kidding, right - how? You're always on time. You never sneak out early. You're willing to work holidays. You don't steal. You clean up after yourself in the break room. You don't masturbate in the produce section —

TIM: Who does that?

LARRY: I'm sorry, that's confidential.

(lowering his voice)

George. We know it's him we just can't catch him. We're readjusting the surveillance cameras.

TIM: (nodding)He always smells like Jergens.

LARRY: Let's try and stay focused here, Tim. The real reason people were . . . suspicious about your blindness is—

(a deep breath)

You're so . . . fucking . . . happy all the time.

(Silence.)

TIM: Why shouldn't I be?

LARRY: You're blind!

TIM: So?

LARRY: *(frustrated)* So . . . so . . . how can you be happy? I have all my senses and I'm fuckin' miserable. Everybody in this store is miserable. This is not a nice place, Tim.

TIM: Then maybe it's better I don't see it.

LARRY: Okay, okay, that's just what I'm talking about. That fucking, "Gosh, ain't life grand" bullshit. You can't see, you got this crappy job—

TIM: I love this job.

LARRY: How the hell can you love this job? Nobody loves this job!

TIM: The pay's decent. I get to talk to people all day. The bus stops right in front. I get tons of pussy. The benefits are good. Paid holidays—

LARRY: Wait a minute, wait a minute—what'd you just say?

TIM: Paid holidays.

LARRY: No, no—Before that. Something about pussy.

TIM: Oh, right. I get laid like crazy here.

(before Larry can react)

Not with other employees and not in the store. Certainly not in the produce aisle. No workplace rules broken. I'm talking about the customers.

LARRY: Which customers?

TIM: I'm not naming names. Let's just say this is a great way to meet women.

LARRY: But you're blind. How do you even know if they're attractive?

TIM: That's the best part. I don't.

LARRY: You mean you're hittin' on the customers when you're supposed to be baggin' their groceries.

TIM: They hit on me. I'm the new taboo. The new forbidden fruit. There's no boundaries anymore, which is terrific. It used to be, "Ohh . . . I'm sleeping with a black guy." Well, nobody bats an eye at that anymore. So now it's, "Ohhh . . . I'm sleepin' with a blind guy." Or a deaf guy. Or a mentally challenged guy. I'm tellin' ya, Larry, we're

---

doin' great. This is the golden age of differently-abled sex. I've got a buddy who's a quadriplegic who has to beat 'em off with a stick. Well, if he could.

LARRY: *(processing)* Women want to . . . sleep with you . . . 'cause you're . . . blind?

TIM: Well, the first time. They come back again because . . . well . . .

(he shrugs)

They love my sensitive tactile abilities. I have great hands, I'm told. And blind people are very good listeners. Comes with the territory. Women love that, trust me. There's been a couple pity fucks. Oh, that poor blind guy. That's usually around Christmas. Kind of a Tiny Tim thing I guess. So, uhh, granted this isn't the most glamorous job in the world but I like it just fine.

(a satisfied smile)

Can't beat the fringe benefits.

LARRY: So . . .

(he picks up a pen)

If I gouged my eyes out with this pen I could get laid, that what you're tellin' me?

TIM: Well, after you heal maybe. Otherwise you look like Oedipus.

LARRY: Who?

TIM: Oedipus. Oedipus Rex.

LARRY: He new here?

TIM: *(starting to rise)*

That all you need, Larry?

LARRY: No. We still have this other problem.

TIM: What other problem?

LARRY: Employee morale.

(moves from behind the desk)

Look, Tim, do me a favor.

TIM: Sure.

LARRY: I really need you to be a shittier employee. Be nice to the customers all you want—fine—do your happy blind guy thing. But with the rest of us could you maybe be a little . . . surly once in a while. Grumble about what a crappy place this is to work. Bag a little slower. Leave a mess in the break room. Maybe come in late once a month.

TIM: I don't know, Larry. I take pride in my work.

LARRY: Pride in your work? What is your problem? Why are you busting my balls?

TIM: I don't mean to—

LARRY: Please, for me, take a little less . . . pride. Oh, and for God's sake don't say a word about what we talked about here.

(off Tim's look)

The fringe benefit thing. They hear about that they'll really hate you.

(Tim says nothing. Larry waits, anxious. Finally, Tim sighs.)

TIM: Okay. I'll try to be a shittier employee.

LARRY: That's all I'm askin'.

TIM: *(rising)*

Can I get back now?

LARRY: Yeah, sure.

(Tim exits. Larry sits there a moment, replaying the conversation in his head. He picks up the pen again, holds it to his eye, realizes he can't go through with it and drops it on the desk.)

LARRY: Lucky blind bastard . . .

(LIGHTS RISE on Tim at his check out line.)

TIM: Hi, Mrs. Carlson. All alone today. Where's the kids?
(he listens)
Right, camp. That time of year again. Sleep away camp?
(he listens)
Wow, no kids for two weeks.
(he smiles)
Must get awfully lonely.

(LIGHTS FADE.)

HOME GOING

Liv Matthews

Produced by Playwrights' Round Table, *Home Going* premiered January 9, 2015, at the Santos Dantin Studio at the Orlando Shakespeare Theater. It was directed by Tara Rewis and Chuck Dent. The cast was as follows:

CAST:
JILL: YaDonna Russell
VALERIE: Kareen Kennedy

CHARACTERS:
>JILL: Late thirties, African-American, A remorseful but hopeful mother.
>VALERIE: Twenty, her disillusioned daughter.

SETTING:
>Present day. An abandoned pre-teen's bedroom. A warm fall morning in Florida.

SCENE ONE
>*A preteen girl's bedroom. Posters of pop and R&B stars from the recent past line the wall. Stuffed animals and dolls lie on the floor. A duffle bag sits on the unmade bed. At the vanity sits VALERIE, twenty, examining her makeup. She is wearing a youthful but sophisticated black dress. As she touches up her blush, her mother, JILL, late thirties, appears in the doorway. Wearing a robe and her hair covered in a scarf, she has just gotten out of bed. With the last moments of sleep escaping her eyes, she looks at her daughter solemnly.*

JILL: Valerie.
VALERIE: Ah! God, you scared me.
JILL: You dont need all that makeup.
VALERIE: I know I don't need it, but I like it.
>*(Jill enters the room, examining the contents on the vanity.)*
JILL: When I'm sending you money, this is where it goes?
VALERIE: No, Mama, Grandma took me shopping before I left for school.
JILL: Of course she did.
>*(A long awkward silence.)*
VALERIE: Good morning.
JILL: Morning.
VALERIE: Why aren't you dressed?
JILL: Just got up. I wanted to check in on you. You ready?
VALERIE: Almost. I'm getting there?
>*(Another silence. JILL begins to straighten out of the*

bed. VALERIE moves to her closet to peruse her shoes. She pulls out two pairs of heels.)

VALERIE: Should I wear my high heels, or my higher heels?

JILL: It's a funeral, not the club . . . You got some flats?

VALERIE: I don't have flats.

JILL: You got the pair I sent you the other month. You don't wear them?

VALERIE: Sometimes. To class, maybe . . . They're in my bag. I'll get them.

(She goes into her duffle bag and pulls out a pair of plain black flats. She puts them and begrudgingly models.)

JILL: Much better. They're more sensible. Besides, you'll be standing a lot at the end. I learned that at your granddaddy's funeral. You wanna be comfortable. Those heels will do you no good. And bring a jacket. It's hot out but it's cold in that church. Got it?

VALERIE: Yes ma'am.

JILL: Good girl.

VALERIE: You know, you don't have to clean my room.

JILL: I know I don't. But I want to. I haven't had to do it in forever. Everything was just sitting there before, stuck in time. When I saw you sitting there, it reminded me of when you used to fool around with your aunt's makeup bag. You'd pick up a brush before you'd pick up your toys. Looking at you, you were my baby girl again, and I used to clean my baby girl's room sometimes . . . Just let me be your mother.

VALERIE: Mr. Fluffins goes on the right side, next to Minnie Mouse.

JILL: Of course he does. I remember now. There we go. That's better, isn't it?

VALERIE: Yes ma'am.

JILL: And I know I'm your mother, but stop with this "ma'am" thing. I'm not that much older than you. A simple "yes" is good enough.

VALERIE: It's just something Grandma taught me.

JILL: I'm sure she had good intentions.

VALERIE: Right.

JILL: How are your grades?

VALERIE: This semester? They're okay, I guess. Everyone's grades are okay right now. School started a month ago.

JILL: Make sure they stay that way. You gotta keep that scholarship, I can help out now with the cafe picking up all, but even that's not much for where you're at . . . I'm proud of you.

VALERIE: Thank you . . . You said the cafe is doing okay?

JILL: Yeah, actually. Everyone lies coffee, and those high school girls really love those frappe things. They come in after school and just talk away. It reminds me of when I used to see you with your friends.

Valerie: Well, I'm glad you're getting to use that business degree.

JILL: Took me long enough to get it. Almost twenty years! Honestly, I'm surprised it's doing so well in a sleepy town like this. Maybe it just needed an espresso shot.

VALERIE: Hmm.

(Another pause. JILL looks around the room to find something to talk about. She chooses a poster.)

JILL: I remember you used to like that group. I got you that shirt that time. I don't think I ever saw you wear it. Did you wear it?

VALERIE: When I could. That's when I started wearing uniforms to school. I wore it on the weekends, though.

JILL: Good! I knew you liked that group. All the young girls did then. I tried to tell your grandma about that, but you know she didn't listen to me.

VALERIE: She took my friends and me to that concert for my birthday that year.

JILL: Oh, right . . .

(Though hesitant, JILL rises and begins to play in her daughter's hair, twirling it around in her fingers and then brushing it down smooth.)

VALERIE: Mama . . .

JILL: I used to do this to you all the time when you were a little girl, a tiny thing. your hair used to be all over the place, wild and puffy. I didn't know someone so little could have that much hair. I tried to tame it with braids and bows for awhile but then I just got so tired. Ha! I just let it be. It still smells the same way, too, like coconuts. You still use that same stuff I used on it, don't you? That hair polish. Just like my little baby . . .

VALERIE: Please don't touch me.

JILL: My bad. I'm sorry.

VALERIE: No, it's fine. I, um, I just did it so I want it to look nice.

JILL: Of course.

(JILL sits back on the bed.)

VALERIE: you're not going, are you?

JILL: What?

VALERIE: You're not going to the funeral.

JILL: Um, I—

VALERIE: You're stalling. Go get dressed.

JILL: I will. Just give me a second . . . it's rough, okay?

VALERIE: The limo will be here soon.

(VALERIE reached for her lipstick on the vanity. She opens the tube. It's a sultry red.)

JILL: Don't wear that.

VALERIE: What?

JILL: You know what I'm talking about. That. Put that away. You'll look just like her.

VALERIE: But Mama—

JILL: I don't want to have to say it again.

VALERIE: No.

JILL: Excuse me?

VALERIE: I said no. I'm wearing it for Grandma Della. That's her thing. I'm wearing it for her. It's in commemoration.

JILL: It's a funeral.

VALERIE: It's a home going service, a celebration. Or at least that's what's going to get me through the day so let me have that.

JILL: I'm not going.

VALERIE: Mama—

JILL: Don't "Mama" me. I said I'm not going.

VALERIE: Okay . . . So we're not gonna talk about it? That's it?

JILL: I don't have to explain myself to you.

VALERIE: And that's fine, but let's not act like it's not a little, a little—

JILL: What?

VALERIE: Selfish. There are a lot of people coming and they want to see you.

JILL: They ain't there to see me.

VALERIE: I understand that but I think we both know why it would be important for them to see you, and maybe even the two of us together.

JILL: If it takes my mother to have a heart attack for them to get that, I don't want anything to do with it.

VALERIE: I know this is a ridiculous concept but has it ever dawned on you in this last week that today may not be about only you? Get dressed.

JILL: Who do you think you talking to?! Look, I'm sure your grandmother had plenty to say about me, I'll promise you most of it is true, but have some sense when you speak to me.

VALERIE: I don't have to do anything. I stopped being your daughter a long time ago.
(VALERIE takes the lipstick again and fills in her lips completely.)

JILL: I said stop it!
(Suddenly, JILL grabs VALERIE by her arms and pulls her out of her seat. She goes to strike the girl across her face, but VALERIE catches her arm and pushes her off.)

VALERIE: And this is exactly what!! What? You thought I was just gonna let you do it again. You sit her getting nostalgic, romanticizing things that came from a nightmare of a childhood, and I'm suppose to be okay? Did you have another flashback? You must have really thought this was like the old times.

JILL: I'm so sorry. I don't know what—

VALERIE: Save the sorry. I'm about to stand in a line and hear a bunch of people who don't know me tell me they're sorry. And for what? I don't even know what they're saying it for. Is it that my angel is gone or because I'm left with you?

JILL: It's all I've got. I've always had to say sorry. That's all I'm good for, a walking apology. I never did anything right, school, boys, work, nothing. I swear, if I had to say it to Mama one more time. I even had to say it about you. And i thought she was gonna be so mad and do something horrible—

VALERIE: Do not twist this on her.

JILL: Dammit, Valerie! Where do you think I got it from?
(A painful pause.)

VALERIE: I'm going to pretend that I didn't say that.

JILL: Pretend all you want. It's true. And it was just me, too, no one else. I was gonna say she stopped because of you. Yeah, I got pregnant with you and she found The Lord. I guess babies and Jesus make you soft. And she seemed straight so when I couldn't do it anymore, I sent you with her. But trust me, I kept an eye on her. Because if it was gonna happen—Anyway, that's why I sent you with her. She was better than me, even to the day she died. She was better than me . . . That's what you want to hear, right?

VALERIE: I've got a story for you, too, since you want to relive the past . . . There was this one time, the last time. Mama, I saw stars. And then a bunch of blood. My lip was fat. And I had to pretend it was a playground accident. Everyone believed it because there was no way Ms. Della Jordan's girl would hit that baby. Jill wouldn't hit that baby. At least not where they could all see it. But Grandma knew . . . How can you even look at me, on the day of her funeral, and accuse her of—She never touched a hair on my head, you understand me? Never. You didn't send me with her. She rescued me. And even if what you're saying is true, which I doubt, it's obviously more than you can say for yourself.

JILL: What else do you want from me?

VALERIE: I don't know but this isn't it.

(Outside, a car pulls up in the driveway.)

JILL: This must be your ride.

VALERIE: You're really not gonna go?

JILL: Valerie, I've messed up since I entered the world. We all have, but I can't lie and say I haven't messed up more than others. My biggest sin, other than the obvious, is lying. I've been lying to myself my whole life and I gotta stop. On the day I should be most reverent, the most honest, y'all want me to stand up in a church, before God, and pretend I felt something about this woman I haven't felt in a long time. I'm not in the lying business anymore. And you shouldn't have to be either . . . So, when you get back, your bags will be packed. Talk to your auntie after the service. I'm sure she'll let you stay with her until you need to go back to school. She'll understand.

(VALERIE begins to collect a few things around the room and puts them in her purse. She crosses to the door.)

VALERIE: All you had to do was keep it to yourself. At least for today.

(She exits. Broken, JILL takes a moment to collect herself on the bed. She takes on of the stuffed animals and holds on to it like a baby for a few moments. Then, she sets it down gently and sits down in front of the vanity, looking at the makeup her daughter left behind. She takes the lipstick and paints her lips perfectly red. Looking in the mirror, she soaks herself in for a few beats. Slowly, she wipes off the lipstick with the back of her hand. And then violently. VALERIE returns and steps at the door for a few moments to watch the red mess.)

VALERIE: Mama.

BLACKOUT.

KILL ME, PLEASE!
Rhea MacCallum

Originally produced by Theatre Encino as part of Valentine's Day Massacre & Other Love Stories, February 19 & 20, 2011. Directed by Eric Ashmore.

CAST:
GLORIA: Shannon Nelson
STAN: Joshua Sterling

Also produced by Artists' Exchange in Cranston, RI, July 25 - August 16, 2014 as part of their 9th Annual One-Act Festival. Directed by Jessica Bradley.

CAST:
GLORIA: Lauren Ferreira
STAN: Michael Shallcross

Melanie Ewbank, Theatre Encino producer, theatre-encino.literary@gmail.com
Jessica Bradley, Artists' Exchange producer, jessica.bradley@artists-exchange.org

CHARACTERS:

> GLORIA: Thirties, modestly dressed.
> STAN: Thirties, wearing a long, dark trench coat.

SYNOPSIS:

> It's late at night. The street is deserted. A serial killer is on the loose. A young woman sits and waits. Expectantly.

SETTING:

> Park bench.

TIME:

> Late at night.

GLORIA, thirties, modestly dressed, is sitting on a park bench. Night. Nearby lamppost occasionally flickers. She's holding a book or magazine, but spends more time checking her surroundings than attempting to read. She smiles and seems almost giddy as a scruffy looking man, STAN, thirties, wearing a long dark trench coat approaches. He looks around before sitting down.

GLORIA: Hello!
  (STAN mumbles something and gives a slight head nod. GLORIA appears eager for something to happen. It does, STAN moves closer. GLORIA smiles.)
STAN: You know a pretty girl such as yourself shouldn't be out so late. All. Alone.
GLORIA: You think I'm pretty?!
  (Stan is thrown.)
STAN: Do you have the time?
GLORIA: Twelve, eighteen and . . . 30 seconds.

STAN: Kinda late.

GLORIA: Yes.

STAN: Pretty dangerous. Neighborhood.

(He moves closer. She is not intimidated by this.)

GLORIA: I know.

STAN: You waiting for somebody?

GLORIA: Yes.

STAN: In this neighborhood, at this hour? Who you lookin' to meet?

GLORIA: The Slasher. I understand this is a favorite haunt of his. You know who I mean, that serial killer who's been in the news lately?

STAN: Yeah . . .

GLORIA: He's done some really interesting work.

(She makes jabbing motions that startle him.)

Totally disembowels his victims.

STAN: Right.

GLORIA: I'm here to meet him. Hopefully.

STAN: Why?

GLORIA: Because.

STAN: Because, why?

GLORIA: I don't want to tell you, unless you're him. Are you The Slasher?

STAN: If I were, would I admit to it?

GLORIA: Why would you deny it? The Slasher is brilliant. His work will be studied for years. There's no question. He's got a real technique.

STAN: So you want to meet him?

GLORIA: Well, if you must know, I intend on being his next victim.

STAN: Really.

GLORIA: *(Throughout she is trying to determine whether or not Stan is The Slasher.)*

Oh, yes. I've read everything about him and I've grown to admire his work. How he makes a small incision at the jugular first, then ties his victims hands behind their back and disembowels them as they writhe. The paper said he uses rope but I'm afraid that'll chaff my wrists

---

so I brought a latex tie.

(She pulls it out of her purse.)

And I went to Super Cuts for a new do and the Clinique counter for a facial. I hope he doesn't mind leaving me face up or seated, seated would be better. I'd like the pictures to look good. I realize I'll never get to see them, so whatever happens, happens, I guess I'll have to be okay with it. I just thought it would be nice, for the newspapers and books and all, to at least be pretty in death.

(Pause.)

So how do you want to do this? Is there a position you want me to get into? Or . . . ? You are The Slasher, aren't you?

STAN: Slasher. Just Slasher.

GLORIA: But in the paper—

STAN: Reporters. Think they're so smart. I signed my letter Slasher. Just Slasher. There's really no need to tack on a definite article. I don't like it. I'm Slasher.

GLORIA: Oh, I kind of liked it. The Slasher.

(He grimaces.)

But Slasher works.

(Pause.)

So, what should I do? Tell me what to do.

STAN: Why do you want to die?

GLORIA: I'm ready.

STAN: Why?

GLORIA: I don't really have anything to live for?

STAN: Family?

GLORIA: Oh, my mother's dead. My father abandoned us when I was a child. I have a half-sister somewhere, but the last time I sent a Christmas card to her it came back—no forwarding address.

STAN: Friends?

GLORIA: There's someone I sometimes eat lunch with at work when I'm running late and have to eat in the cafeteria.

STAN: Okay.

GLORIA: But I don't really like her very much. I'd be happier eating alone, but every time she sees me in the cafeteria she waves me over and I go because it would be rude to just ignore her.

STAN: Neighbors?

GLORIA: Eh. Most are closed doors and TV hums through hallway walls. There is an old man with a cat who lives downstairs. He looks at me funny. The only conversation, if you call it that, we ever had, he offered that he'd let me pet his pussy, if I let him pet mine. Needless to say, he gives me the creeps.

STAN: But I don't?

GLORIA: No.

STAN: Even though I'm Slasher.

(She shrugs.)

GLORIA: Can we do this now? Will you kill me? Please.

STAN: No.

GLORIA: What?

STAN: I don't think so.

GLORIA: But I'm here and you're here and I'm ready.

(Pause.)

This is so typical. I never get what I want. Nothing ever works out for me. Why won't you kill me? I'm here. I'm ready. I'm willing.

STAN: You're not scared!

(Quieter.)

STAN – cont.: I need you to be afraid. You're a lot of things but afraid isn't one of them.

GLORIA: I could be afraid.

(He scoffs.)

Here, let me try.

(She makes a face. He shakes his head. She tries again. He's unmoved.)

Maybe if you pulled out your knife.

(He does so.)

Ooooooo, shiny!

STAN: Oh, geez.

GLORIA: What? It's pretty.

(Uses it to look at herself, fixes her hair, then nicks her finger.)

And sharp! Bet that's handy.

STAN: Ginsu. Doesn't just cut through aluminum cans. This baby breezes through cartilage, small bones—

GLORIA: Cool.

STAN: No, not cool. Big shiny knife is supposed to scare you, but there's no fear here. I prey on the unsuspecting. That's my joy. But you! You saw me coming. I lean into you.

(He does so, she smiles.)

And you smile. What is up with that? I'm creepy. I haven't showered in days. My smell should repulse you. I'm wearing a trench coat. It's not cold out. I don't need the layers. It's dark, it's late, you're a woman, I'm a man. You're supposed to be afraid of me.

(He gets in her face.)

GLORIA: You have the most beautiful eyes.

STAN: What?!

GLORIA: Has anyone ever told you that?

STAN: My eyes have seen unspeakable horrors, the like you can't even begin to imagine.

GLORIA: Oh, I'm sure. Abusive mother, alcoholic father—

STAN: Nonono. Well, yes, but I mean horrors of my own creation. I have done things to the human body no one should ever do.

GLORIA: Don't doctors and scientists dissect bodies? I bet with a better up bringing you could've been a doctor.

STAN: No, it's not the same. Wait. Really? You think I could've been a doctor.

GLORIA: Totally. The paper said your cuts are clean and precise. Like a surgeon.

STAN: Really? What paper was that in?

GLORIA: Press Telegram.

STAN: Damn, I missed that one. Do you remember what date that came out?

GLORIA: *(Pulling a scrapbook from her purse.)*It was a couple weeks ago.

(Flips through pages.)

See, right there.

(Pointing it out to him.)

Like a surgeon.

STAN: Well, I'll be.

GLORIA: That's part of what helped me decide that you should be the one to kill me. I figured if that was true, you must really care about your work.

STAN: *(Flipping through the book some more.)* I'm so perplexed.

GLORIA: Why?

STAN: I'm not sure if I should kill you or marry you.

GLORIA: Marry!

(Stands up. Truly offended.)

I came here to die, not to be tortured!

STAN: Settle down. It's just . . . I don't think anyone's ever shown such an interest in me, my work, before. I mean, not like this.

(Waves scrapbook.)

GLORIA: Oh, well. That's just a hobby of mine. Scrapbooking.

STAN: Yeah?

GLORIA: Only most of my scrapbooks are of places, not people.

STAN: Your vacations?

GLORIA: Not exactly.

(Pause.)

I've never been anywhere. I just like to collect pretty pictures of places and group them together.

STAN: Places you want to visit?

(She nods.)

Like where?

GLORIA: The African Safari. Castles in Ireland and Scotland, where everything is so green. France. The countryside, not Paris. Paris is so . . . overdone.

STAN: Why don't you go to one of those places?

(Pause.)

Just pick one and go.

GLORIA: By myself?

(He shrugs, why not.)

That just seems . . . too . . . sad.

STAN: Maybe you'd meet someone along the way.

GLORIA: I couldn't.

STAN: Why not?

GLORIA: I'd rather die.

STAN: Damn.

GLORIA: What?

STAN: I don't want to kill you, but . . . You can identify me. That's a problem. I kinda can't let you live at this point, can I?

GLORIA: So you'll do it?

STAN: No.

GLORIA: But . . . you just said.

STAN: I know. But I can't. I like you. You're so . . . you. And this is probably the longest conversation I've had with a woman in months.

GLORIA: Then that's it then? I'm not going to die tonight.

STAN: Not by my hand. I hope not at all.

(She laughs.)

What?

GLORIA: You want me to live. A serial killer wants me to live.

STAN: I think I'd like to see you again.

GLORIA: Really?

STAN: If that's not being too forward. You know, maybe, somewhere with better lighting. Earlier in the evening. Indoors. Maybe with food.

(Pause.)

Do you think that's possible? That we could, you know, do that some time?

GLORIA: You're asking me out on a date? An actual date.

STAN: Yeah.

GLORIA:

(Pause.)

Okay.

Lights out.

LOVE, THEATRE, AND DAMN YANKEES

E. Scott Icenhower

ORIGINAL PRODUCTION:

Performed at the Weathervane Playhouse, 1301 Weathervane Lane Akron, OH 44313-5186 Telephone: (330) 836-2626 info@weathervaneplay-house.com as part of their 2014 8x10 Theatrefest, July 11 – 13, 2014.

Directed by Mathew King, featuring Abby Schramp and Mary Mahoney.

PRODUCER:

Eileen Moushey, coordinator of Weathervane 8x10 Theatrefest

John Hedges, Executive Director Weathervane Playhouse.

CHARACTERS:

> REBECCA BRADY: Twenties. An overly dramatic artistic type who will suffer for her art so she can write a romance novel.
> KAREN BRADY: Twenties. Rebecca's older and less artistic sister who is an FBI agent.

SETTING:

> Interior of a rustic vacation cabin in an isolated area of the mountains. Present day, afternoon.

AT RISE: REBECCA BRADY is alone looking through an ornate box of memories recalling the few precious months she shared with her boyfriend before he left due to illness. Today is the one year anniversary of his departure, and she believes he is dead. She over reacts to each item she takes out of the box. After looking at a picture, then a letter, she pulls a jump rope out of the box.

KAREN:
(KAREN BRADY kicks the door open. She is on duty and has pulled her gun. REBECCA screams.)
FBI, nobody move. You're all under arrest!
(She looks around and recognizes her sister, but keeps her gun drawn on REBECCA.)
REBECCA?: Are you alone?
REBECCA: I wanted to be, but you ruined that didn't you?
KAREN: Have you seen anybody since you've been here?
REBECCA: No, I believe that's the definition of alone isn't it?
KAREN: We've got an APB on some thieves in the area. So, when I saw the lights on I . . . I thought you'd be here tomorrow.
(She sees REBECCA clutching a jump rope and thinks she might use it to hang herself.)
What are you doing?
REBECCA: None of your business.
KAREN: It's that jerk you dated isn't it?

REBECCA: He has a name—Steve. Have some respect for the dead.

KAREN: He's not dead Becky. He just broke up with you and took your money.

REBECCA: He needed that money for the experimental medicine in Canada.

KAREN: I can't believe we're related.

REBECCA: Will you leave me alone? I want to cherish his memory.

(She hugs the jump rope and starts to cry quietly.)

KAREN: Why are you holding that rope?

REBECCA: It's a jump rope.

KAREN: What are you going to do with it?

REBECCA: *(Reminiscing.)* We were walking in the park and Steve started jumping rope with this little girl. "Cinderella dressed in yella"—he was so cute playing with her. He would have made a wonderful father.

KAREN: So why do you have the rope?

REBECCA: It's a keepsake, a precious memory of our limited time together.

KAREN: No, I mean why do *you* have the rope? It belonged to that little girl. He stole a jump rope from a little girl?

REBECCA: Shut up! I'm grieving.

KAREN: Don't grieve with a rope.

REBECCA: I'll grieve any way I want to. You're not going to tell me . . . do you think I'm going to hang myself with this? *(Attempting to irritate KAREN by playing along and then showing her how wrong it is.)* Yes, that's a good idea. I can use this rope. I'll wrap it around my neck and throw the other *two feet* over a tree limb.

KAREN: Just put the rope down and step away. Let's talk.

REBECCA: You're an idiot.

KAREN: It doesn't have to end this way.

REBECCA: No, it's supposed to end this way. *(REBECCA stands up and starts to skip rope.)* Cinderella dressed in yella went upstairs to kiss her fella. By mistake she kissed a snake. How many doctors will it take? 1, 2, 3 . . .

KAREN: *(Speaking over REBECCA.)* Stop it Becky. Put the rope down. Just think about what you're giving up. Becky, I'm warning you. Stop it or I'll—

REBECCA: *(Stopping.)* Or what, you'll shoot me? So, to keep me from committing suicide with a jump rope you're going to shoot me? Do you realize how stupid that sounds? Did mom put you up to this?

KAREN: She may have said something about Steve leaving you a year ago this weekend and that you might over react like you always do.

REBECCA: No I don't.

KAREN: Yes you do. Remember when Bobby Thompson pulled the head off of your Barbie doll? You had an elaborate funeral service, cremated the body in the fireplace and put the head in the freezer so technology could cure her in the future.

REBECCA: I was a child.

KAREN: Three years ago you were so heartbroken you tried to overdose on fudge ripple ice cream and Snickers.

REBECCA: That wasn't an overdose; it was comfort food. But you're right. I did overdo it. For the next six months my thighs couldn't pass each other without stopping to chat.

KAREN: Normal people don't do things like that.

REBECCA: Normal people don't threaten their sisters with a gun for jumping rope.

KAREN: Just give me the rope.

REBECCA: You want this rope? I'll trade you for your gun.

KAREN: You're out of your mind. That would explain it. You shouldn't be left alone.

(She starts to exit to the kitchen.)

REBECCA: So you're leaving?

KAREN: Checking out the kitchen.

REBECCA: It's an electric stove.

(KAREN stops.)

REBECCA: And there are no sharp knives. I could spatula myself to death. You might want to hide that.

KAREN: Gas logs?

REBECCA: No. You have to chop your own firewood.

KAREN: Where's the axe?

REBECCA: You're kidding.

KAREN: Just let me be in charge of the axe.

REBECCA: You really think I might try to behead myself?
Seriously, what are you doing here?

KAREN: Kyle left.

REBECCA: I'm so sorry.

(She gets up and they hug.)

Come here. Sit by me and tell me what happened?

(They sit together on the couch.)

KAREN: Maybe he needs his space or more time. I don't
know.

REBECCA: What did he say?

KAREN: "Karen, I need my space or more time. I don't know."

REBECCA: Oh.

KAREN: Do all these theatrics you do really help you get
through this?

REBECCA: They're not theatrics to me. It's just who I am.
It's how I cope.

KAREN: So what were you doing?

REBECCA: I'm going to write a tragic romance novel inspired by my fated love with Steve. I was remembering
so I could get myself in the mood to write.

KAREN: Sorry I broke your mood.

REBECCA: Don't you worry about that. You'll just have to
find you own way to cope. Ooh, maybe you could put
everything he gave you in a box and have that friend of
yours on the bomb squad blow it up for you? Would that
be too much?

KAREN: No, it helped a little. But the sadness came back as
soon as the smoke cleared.

REBECCA: Wow, that would have done it for me. Ok then,
we go the other way. We embrace our sadness. We feed
it 'til it builds up in us so much that we have to release it.

KAREN: Are you talking about a fudge ripple and Snickers
binge?

REBECCA: No. What say we get all dolled up, go downtown

---

and see that new play about suicide?

(She holds up a magazine or newspaper or something similar.)

It got great reviews in this offline application.

KAREN: No, theatre's not natural. I just can't believe it when people break out in song and dance.

REBECCA: Well this is a play, not a musical, and it's about suicide. So, I doubt we'll even see one set of jazz hands on the stage. What do you say?

KAREN: Going out and being around a lot of people does sound good, but . . . what about a baseball game?

REBECCA: No, baseball's not natural.

KAREN: It's as natural as apple pie.

REBECCA: Apple pie's not natural. You have to bake it.

KAREN: You know what I mean. So what's so unnatural about baseball?

REBECCA: Well, you have all these strangers sitting together outside when suddenly they break into song.

(She sings the first line of "Take me out to the ball game.")

Why, because someone brought a pipe organ to the stadium. Then there's the da da da dat ta da CHARGE! More singing. And if that's not enough. Everyone does the wave.

(She raises her arms, stands and sits while "whooping" several times to demonstrate.)

Choreography on a grand scale. People breaking out in spontaneous song and dance—unnatural.

KAREN: Point taken. I only mentioned it because Paul said he was going to the ball game.

REBECCA: Paul?

KAREN: My friend on the bomb squad.

REBECCA: Then we should go. Do you think we could find him there?

KAREN: I don't know if I want find him.

REBECCA: I get the impression you kind of like him. Why wouldn't you want to find him?

KAREN: He may have a speech impediment or a weird accent. Every time I see him he's covered in a bomb proof suit with full head protection. I never really heard his voice until today when he took his helmet off—

REBECCA: Is he good looking?

KAREN: His visor is clear. I've always been able to see his face. And yes he's good looking. But when he removed his helmet, he asked me if I wanted to go see dem Yankees tonight, to take my mind off Kyle.

REBECCA: That's considerate. So what's the problem? Is it too soon?

KAREN: He said "dem" Yankees, not "those" Yankees or the more appropriate "the" Yankees.

REBECCA: You're still an idiot. Not going out with a considerate nice looking man because of his use and pronunciation of the adjective used before the word Yankees. I'm glad I didn't give you the jump rope.

KAREN: I know. It doesn't make sense.

REBECCA: Yes it does. You're scared and you're looking for excuses. You're afraid if you move on; Kyle won't have a place in your heart to come back to.

KAREN: Hey, that's good.

REBECCA: Thanks, that's what I wrote for the book jacket cover.

KAREN: You've finished the book? I thought you were—

REBECCA: No, people always read the book jacket cover before they buy the book. If I can hook 'em there, I've made a sale and no refunds. It takes the pressure off writing a blockbuster.

KAREN: I should let you get started on that non blockbuster. Thanks for listening Sis.

(She starts to exit.)

REBECCA: You're not leaving. We're going out. It doesn't have to be a ball game or the theatre . . .

(She looks at the magazine/newspaper)

It can be both.

KAREN: What?

REBECCA: Paul didn't ask you to a ball game. He asked you to go to a revival of the musical "DamnYankees."

(KAREN just stares at her.)

REBECCA: It's a musical about baseball.

KAREN: Oh, I get it. He's gay.

REBECCA: No. Not necessarily. Here's what we do. Call him back and say you decided to go, but you'll meet him there. Tell him you're bringing a friend and he should do the same. Then we can all go out for drinks after the show.

KAREN: And if he brings a guy friend, then we'll know he's gay.

REBECCA: He may be bringing a guy friend for me so it can be a double date. Do you really work for the FBI?

KAREN: Yes. Do you want to see my gun again?

REBECCA: Don't take that to the theatre. They'll think you're a critic from the NRA.

KAREN: I don't get it. You are so weird. Am I even going to like this musical?

REBECCA: Of course you will; it's got the Devil in it.

KAREN: As long as he doesn't sing.

REBECCA: Ok.

END

ORIGINAL PRODUCTION

Mistress Marlene was produced by Artistic New Directions @ Theatre, 54 - 244 West 54th Street, NYC Seventh Annual Eclectic Evening of Shorts: Boxers & Briefs

April 10 – April 13, 2014

Directed by Alex Dmitriev

CAST:
BILL: Tim Barker
SANDRA: Susanne Marley

BILL: Electrician, average looking working class guy, thirty-five to forty.

SANDRA: Woman of the house, any age between forty to sixty.

TIME

Present Day, 9A.M. sharp.

PLACE

Average American living room.

(LIGHTS UP, SANDRA ENTERS talking on cellphone and dragging a vacuum cleaner behind her.)

SANDRA: Yes, honey, I'll pick up your shirts. I will. This afternoon. The electrician is coming back to finish this morning. Larry, I know it's expensive but that job has got to get done. It's dangerous, for God's sake. *(DOORBELL rings)* Gotta go. That's probably him at the door. Bye.

(SANDRA answers door. BILL ENTERS)

SANDRA: Good morning Jim.

BILL: Bill.

SANDRA: Oh right, Bill. Sorry.

BILL: S'ok.

SANDRA: Bill. *(checks time)* Ooo, 9A.M. sharp! That's pretty good.

BILL: I aim to please.

(BILL formally bows to SANDRA)

SANDRA: (surpised by the bow)

Oh. Ah, so, do you need anything?

BILL: No, I've got my tools here. I'm ready to finish up.

SANDRA: Ok well, you know where everything is.

BILL: Yes I remember. Thank you.

(BILL bows again)

SANDRA: I . . . *(She giggles and attempts to bow herself)*
There! Well.
(BILL stands still. Awkward moment. BILL has an envelope in his hands.)
You don't need anything?
BILL: No thank you. No.
(He doesn't move)
SANDRA: . . . So!
BILL: I have something for you.
SANDRA: You do?
BILL: Yes.
(BILL holds the envelope delicately)
SANDRA: It's the bill already?
BILL: No.
(BILL holds the envelope up)
SANDRA: What?
BILL: This is for you.
(BILL offers SANDRA the envelope)
If you don't mind, I'd like you to read it.
SANDRA: Now?
BILL: If you don't mind.
(SANDRA opens letter and reads a sentence or two then looks up questioningly at Bill)
SANDRA: Really? (SANDRA looks at BILL in disbelief)
Wow! You don't . . .
BILL: What?
SANDRA: I just—That's—I never—I wouldn't have known.
BILL: Well. Do you have any problem with this?
SANDRA: Ah, nooo. I . . . I don't.
BILL: You might want to read the entire letter in order to get the whole idea.
SANDRA: Ok. Uhm, yah, yah I will. Just . . . ah, why don't you start the job and, ah, I'll read the rest of the letter in a little bit? I, have, ah . . . I need to eat something and . . .
BILL: Yes, of course, I'll get to work. No problem. After reading it, though, if you have any questions I'd be happy to answer them for you.
SANDRA: Yah, ok, sure. Just—

BILL: I'll get to work.

(BILL EXITS. SANDRA thinks for a moment then picks up phone and makes a call.)

SANDRA: Larry? Me again. I know but . . . there's something really . . . He gave me a letter. The electrician! Yah. No, he's downstairs. Listen, this is the first sentence. *(reading from letter)* *"Hello, my name is Mistress Marlene and I control the male who just gave you this letter."* Mistress? Larry, do you think he's a transvest . . . a cross dress . . . is he a woman inside? What? No. He looks real normal; like an average, normal guy. Nothing special, nothing weird. Just a guy.

(BILL calls from OFFSTAGE)

BILL: Ma'am?

SANDRA: Oh no, he's coming upstairs. I'm putting the phone down.*(calling off)* Yes.

(BILL ENTERS)

BILL: So sorry to bother you. Your receptacle is hot.

SANDRA: Huh?

BILL: Two hot wires are energizing the plug. You're not wired properly.

SANDRA: Oh, the recept . . . it's . . . ok, ah . . .

BILL: Would you like me to replace it?

SANDRA: Yes please.

Bill: I'm on it.

(BILL EXITS)

(SANDRA picks up phone and reads on.)

SANDRA: Larry? Listen to this. *(reading from letter)* *"Bill and I live the lifestyle of Female Supremacy. In Matriarchy women issue direction and men obey."* What? Whadaya mean? He's not? Oh my God, *Mistress* Marlene. She's Bill's dominatri—Agh! Oh, dear. What? *(Larry is asking her to get back to the letter)* Oh, ok, ah. *"My objective is to modify his behavior until it is completely natural for him to give women priority in all situations."* Modify? How do ya do that? Wow. Larry, I'm reading word-for-word. It's right here in front of me. Wait. *(reading on)* Uh oh. *"To obtain the best service, order this male to give you his key. Keep the key until you are*

completely satisfied with his attitude and his work. Use him as you wish, he must obey."
What the—Larry, what should I do? Whadaya mean? Give me a break. Come on. I didn't do anything. Huh? *(looking down at her attire)* I am wearing my grungy pants and slippers. Oh yah, these hot pink, fluffy slippers must have started the whole thing. Geez.

BILL: *(from Off)*Ma'am?

SANDRA: He's coming upstairs. Wait, no, yah. Ok. Bye.

BILL: Hello?

SANDRA: Hi.

BILL: Have you had a chance to read it?

SANDRA: A little.

BILL: Do you have any questions?

SANDRA: No?

BILL: None?

SANDRA: No. Well, yes.

BILL: Ok.

SANDRA: Do you give this letter to all of your customers?

BILL: No.

SANDRA: Hmm. *(pause)* Why me?

BILL: It's the way you stand. The way you address me.

SANDRA: I can't help the way I stand.

BILL: You're direct and assertive and you tell me what you want.

SANDRA: Look, I'm supposed to tell you what I want. I hired you to do electrical work. *I want the ceiling lights replaced in the basement and I want the shutters on this fan freed up.* Simple. Geez.

BILL: You are beautifully confident.

SANDRA: Please . . . oh never mind. Just get back to work.

BILL: Of course.

(BILL starts to exit.)

SANDRA: Wait. One more question.

BILL: Yes ma'am!SANDRA: Is Marlene a real person?

BILL: Mistress Marlene.

SANDRA: Right.

BILL: Yes, I live with Mistress Marlene. I serve her.

(Bill reveals a key on a chain around his neck. He

---

is also wearing a spiked black-leather dog collar.)

SANDRA: Ahh.

BILL: This is my house key.

SANDRA: Ok.

BILL: You keep it until I've satisfied you completely. I must obey.

SANDRA: She won't let you into your house?

BILL: No. Not without the key.

SANDRA: Look, I'm sorry, but I don't think I'm interested in any of this.

BILL: You don't *think*?

SANDRA: I . . . what?

BILL: You didn't say *no*.

SANDRA: Well, that's what I meant.

BILL: So you are not interested?

SANDRA: I do not want to be deliberately mean to you or to anyone.

BILL: Is that what you think Female Supremacy is?

SANDRA: Well, aren't I supposed to *(she reads from letter)* order you into submission?

BILL: You command me and I respond to your loving voice. I become a boy to your powerful Goddess self.

SANDRA: I am not a Goddess.

BILL: Oh you are.

SANDRA: I am not.

BILL: And strong.

SANDRA: Stop it.

BILL: You are a powerful woman.

SANDRA: I am?

BILL: Oh yes.

SANDRA: I don't get it. You want someone to degrade you?

BILL: I yearn to lovingly surrender to powerful women. You are one of those women.

SANDRA: Women? You actually have other customers who do this? Go along with this? *(BILL shrugs yes)* Oh God.

BILL: Your commands can touch my submissive self and in return you become the Goddess that you truly are. If you wanted me to I would get down on my hands and knees right now and beg like a dog. Whimper.

SANDRA: Please don't do that.

BILL: If you wanted me to I'd do your vacuuming for you.

SANDRA: My vacuuming?!

BILL: Order me.

SANDRA: Wait a second. You'd actually clean my house for me?

BILL: Absolutely. If you want me to.

SANDRA: *(Wistfully)* Do my housework? *(thinks for a moment then . . .)* Just finish the electrical job, ok?

BILL: Yes Ma'am. One more thing.

SANDRA: What?

BILL: If you could fill out the survey part of the letter I would really appreciate it. Mistress Marlene expects it.

(SANDRA looks at survey)

SANDRA: A survey?

BILL: I need it.

SANDRA: She expects you to come home with a survey?

BILL: If I don't I'm in big trouble.

SANDRA: Geez.

(Reads aloud)

As part of his training I have ordered this male to follow directions. Please answer these questions and return this form to your servant.

God.

(BILL hands SANDRA a pen)

BILL: Please?

SANDRA: Ugh.

•   Did he address you respectfully?

•   Would you recommend this type of service to another woman?

You're kidding me?

BILL: No.

SANDRA: Suggestions or comments? Please send an email to MistressMarlene@yahoo.com.

Oh boy. Oh, all right, fine. Just get this job done as soon as possible! Ok?!

BILL: Whatever you wish.

SANDRA: Just do your job!

BILL: The lights downstairs have been remounted. I can now attend to your air system here.

SANDRA: Yes.

BILL: What's the problem?

SANDRA: WHAT!?

BILL: With the fan.

SANDRA: Oh, it's well, the thingy, the shutter thing opens but then no air is pulled through.

BILL: That should be easy to fix.

SANDRA: Good.

BILL: Anything else? (Pause)

SANDRA: (abruptly)Tighten those knobs!

BILL: These?

SANDRA: Yes.

BILL: Like this?

SANDRA: (with confidence) Yes.

BILL: Ok!

SANDRA: And those shutters are filthy. Clean them.

BILL: Yes Ma'am.

(As BILL is working SANDRA goes to cupboard and takes out cleaning supplies. She places them in a tableau next to the vacuum cleaner.)

SANDRA: And after that, this is your next job ok.

(BILL looks at her affectionately and nods yes)

BILL: Yes.

SANDRA: Yes what?

(SANDRA holds out her hand and BILL places his key in SANDRA's hand)

BILL: Yes Mistress Sandra.

END OF PLAY

NEW YEAR'S EVE
David MacGregor

ORIGINAL PRODUCTION:

NEW YEAR'S EVE was originally produced by Tipping Point Theatre (Northville, MI), June 28, 2013.

Directed by Amanda Ewing

CAST:

MR. HOLLINS: Clement Valentine
LAURA: Tara Tomisck-Husak

The play was subsequently produced by Santa Paula Theater Center (Santa Paula, CA), May 30, 2014

Directed by John McKinley

CAST:

MR. HOLLINS: Braden McKinley
LAURA: Erin Hollander

CHARACTERS:
>MR. HOLLINS: Man over sixty.
>LAURA: Caretaker in her twenties to thirties.

SETTING:
>A retirement home.

TIME:
>Now and then.

MR. HOLLINS hobbles onstage with a cane or walker, helped by LAURA. She gets him to a chair and he sits down. She stands behind him as he looks around.

MR. HOLLINS: This is complete and utter bullshit.

LAURA: Let's try and keep a positive attitude.

MR. HOLLINS: You know when people tell you to keep a positive attitude? When things are complete and utter bullshit.

LAURA: You don't have to talk so loudly.

MR. HOLLINS: I'll talk as loudly as I goddamned want.

LAURA: You'll disturb the others.

MR. HOLLINS: They need to be disturbed. Any kind of brain activity at all would be a blessing to most of them.

LAURA: Don't say that.

MR. HOLLINS: You know it's true. I know you're paid to pretend it's not true, but it's true and that's that.

LAURA: Other people are enjoying themselves. Look at Mrs. Davis.

MR. HOLLINS: Mrs. Davis would enjoy herself if you parked her in front of a brick wall for six hours. Although fifty years ago, that's a piece of tail I'd have been all over.

LAURA: I'm going to pretend I didn't hear that.

MR. HOLLINS: Exactly. That's your job—pretending. Pretending you don't hear, pretending you don't see, pretending you don't think. And you're pretty damned good at all three.

LAURA: My job is helping. My job is being kind and considerate and understanding.

MR. HOLLINS: And ass wiping. Don't forget the ass wiping. I'll bet that's what you hoped you'd end up doing when you were in school, wiping the wrinkly asses of geezers who can't reach back there without falling off the damned toilet.

LAURA: Is this really necessary?

MR. HOLLINS: Is what really necessary?

LAURA: Being this unpleasant. It's New Year's Eve. Tomorrow is a new day, a new year . . .

MR. HOLLINS: Go on. What else? *(off her silence)*

I'll tell you what else. A new goddamned nothing, that's what else. You want to ask the people here for their New Year's resolutions? Half of them will be "to die in my sleep tonight."

LAURA: No, they won't! This is a vibrant community of senior citizens who have led full, productive lives, and who are entitled to enjoy all the benefits of their golden years.

MR. HOLLINS: Jesus Christ. What . . . did you memorize that from the brochure? You must have. No normal human being would talk like that.

LAURA: What I'm saying is, no one here is going to make the kind of New Year's resolution you just mentioned.

MR. HOLLINS: Oh no? Every time the EMS unit shows up, people can't wheel themselves into the lobby fast enough. Who is it now? They're like a bunch of seals watching one of their own being dragged into the surf by a killer whale. There goes Marge. Oh, they got Joe this time. They're all jostling around in their electric scooters, trying to see who's getting carried out of here, knowing that any day now it's going to be them on that stretcher.

LAURA: That's a little morbid, don't you think?

MR. HOLLINS: No. What's morbid is, every time the lobby fills up with those flashing red and blue lights, and every time you hear the EMS guys squawking on their radios, half of these poor sons of bitches wish it was them with a sheet over their face.

(off her silence)

What's the matter? Nothing perky and upbeat to say?

LAURA: I don't understand why you have to be like this.

MR. HOLLINS: Because I'm pissed off, that's why! It's New Year's goddamned Eve and look at me! Am I dressed up? Am I dancing? Am I popping open a bottle of champagne? No, I'm sitting in the lobby of the god-damned Parkview Retirement Home with a limp pecker and a clear head. Son of a bitch!

LAURA: Mr. Hollins . . . can I get you a brownie or some nuts?

MR. HOLLINS: And what time is it? Please be so kind as to tell me what goddamned time it is.

LAURA: It's ten minutes to twelve.

MR. HOLLINS: Oh, that is good. Ten minutes to twelve she says.

LAURA: What do you want me to say? That is the correct time!

MR. HOLLINS: Technically, yes. But not really, and you know it.

LAURA: I think the Barry Manilow impersonator is about to start. He's opening with "At the Copacabana."

MR. HOLLINS: It's ten minutes to goddamned noon! Not midnight. Noon! You think I don't know that? It's the middle of the goddamned day!

LAURA: I'm aware of that.

MR. HOLLINS: Then why are we here? The new year isn't for another twelve hours, so why are we here pretending it starts in ten minutes?

LAURA: I'm not going to let you bait me. You know very well why.

MR. HOLLINS: Because we're old. Because we can't stay up that late. Because our medications will get out of whack.

LAURA: Right. And instead of having no New Year's cel-ebration at all, we thought it would be nice to have it at noon instead. Lots of retirement places do this.

MR. HOLLINS: You know something? When you get to a point in your life where you have to celebrate New Year's

Eve at noon, someone should have the decency to just put a goddamned bullet through your head.

LAURA: Stop that! This is a good thing! Other people like it! They think it's fun! They get a treat, they have some sparkling grape juice, they get a paper hat . . . it's fun!

MR. HOLLINS: What are you doing tonight?

LAURA: I'm going to a party.

MR. HOLLINS: With who?

LAURA: My boyfriend.

MR. HOLLINS: Are you going to drink?

LAURA: In moderation.

MR. HOLLINS: What are you going to drink?

LAURA: I don't know . . . champagne, I suppose.

MR. HOLLINS: And what are you going to eat?

LAURA: You want me to run through the entire menu?

MR. HOLLINS: Yes. I want you to run through the entire menu. What are you going to eat?

LAURA: I'm not sure. Probably some shrimp, maybe some caviar, cheese . . . you know, appetizer, finger-food type things.

MR. HOLLINS: Okay, so you eat, you drink, it's midnight, the ball drops in Times Square, and then what happens?

LAURA: Well, we'll probably—

MR. HOLLINS: Are you going to get laid?

LAURA: I am not answering that!

MR. HOLLINS: Why the hell not?

LAURA: Because that's . . . because it's none of your business, that's why not!

MR. HOLLINS: I'd just feel better about this whole New Year's Eve business if I knew one of us was getting laid.

LAURA: You're trying to goad me and I'm not going to let you. Here, let's blow our noisemakers.

(LAURA holds out a noisemaker to MR. HOLLINS as she blows on her own noisemaker for all she's worth. MR. HOLLINS stares at her like she has lost her mind.)

LAURA: All right then, how about a hat?

(She holds up a paper Happy New Year hat.)

MR. HOLLINS: You're kidding me.

LAURA: Other people are wearing hats.

MR. HOLLINS: Other people are wearing diapers too.

LAURA: Fine. Don't wear a hat.

MR. HOLLINS: I'll wear the hat if you'll answer one question.

LAURA: What's the question?

MR. HOLLINS: First the hat, then the question.

(LAURA puts the hat on him.)

LAURA: There.

MR. HOLLINS: Thank you. Now I look as stupid as everyone else.

LAURA: What's your question?

MR. HOLLINS: This boyfriend of yours, is he any good in the sack?

LAURA: Give me that!

(LAURA grabs for the hat and they tussle for it, until MR. HOLLINS wins and puts the hat on his head.)

MR. HOLLINS: We had a deal!

LAURA: No, we didn't!

MR. HOLLINS: One hat equals one question.

LAURA: I'm not responding.

MR. HOLLINS: It's a funny thing with men. Some guys, they get it up and they can go all night. Other guys . . . one shot and they're done. Straight to sleep. Which one is your boyfriend?

LAURA: I said you could ask a question. I never said I would answer it.

MR. HOLLINS: Straight to sleep, huh?

LAURA: Listen, instead of worrying about my sex life, why don't you hook up with Mrs. Cavanaugh tonight? She got her hair done, her nails done, and best of all, she's got Alzheimer's, so she won't remember whether or not you could get it up.

(mortified at what just passed her lips)

I shouldn't have said that.

MR. HOLLINS: No—

LAURA: I'm sorry. That was a horrible, horrible thing to say.

MR. HOLLINS: It's all right—

LAURA: Please don't tell anyone I said that.

MR. HOLLINS: No, no. This is just between you and me.

LAURA: Thank you.

MR. HOLLINS: I'm not some blabbermouth.

LAURA: I appreciate that.

MR. HOLLINS: I still have some common sense, you know.

LAURA: I know you do.

MR. HOLLINS: And I like the way you think.

LAURA: Oh my God . . . please . . . you can't . . . Mrs. Cavanaugh—

MR. HOLLINS: Relax. I have about as much interest in banging Mrs. Cavanaugh as I have in banging a dried out gourd.

LAURA: Good . . . I mean, no, that's not good. I mean, it is, but it isn't.

MR. HOLLINS: Let me tell you something. When I was twelve years old, what I wanted more than anything else in the world was to bang a beautiful eighteen-year-old girl. And when I was eighteen, same thing. Twenty-eight, same thing. Fifty-eight, same thing. And today . . . same thing. You think that feeling will go away. And then after a while, you pray to God it will go away. And eventually you pretend that it has, you know, just to make everyone feel better. But it never goes away . . . it's a helluva thing . . . to want to live when you should already be dead.

LAURA: Mr. Hollins . . . I don't want you to feel this way.

MR. HOLLINS: That makes two of us.

LAURA: What do you want?

MR. HOLLINS: Want? I want to feel that little burn of the bubbles as the first glass of champagne slides down my throat . . . maybe some caviar on toast . . . I want the girl I'm with to edge closer to me, so I can feel her warmth, smell the sandalwood perfume she has on, and feel her fingers curling around mine when midnight is a minute away. And I want to know that this year, more than any other year, this year is gonna be the best goddamned year of my life. That's what New Year's Eve is about.

Not this . . . it's not this.

(They look at one another and LAURA opens her mouth, platitudes ready to spring forth, but they die on her lips as they hear the sound of a siren, which dies as red and blue flashing lights fill the space.)

LAURA: Oh no.

MR. HOLLINS: I don't want to see this.

(He struggles to his feet as LAURA helps him. He takes his hat off, tosses it on the chair. He starts to walk off, assisted by her.)

MR. HOLLINS: I want you to have a good time at your party.

LAURA: I'll do my best.

MR. HOLLINS: I want you to appreciate it.

LAURA: I will.

MR. HOLLINS: Promise me you won't listen to Barry Manilow.

LAURA: I won't listen to Barry Manilow.

(He pauses and turns, shaking his head at what he sees.)

MR. HOLLINS: Goddammit.

(He looks at her for some glimmer of connection and understanding.)

LAURA: I'll bring you back some of that champagne.

MR. HOLLINS: We're not supposed to have champagne.

LAURA: That is complete and utter bullshit.

(He smiles at her and she smiles back. She puts her hand on his arm and they exit together.)

END OF PLAY.

ONE MONKEY MORE OR LESS
Rod McFadden

ORIGINAL PRODUCTION

Santos Dantin Studio Theater, John & Rita Lowndes
Shakespeare Center
812 E. Rollins St., Orlando, FL 32803

January 9-18, 2015

Directed by Buddy Fales

CAST
SIMON: PJ Metz
GEORGE: Russell Trahan

Produced by The Playwrights Round Table,
Orlando FL
Producers: Al Pergande & Jim Cundiff

CHARACTERS:

> SIMON: a monkey, any age but ideally mid-forties or older.
> GEORGE: another monkey, similar age as SIMON.

An undefined space. Muffled sounds of random typewriter clacking, and of pensive.

The lights come up to reveal two monkeys, SIMON and GEORGE, each seated behind a typewriter, next to a wastebasket. Around them just outside the light are many other typing monkeys (which could be actual actors or simply cardboard cut-outs or pictures attached to flats, etc.) The effect is that of a large crowd of monkeys at typewriters.

The sounds of typewriters and monkeys continue beneath the dialogue.

SIMON and GEORGE tap a few keys, but without purpose, choosing keys at random. Neither seems aware of the other.

GEORGE stops and looks at the paper in his typewriter. He reads it to himself, then sighs heavily, pulls it from the typewriter, and crumples it. He tosses it at his wastebasket, but misses and it bounces into SIMON's peripheral vision.

SIMON looks up from his typing, at the wadded paper, following its trajectory back to GEORGE.

SIMON: Oh. I forgot there was anyone else here.
GEORGE: Yes. It's easy to become . . . absorbed. In the task.
SIMON: Yes. I'm Simon.
GEORGE: George. Sorry to have, um . . . disturbed you. You'd think after throwing so many pages into that basket, I could dunk one in my sleep by now.
> *(SIMON goes to pick up the wad of paper.)*
SIMON: No bother. Truth is, even a short break is welcome.

(SIMON picks up the wadded paper and starts to open it.)

GEORGE *(continued):* Hey! Don't. Just put it in my basket. I don't want you looking at it.

SIMON: I'm just curious, George. I mean, here we are, all of us monkeys, typing away for . . . well, it does seem like forever, doesn't it? And there's all these wadded up papers in our baskets, so . . .

(SIMON makes another furtive scan around to ensure no one is looking.)

SIMON *(continued):* . . . I just wondered what kind of stuff you were getting.

GEORGE: The fact I threw it in my basket should tell you. It's crap. More gibberish. More . . . failure.

SIMON finishes opening the paper, and looks at it.

(GEORGE approaches him.)

GEORGE (continued): You have no right. Give that to me.

SIMON: Wait, no. This is pretty good, George. It's . . .

GEORGE: I said give me that.

SIMON fends off GEORGE's attempts to get the paper.

SIMON: These are real words, George. These. . . almost make sense.

GEORGE snatches the paper away and rips it up.

GEORGE: It doesn't matter. None of it matters.

(SIMON reaches into GEORGE's basket and takes out a couple of other paper wads.)

SIMON: What else have you written?

GEORGE: Get out of there. Give me those. Right now.

SIMON avoids him and opens a page and reads it.

SIMON: (reading)Now is the wiener of our discontent made glorious simmer by this song of Pork.

GEORGE: Shhh. Stop it.

SIMON: (reading another)But soft! What light through blunder window beaks? It is the beast, and Ju-ju-bee is the Sin.

(GEORGE catches hold of SIMON, and almost violently pushes him to the ground.)

GEORGE: Stop reading that! I tell you, be quiet.

(GEORGE grabs the pages and rips them up.)

SIMON: How can you . . . ? Are there others like this?

GEORGE: You mean more gibberish?

SIMON: But it's not. Here. Look at this.

(SIMON yanks the page from his typewriter, and hands it to GEORGE.)

SIMON *(continued)*: Read that. Go ahead.

GEORGE: Why? What difference will it make?

SIMON: Here. I'll do the honors.

He takes the page, and strikes a dramatic pose.

SIMON *(continued)*: *(reading)* Yerf hak looom. Twe ffff dop ass nug.

(SIMON shoves the page back into GEORGE's hands.)

GEORGE: So. What's your point?

SIMON: That is gibberish. That is unreadable. And I was thinking it was pretty good. I mean, look. I got a real word. Ass. Three whole letters, too. A-S-S. I've gotten real words before. "A" and "I" and once I even got "if". But Ass is a long word. I was proud of my ass. Not to mention, all but one of the words have a vowel – that is, if they were words, which they aren't. But they could be words, because they all have an appropriately placed vowel. This page may well be my best effort yet. And then I see what you're throwing away, and I realize, I'm not even in the same league as you!

GEORGE: No, we're not in the same league. Because I'm quitting the league altogether. I'm done with this.

SIMON: What? You can't quit. We're. . . we're not allowed to quit.

GEORGE: What does it matter? One monkey more or less isn't gonna make a damned bit of difference.

SIMON: Of course it makes a difference. It's part of our company mission. It's right up there, so we never forget it.

SIMON points to a sign hanging on the 4th wall.

GEORGE: No. I don't need to be part of it anymore.

SIMON: Hey, come on now. Read it. Go ahead. Out loud. Come on. I'll start and you join in.

(reading the sign)

"At Infinite Monkeys Incorporated, time and total team-work make the impossible possible."

(to GEORGE)

You didn't join in. That's hardly total teamwork, is it?

GEORGE: They don't need total teamwork. They have an infinite number of us, typing away, for an infinite amount of time.

SIMON: And that is why it's certain we'll reach our goal. As a team, we will recreate one of Shakespeare's plays in its entirety, as impossible as that seems. But if you . . . leave, well . . . the whole enterprise is compromised.

GEORGE: And what if it is? So what?

SIMON: So what? How can you ask that?

GEORGE: What's so important about a monkey tapping out a copy of Macbeth or King Lear?

SIMON: The mission, George. Look at it. Making the impossible possible. If we don't do this, the overwhelming gloom of impossibility will blanket everyone and everything. The hopes and dreams of our universe will disappear.

GEORGE: My part in it is meaningless. If I leave, there'll still be all of the rest of you.

SIMON: We need an infinite number of monkeys for this to work. If you leave, there'll only be an infinite number of monkeys, minus one.

GEORGE: Which is still an infinite number of monkeys. That's how infinity works. Don't you see? None of us make any difference in this. I'm leaving.

SIMON: But you can't. We each make a difference. What if you're the monkey. I mean, the monkey.

GEORGE: And maybe you are, Simon. It's just random chance, which one of us will get it right, if any of us ever does.

SIMON: George, it ain't gonna be me. I typed the word "ffff"—four F's in a row. But you . . . .

(SIMON grabs another paper wad from GEORGE's basket and opens it.)

SIMON *(continued)*:
>*(reading)*
>To be or not to be, that is the question: Whether 'tis nobler in the mind to suffer the slings and arrows of outrageous fortune cookies, or to take arms against a sea of bubbles, and by opposing, end ham.

GEORGE: Yes, I know. From Omelette, Blintz of Denmark. I fail every time, Simon. I can't take it anymore.

SIMON: You can, George. You must. You must . . . suffer the outrageous fortune cookies, because if you don't, then none of us has any hope at all.

GEORGE: But every try . . . They're wrong. Yes, I can see that I get really close, but it's always wrong in the end. It's no better than four F's, or a whole page of F's. Either way, it's still wrong. It's still failure.
>*(beat)*

GEORGE (continued): You should quit, too. Come with me, and we'll—

SIMON: We'll what, George? Run away? From our responsibility? From our hopes for the future, just because it seems so impossible? No. I need to stay, George, because someday, I might—I mean, I will type a word with four letters, or even more. And, George, you need to stay, too.

GEORGE: So I can fill my basket with more failures?

SIMON: Yes, because you do matter. Because all our failures are successful steps toward the goal. Because Infinity minus one might still be infinity. But what about infinity minus ten, or a hundred, or a thousand, or a hundred thousand? What if we all got up and left, George?

GEORGE turns away. He stands over his waste basket, and then reaches in and takes out a paper wad. He opens it, and laughs to himself.

GEORGE: *(reading)* Not marble nor gilded monuments Of princes shall outlive this pow'rful rime. But you shall shine more bright in these contents.

SIMON: Wow, George. That one . . . what was wrong with that one?

GEORGE: It's not a play, Simon. It's one of the sonnets.
(GEORGE looks at it again.)
GEORGE *(continued)*: But, it's a good try, huh? Even if it's the wrong genre.
SIMON: You're darn tootin'. It's inspiring, Georgie. It makes me wanna get back to my typewriter, and take another shot.
SIMON goes to his typewriter, but GEORGE remains where he is. He looks at the wrinkled page in his hand, and then into his wastebasket.
SIMON (continued): What about you? Come on. I bet you get real close on your next try. It doesn't have to be Hamlet, you know? I'm sure they'd be just as happy with King John, or Cymbeline.
(GEORGE looks up at the Mission statement.)
SIMON *(continued)*: Yeah, that's it. Let's read it.
(reading)
At Infinite Monkeys Incorporated . . .@
(to GEORGE)
George?
(SIMON goes to him, and stands by his side.)
SIMON *(continued)*:
(reading, slowly)
"At Infinite Monkeys . . ."
GEORGE: *(after a long pause)* "Incorporated"
SIMON /GEORGE: "Time and total teamwork make the impossible possible."
SIMON: Atta boy! Now, let's type some Shakespeare.
(SIMON and GEORGE go to their respective type-writers, and begin typing again.
The lights fade, leaving only darkness and the sound of typewriters and an infinite number of determined monkeys.)

END OF PLAY

A Piece of Advice

Samuel Toll

Original Production

The Colonial Playhouse, Aldan, PA
June 2014,

Cast:

Gene Harris: Ted
Jim Copeland: Bob

Directed and Stage Managed by Jim Brennan.
Lighting Design by James Meinel.
Lights and Sound by Alex Plasmeier.

CHARACTERS:

> TED: Thirty-three, a cynical, glib man. The world is not his oyster.
>
> BOB : Twenty-eight, a romantic man/child who's searching for love in all the wrong places.

SETTING:

> Small office with two desks, laptops.

TIME:

> Present. Late afternoon.

AT RISE: Two young men sit at opposing desks, work at their laptops. After a few moments, Bob hits his desk. Ted looks up.

BOB: This is driving me nuts!

TED: What, the Carter account?

BOB: No . . . this damn Thanksgiving . . . card thing. I don't know how to . . . you know . . . say what I . . . feel. What I wrote . . . It sounds stupid.

TED: That's because Thanksgiving is stupid.

BOB: That's a big help.

TED: It's all about consumerism. Buy cards, buy this, buy that. It's all about buying things. To validate your affection for another person. The more expensive the thing, the more you love them. Crass consumerism! Ought to be banned . . . They ought to ban all holidays for that matter, including Thanksgiving. They interrupt the natural flow of life.

BOB: Are you finished?

TED: Let me hear what you wrote.

BOB: There's not very much . . .

TED: Okay . . .

BOB: *(Reads.)*

> "Dear Janice, I'm not good at this so I'll do my best . . . From the first time I laid my eyes on you . . . my

heart jumped out of my chest. And that hurt." Thought I'd throw in some levity. "All kidding aside, I'm glad we met . . . "

(Pause)

TED: That's it?

BOB: That's it . . . so far . . .

TED: You better stick with car and furniture ads.

BOB: . . . I can't . . . I mean . . . wanted to tell her . . . didn't just wanted to mail her a card. I wanted to write her a letter and give her a dozen roses. But the words are stuck in my brain.

TED: Well, let me get some background before we pluck your new lady's heart strings. Is this the Jersey woman you've been seeing?

BOB: Yes . . .

TED: How long?

BOB: About a month.

TED: Not very long.

BOB: But it seems like I've known her for a lifetime.

TED: Sleep with her yet?

BOB: That's very personal.

TED: Did you?

BOB: Come on, Ted.

TED: How can I help you compose your love letter if I don't have all the facts?

BOB: Okay, yes!

TED: Now I have something tangible to work with . . . How many times?

BOB: Forget it. I'll figure it out on my own.

TED: No you won't.

(Bob looks at his computer screen for a few beats, sighs.)

BOB: Three . . .

TED: Were they passionate . . . or clinical?

BOB: Both . . . I mean . . .

TED: Elaborate or simple?

BOB: It's never that simple . . . but if I'm pressed . . . a notch or two above simple.

TED: I see . . . Did you do all the work, or was she a team player?

BOB: Somewhere in between . . . I guess . . .

TED: Words spoken or a deep, languid silence?

BOB: All of the above . . . But not at the same time.

TED: Interesting . . .

BOB: I haven't felt this way since . . .

TED: Black Magic . . .

BOB: Yeah . . . she *was* a killer . . .

TED: She killed me too, Bob. I suffered for you.

BOB: Wicked woman.

TED: Cast a spell then . . .

BOB: Vanished . . .

TED: Leaving behind a broken heart . . . a shattered ego . . .
    (Pause)

BOB: But great sex!

TED: The whole Kama Sutra you said.
    (Bob sighs.)

BOB: But Janice is different. She's a true heart.

TED: Sorry bro, but sounds familiar.

BOB: No way. She's got integrity!

TED: She may be bangin' another dude . . . just like Black Magic.

BOB: No way, Ted. She told me . . . she said . . .

TED: She loves you?

BOB: In so many words . . .

TED: How many?

BOB: "How many?"

TED: Yes, give me a number . . . the classic three, or about five . . . ten . . . fifteen!

BOB: Maybe . . .

TED: Where she actually said the words . . . I love you . . .

BOB: One. She said one word.

TED: One?

BOB: One.

TED: Which one?

BOB: "I."

TED: I?

BOB: She was about to say I . . . I mean, she said "I" . . . then she started to have an orgasm . . . multiple orgasms, in fact, which mixed the word *love* with the all the "ahs" and "ooh's."

TED: You sure? You could distinguish the L word in a gush of ahs and oohs?

BOB: I'm sure she was saying "love." Yes . . . I'm pretty sure . . .

TED: Did you say it?

BOB: What?

TED: The "L" word?

BOB: Yes . . .

TED: Before or after she allegedly said it?

BOB: After.

TED: You lie. I know you, Mister Mush. You surrendered to Cupid after the first stroke!

(Beat)

BOB: I did. I'm weak.

TED: You're a disgrace to the male gender.

BOB: I know . . . but she's so beautiful . . . and so sensitive to my touch. No one has ever responded to me like her. I mean . . . when I embrace her . . . she swoons. It's so exciting it's hard to breathe.

TED: You wimp.

BOB: I can't help it. I just love women. I love Janice.

TED: I've been in more pussy than a tomcat and I never said "I love you" first. That's unmanly.

BOB: That's because you're a control freak.

TED: True . . . but . . .

BOB: But what?

TED: They won't respect you in the morning . . . if you de-clare your feelings so fast.

BOB: That ridiculous.

TED: They want to hook you and then reel you in slowly. They want a catch who fights a little, or in some cases a lot . . . like a fisherman reeling in a powerful dolphin.

BOB: Ted, I'm not a damn fish!

TED: Okay, I think I know what I'm working with . . . Oh, how old is she?

BOB: I don't know.

TED: What do you mean you "don't know."

BOB: I don't. Age never came up in any of our conversations.

TED: Well . . . can you give me a guesstimate ? Is she in her thirties, twenties . . . jailbait?

BOB: I'd say thirties . . . late thirties . . .

TED: And you just had your twenty-eighth birthday. She's robbing the cradle!

BOB: So what . . . She can open up new vistas for me. I can learn from her experience.

TED: She's a cougar! You're just fresh meat for her. As soon as she finishes the meal, you're history.

BOB: Man, you are one cynical, bitter guy. I'm taking it one day at a time. Whatever happens, happens. Right now I'm leaving my armor in my closet.

TED: It's your funeral.

BOB: I'll take that risk. Now are you going to help me write this letter or not?

TED: Sure. You're my friend. I see your ugly mug every day. I want you to be happy! I'm also a single guy like you. I know all the games, every trick in their purse.

BOB: How come you never married?

TED: Marriage is an institution. Why would I want to spend my life in an institution?

BOB: You'd make a great dad.

TED: I have a dog . . . who won't go to college and put me into debt for the rest of my life . . . besides . . . I don't want the state looking over my shoulder . . . and I don't want to go through a divorce, which is inevitable in most marriages.

BOB: Yes, but . . .

TED: Let's get back to the job at hand. I'll leave "love" to suckers like you. Okay: you both allegedly love one another; you have great sex; she's sensitive to your touch and so on . . . Oh, has she cooked a meal for you yet?

BOB: No. Why?

TED: Because food is sexy and romantic. A woman can express her affection through her cooking.

BOB: I don't think she cooks for herself. Eats out all the time. Is that a problem?

TED: Not necessarily. But eating out every night is expensive, and if you're paying the bills, that's digging a big hole in your pocket.

BOB: I can handle it.

TED: Not on what they're paying you here. What does she do for work?

BOB: She's . . . a dancer.

TED: Uh oh . . . What kind?

BOB: Exotic. She dances to put herself through law school.

TED: You're kidding me. She really goes to—

BOB: That's what she said . . . Something legal . . . Or maybe it was paralegal school. Or maybe it was—

TED: Maybe it was thong school? They're legal!

BOB: Very funny, but you'd change your tone if you ever saw her dance . . . wrap herself around a pole like a seductive serpent. That'll put a tent in your pants.

TED: How'd you meet, at a lap dance?

BOB: No. She smiled at me when I stuck a five dollar bill in her G-string and my finger got caught and almost yanked her costume off. The bouncer tried to throw me out but Janice intervened. Then, after I saw her act a few more times she handed me her number and the rest is history.

TED: My dates won't pole dance for me. I'm jealous.

BOB: Look . . . I just wanted to send her a romantic letter. A Thanksgiving letter!

TED: Just trying to watch your back. You're my friend. Friends watch out for each other. And I know how fucked up you get after your fall from bliss into hell!

BOB: I appreciate that.

TED: Before Black Magic there was the Scorpion; Pretty Poison; and the Venus Fly Trap. They all ripped your heart out and left you with the emotional wreckage. Now you're involved with a Serpent!

BOB: Maybe Janice is . . . different . . . You need hope,

don't you? You can't waltz around life without hope.
Without thanks for the gift of life. You'd die . . . Despair
. . . then die . . .

TED: You're right. I'm sorry if I—

BOB: Don't apologize. I do have a lousy track record with
women. I am a fool. A cynical fool.

TED: Stop it! You're not a fool . . . just hopeful. Let's get
back to the letter.

(Beat)

BOB: Maybe I should rethink this relationship.

TED: I'm sorry . . . I didn't mean to burst your balloon . . .
but you have to protect yourself.

BOB: Maybe I'll worry about the letter later.

TED: I'm glad to help anytime. Like I said . . . I got your back.

BOB: I appreciate that.

TED: Women can be very dangerous, Bob. Don't wear your
heart on your sleeve. Keep it hidden till you're absolutely
certain she's true and blue throughout.

(Pause)

BOB: I think I'll send her a card instead . . .

TED: Sounds like a plan . . .

(Beat)

Where did you say she dances?

(LIGHTS FADE)

END OF PLAY

2012, presented by Turnip Theatre Festival, produced by Dirt Theatre Company

Directed by Carter Jackson

CAST
TOMMY: Dean Imperial
AMBER: Annie Meisels

Producer Contact: jacksoncarter@gmail.com

2014 produced by Core Artists Ensemble

Directed by Jenna Worsham

CAST
TOMMY: Dean Imperial
AMBER: Rachel Casparian

Producer Contact: coreartistensemble@gmail.com

TOMMY: (M) any age, any ethnicity. Amber's husband. Well meaning. Sexually frustrated to the point of desperation.

AMBER: (W) any age, any ethnicity. Tommy's wife. Determined to avoid the elephant in the room.

Setting:

A bedroom of a rent-stabilized New York City apartment. Shabby around the edges.

Time:

Now.

A bedroom. A made bed. Empty black garbage bags in a corner. TOMMY, in shorts and T shirt, folds a stack of clothes on a tarp on the floor over and over again nervously. Off stage the noise of door being unlocked.

TOMMY: Amber?
  (Amber enters carrying a full garbage bag. She wears her hair up and is sweating. A lot.)
AMBER: I have seen the fires of hell.
TOMMY: God.
AMBER: It's not your fault. You did your turn.
TOMMY: I'm sorry. I didn't mean for you to get the worst of it. You look like you've been in a sauna—
AMBER: It's like 110 degrees down there. Seriously. It's like 104 outside and 110 degrees down in the basement. And I don't know if you know this? But a dryer? It generates heat.
TOMMY: Well. Nothing will live through that?
AMBER: The good news is this is the last of it.
TOMMY: That is good news. That's the best news I've heard.
AMBER: Yeah, one more bag and we are back to—
  (seeing the bed)
  You made the bed.
TOMMY: Yeah.

AMBER: Did you—

TOMMY: I did everything. Don't—

AMBER: Don't what?

TOMMY: Look at it like it's done something to you.

AMBER: I feel like it did.

TOMMY: It didn't.

AMBER: Your grandmother gave us that mattress for our wedding. Your aunt gave us the sheets.

TOMMY: I have something for you.

AMBER: Wait. Let me just finish and put this to—He presents her with a bottle of wine.

AMBER: What's this?

TOMMY: You tell me.

(She unwraps it.)

AMBER: Oh my God.

TOMMY: Did I do okay?

AMBER: Oh my God. This is totally. From the night we went out w Tony and Magdalena.

TOMMY: I called the bar and got the name. I talked to Katrina—

AMBER: This is like a $150 bottle of wine.

TOMMY: So?

AMBER: So. It's like a $150 bottle of wine.

TOMMY: I thought we deserved it.

AMBER: Wow.

(He pulls out glasses and an opener.)

AMBER: Wow.

TOMMY: I am a full service operation.

AMBER: Wait. Just let me put these away—

TOMMY: No. No "just letting you". Stop. Stop.

(He pours.)

TOMMY: To new beginnings

AMBER: To total death and annihilation.

TOMMY: Okay. To that too.

(The clink at that. Taste.)

AMBER: Gorgeous

TOMMY: Yes.

(He goes to kiss her.)

AMBER: I'm sorry. I'm sorry. This is so nice. It's just. I just feel so dirty.

TOMMY: I like you dirty.

AMBER: Please just let me change my—

TOMMY: Amber—

(She dumps out the garbage bag. Clothes. She stares at them.)

AMBER: This was all the bags?

TOMMY: That better be all of them.

AMBER: And you put everything back in the drawers—

TOMMY: Yes! I told you—

AMBER: Okay. My underwear is totally missing.

TOMMY: Oh. Oh?

AMBER: Like it's gone. All of it. I don't have a single pair. I didn't want to wear any now because I wanted to wash—

TOMMY: Well. Are you sure you—

AMBER: Yes I'm sure!

TOMMY: Okay!

AMBER: It's my underwear! I know when my underwear is missing! Jesus, my underwear is missing. That is so frickin—

TOMMY: Okay. Well. Maybe you could go without it?

AMBER: What?

TOMMY: You know. It's sexy. Short dress. It's hot outside.

AMBER: It's sexy. To go without my underwear. Forever.

TOMMY: No. I meant—

AMBER: Okay. I'm going back down to look—

TOMMY: Don't—

AMBER: No! This is too weird.

TOMMY: It's not.

AMBER: Of course it. Wait. What?

TOMMY: Okay, okay. Um. . .you know Jack. From around the corner.

AMBER: The sushi guy?

TOMMY: Yeah.

AMBER: Why are you talking to me about Jack the sushi guy?

TOMMY: I ran into him.

AMBER: Okay

TOMMY: Okay. And I was carrying our laundry and I stopped to talk to him and. And your underwear was kind of on top—

AMBER: Oh my God! Why would you ever put my dirty underwear on top—

TOMMY: And he looked and said. . . he thinks you're really pretty, like really pretty. Which of course you totally are. *(He kisses her. She doesn't respond. He goes to kiss her again.)*

AMBER: What the hell does this—

TOMMY: Oh. So. So he. I kind of. Well. I sold them if you must know. I sold your underwear. To him. *(Amber stares. He's unnerved by it.)*

TOMMY: I did. He made me a kind of insane offer and I was just in the moment and. Anyway. (seductive)What do you think he's going to do with them? *(Amber dumps her glass of wine on him.)*

TOMMY: Hey! *(She dumps the whole bottle of wine on him.)*

TOMMY: Are you out of your mind? Do you have any idea—

AMBER: What kind of a person are you!

TOMMY: What? I just thought—

AMBER: What kind of person sells his wife's underwear to a sushi guy?! Oh. I'm sorry. I know that guy. That's the kind of guy who insists we park on the street instead of paying for a garage.

TOMMY: Wait what?

AMBER: And then ends up floating New York City with all the parking tickets he wracks up—

TOMMY: Hey!

AMBER: —and puts them on overloaded credit cards and decides we subsequently have to live in his horrible decaying rent stabilized apartment—

TOMMY: Oh so we should kiss up to your dad instead so we can live in his place and totally be—doormen buildings get bedbugs too!

AMBER: Doormen buildings at least pretend to be clean you idiot!

TOMMY: Oh. I'm an idiot? That's what you think?

AMBER: No.

TOMMY: Oh my God. You think I'm an idiot.

She doesn't say anything. Tommy takes out a bag from the back of his shorts. He opens it.

AMBER: What's that? Some kind of stupid peace off—He throws a dozen panties at her.

TOMMY: There! Happy?

AMBER: . . .did he give them back to you?

TOMMY: I made it up. You idiot.

AMBER: What!

TOMMY: Yeah! I was under the misguided idea that you might think it was sexy.

AMBER: Okay. Okay. So just to rehash, you thought that I would think it's sexy to tell me that the Jack the sushi guy bought my underwear from you—

TOMMY: You told me I was boring. The last time we. . .

AMBER: Oh.

TOMMY: Yeah. Remember that?

AMBER: I didn't. . .

TOMMY: You didn't what? Mean it? The way you didn't mean I was an idiot.

AMBER: *(struggling)*. . .I just. . .I wanted you to throw me up against a wall. Or something.

TOMMY: Did you say that?

AMBER: Well—

TOMMY: Am I a mind reader? Oh no I'm sorry. I'm an idiot.

AMBER: Tommy stop—

TOMMY: Why won't you sleep with me?!

AMBER: We had bedbugs! Excuse me if I don't want little creeping disgusting crawling itching—

TOMMY: It was before the bedbugs and you know it. *(she grows quiet)* It's been four months. Do you know that? You're too busy or you're too tired or you're going to yoga—

AMBER: Don't throw—

TOMMY: Or you're working late at the restaurant or you have to go to therapy or you have to see Blair because she's had three miscarriages.

AMBER: Stop it!

TOMMY: You know what? This isn't working.

AMBER: What?

TOMMY: I can't do this anymore. I'm a guy. I'm a man.

AMBER: What do you mean? Tommy. Tommy. What do you mean? What do you mean? What do you mean you can't do this anymore?

He doesn't answer. They sit with that for a while. Suddenly she licks his arm.

TOMMY: What the hell?

(She licks it again. It's just plain weird.)

AMBER: Mmm. Tastes better than in a glass.

TOMMY: Stop it. That's just. You're like a spaniel or something. Jesus.

(They sit. Tommy begins shaking his head.)

TOMMY: I'm just gonna—

AMBER: (quietly) Maybe he. . .he smelled them.

(A loaded pause. He turns. She tries to say something more. Doesn't. He starts to get up. She grabs him.)

AMBER: Maybe he. Maybe he was. Knowing I wasn't wearing any panties. Because he had all of them. You know. So I was . . . I was

TOMMY: What.

AMBER: Crossing my legs. With nothing. There. Maybe he was thinking about how I would be . . . moist. And. . . hot. And I would smell. A lot.

TOMMY: . . .yeah?

AMBER: I would smell like like sushi. But hot wet moist sushi. Between my legs.

TOMMY: Yeah

AMBER: Yeah. Maybe he would take his finger and touch me and then lick it, lick his finger

TOMMY: Yeah?

AMBER: And while he would he would put his hand all the way up me. His fist . . .

(He does.)

AMBER: Oh God.

TOMMY: You really aren't wearing underwear.

AMBER: And he would grab me. Oh. And he would hoist me He does.

AMBER: And he would fuck me for all I'm—

They are all over each other. They can't stop. It's messy, hot, wild. Clothing starts to come off. Tommy throws her on the bed, throws himself on top of her. *Beat.*

AMBER: *(in between kisses)* Oh my God. The bed.

TOMMY: *(into it)* The bed.

AMBER: We're on the bed.

TOMMY: *(raunchy)* You're on the bed. I'm on—

AMBER: The bed! The bed! We're on the bed!

They both scream, recoil, scramble to the other side of the room. Slowly, warily, they turn towards the bed. And stare. After an interminable amount of time, Tommy turns to Amber.

TOMMY: . . . maybe we could try the futon?

END OF PLAY

RAGHEAD Premiered on 9/5/14 as part of the Pittsburgh New Works Festival, produced by McKeesport Little Theater.

Directed by Mark A. Calla

CAST
NICK: John Siciliano
SARAH: Jennifer Luta

Stage Manager: Rose-Lorene Miller
Producer: Linda L. Baker

    SARAH: Female, twenty to thirty-five, Italian-American. Nicely dressed, hip, she wears a pretty headscarf in an Islamic hijab style. Method actor.

    NICK: Male, twenty-two to thirty-five, Italian-American, firefighter. A regular, normal guy. Nicely dressed.

SETTING:

    Cozy bar in New York City. Rainy day. Table for two.

TIME:

    The Present.

Cozy bar in New York City. Rainy day. A blind date. Nick sits at a table for two, beer in front of him, reading a text on his cell phone. Smiles. Texts back. Gets a text. Laughs. Gets another text. Sarah enters wearing a rain coat with a hood. Umbrella. Under her hood she wears a pretty headscarf in an Islamic hijab style. She texts. Nick gets text, raises his hand, she waves. She rushes to table. Nick stands, smiling, a gentleman.

SARAH: Thank you, thank you, thank you for waiting. I'm so sorry.

NICK: Hi.

(She hands him her umbrella)

SARAH: Stand back!

(He stands back.)

I'm soaked!

(She gives a little shake, shedding raindrops. He smiles. She sheds purse, raincoat. Her headscarf is revealed. Nick stops smiling.)

I ran all the way from the stop. I was stuck in the subway car for like twenty minutes. Not moving. It was nothing but you never know, right? I thought god, please don't let there be anything happening. Like last month, that guy who jumped in front of the train. Crazy. I'm totally babbling aren't I? I'm sorry, this has been a really weird day. Babbling is my first line of defense.

(She sits)

Anyway, so, hi! How are you?

NICK: Uh, listen, I'm really sorry, I think maybe you've got the wrong table.

SARAH: But..you're Nick right? Nick, Jen's cousin the fireman?

NICK: Right . . . but . . . who are you?

SARAH: Sarah! *(Indicates phone)* We've been texting?

NICK: You're Sarah?

SARAH: Appearing before you live, in the rain-soaked flesh.

(Takes umbrella)

Sit!

(Nick slowly sits)

What are you drinking? Bud Light? And you call yourself a fireman.

NICK: Firefighter.

SARAH: Really? Firefighter?

NICK: That's what we call ourselves.

SARAH: I like that. Action word. Sexy *and* PC. Graphic! Is there a waiter? I could totally kill a double black rum OJ with a splash of vodka . . . I'm kidding, I'm kidding! I'm a pinot grigio girl.

NICK: You drink alcohol?

SARAH: Does pinot grigio actually count as alcohol?

NICK: I thought Muslims didn't drink.

SARAH: Seriously? I know lots of Muslims that drink. Lots! If their waiter shows up.

NICK: Waitress. Allison. She was just here.

SARAH: Allison. You come here a lot?

NICK: Yeah. Close to the station. I just got off.

SARAH: Is this like a firefighter hotspot?

NICK: Sort of.

SARAH: Good place to hook up some burning, burning love? Or do firemen all use match.com?

NICK: Jen said you were funny.

SARAH: Oh god, I'm sorry, sorry. I swore I wasn't going to

---

make any fireman jokes. Firefighter. I'm being an idiot. Post-audition adrenalin frenzy. Plus I'm really nervous. Plus . . . Sarah, stop speaking, just close your mouth. *(She does.)*

NICK: You were at an audition?

SARAH: Disaster. Don't ask.

NICK: Sorry.

SARAH: Humiliating. Maddening. Made me want to kick the director's balls up into his ivy-league esophagus.

NICK: *(Pause)* You're not what I was expecting.

SARAH: You weren't expecting a babbling, bitter, soggy, wall of sound?

NICK: You don't look like your photo.

SARAH: That's what they said at the audition! Didn't have the Juliette look. Wait, what photo? Oh my god, she didn't show you the Spring break whipped cream motel room? That's not me!

NICK: I mean, I didn't expect . . .

(vaguely indicates the veil, embarrassed)

SARAH: Ahh, right. I get it. That was a veiled reference.

NICK: No, I mean..I guess it is.

SARAH: You're freaked out.

NICK: Surprised.

SARAH: Maybe you think a veiled women shouldn't be in a bar?

NICK: I didn't say that.

SARAH: Or god forbid at an audition. Women of Juliette's day WORE veils! Can I ask you something?

NICK: Sure.

SARAH: Do men find veiled women sexy?

NICK: Seriously?

SARAH: The director said he wanted a sexy Juliette.

NICK: Ah.

SARAH: So when you, you being all Western men, see a veiled woman, like me, on the street, don't you wonder what she looks like under all those clothes.

NICK: Well . . .

SARAH: Come on . . . the mystery of the hidden. Salome

and her seven veils, the nine parts of desire. Don't you want to rip my clothes off with your teeth?

NICK: That's a trick question.

SARAH: A taxi driver said that to me this very morning.

NICK: Oh. Honestly?

SARAH: Speak your heart.

NICK: Then no, oppressed isn't sexy.

SARAH: Now I'm oppressed?

NICK: Look, all I really know about veils is what I see on TV.

SARAH: So, I should go on Dr. Phil? Call Oprah?!

NICK: Come on.

SARAH: Do I *seem* oppressed to you?

NICK: Jen said you were warm, caring, and smart.

SARAH: I knew I liked her. BFF!

NICK: That you were pretty.

SARAH: Aw shucks! She told me that while you might not exactly be the nudie calendar kind of fireman, you were the kind who would carry women and children out of a burning building.

NICK: That you had real talent.

SARAH: That you had, in fact, carried women and children out of a burning building! And that you were quiet. The strong, silent type. Which is good, right? Opposites attract?

NICK: That you would be a wonderful mom.

SARAH: That you listened. And sometimes I think that's all I really want from life is someone to listen.

NICK: She didn't say that you were Muslim.

SARAH: She didn't?

NICK: Somehow I got the impression that you were . . . well Catholic.

SARAH: Oh.

NICK: Like me. And it's not like I'm Opus Dei or anything but I think that in terms of love and marriage..and my mother, Muslim and Catholic don't mix. Water and oil. Irreconcilable differences. So, no offense, I'm sure you're a wonderful girl, but dating-wise, you're a wonderful Muslim girl and I just don't think this is gonna work out. I'm sorry.

(He starts to get up to leave.)

SARAH: Ok, ok, wait . . . listen . . . I'm not Muslim.

NICK: You're not?

SARAH: I am Catholic. Born and raised, fish every friday.

NICK: I don't get it. So this is what? Some kind of joke?

SARAH: No! More of a social experiment. It's research for a role . . . for a play reading. I'm playing a Palestinian woman.

NICK: So, you don't wear a veil?

SARAH: In the play I wear one. So, I wore this all day to see what it's like. *Serious* eye-opener.

(Nick laughs at a memory)

What?

NICK: When you first took your hood off, I thought, oh my god, she's had brain surgery.

SARAH: Ha, ha! Do you know how long I practiced putting this on. YouTube all-nighter. I wasn't gonna wear it here but . . . I wanted to see how you would react.

NICK: Thanks, I always wanted to be a social experiment.

SARAH: After today, somehow it became important to see how you would react.

NICK: I can't believe you wore that to an audition.

SARAH: The whole freaking day.

NICK: More?

SARAH: Oh my god, first, the gym, I mean I go there three times a week and now people wouldn't even look at me. Or else they totally stared, like I was wearing panties on my head. One woman asked me if I wear my veil in the shower!

NICK: Did you?

SARAH: No, my Al Queda shower cap, smart ass. Then lunch shift at the restaurant. My owner, who barely speaks English, had a little after work chat with me about proper dress and how a hostess wearing a veil might freak out the customers. Look "un-American." In a Mexican restaurant! Then at the post office I got the other extreme, this lady speaking reeaally slowly, trying to be soooo helpful like I can't find my way to the counter. Followed by that pig taxi driver. Followed by audition megaflop. Then..well..

NICK: The subway.

SARAH: Yeah, the subway.

NICK: So take it off, let your hair down. You did your homework. Relax and have a drink.

SARAH: I would if Casper the friendly waitress would appear.

NICK: Maybe if you took your veil off.

SARAH: What do you mean?

NICK: I don't know, I just think . . . well, I know she had a brother who was a first responder on 9/11. He died in the tower.

SARAH: A firefighter.

NICK: His photo's on the wall at my station.

SARAH: And she what, thinks I had something to do with it?

NICK: Painful memories. I don't know. I'm just guessing. I know she's not the only one in here feels that way.

SARAH: So I have to sit here with no drink because I have a piece of cloth on my head?!

NICK: Come on, chill. You're not Muslim, you don't wear a veil. You're just pretending.

SARAH: What if I was a Muslim?

NICK: Look, maybe we should just go somewhere else?

SARAH: How is a veil different than a hat?
(Indicating Nick's NY Yankees hat hanging on the back of his chair.)
What if I wore my Red Sox hat in here?

NICK: You probably still wouldn't get served.

SARAH: What about nuns? They wear veils. Would they get served?

NICK: Come on, there's a good falafel place around the corner.

SARAH: So, you don't personally like the veil?

NICK: I'd prefer to talk to the real you.

SARAH: Would it be different if I wore it around my neck? Or around my waist like a little gypsy? Maybe you'd like it if all I wore was this scarf?

(She starts unbuttoning her blouse.)

NICK: What are you doing?

SARAH:

(Continues to unbutton blouse)

Another social experiment?

NICK: Seriously?

SARAH: Come on, a blouse is just another piece of cloth.

NICK: Not sexy.

SARAH: No?

NICK: No, just nuts. I'm sorry but I'm out of here.

(Nick gets up to leave, putting coat on, etc. during the next lines)

SARAH: Raghead.

NICK: What?

SARAH: Hey raghead, show us your tits.

NICK: Jen forgot to say you were wacked.

SARAH: Someone..someones..said that to me while I was waiting for the subway. On the platform. On the way here. It's affected my outlook.

NICK: I'm sorry.

SARAH: Group of guys, college guys, baseball hats, drunk, coming from a game or something. Regular, normal guys.

NICK: Arrested development.

SARAH: Snide, sneaky stage whispers . . . "Hey, do you fuck camels?" "Show us your humps."

NICK: And what, you tried a social experiment on them?

SARAH: I wanted to try a rectal experiment on them but instead I walked away . . . and one guy shouted after me "Go back to your own fucked up country, you sand nigger bitch." *(pause)* Nobody else on the platform said anything, nobody did anything. Just looked away.

NICK: Men can be real scumbags. I'm sorry.

SARAH: Jen said you were a regular, normal guy.

NICK: Now you're comparing me to these assholes?

SARAH: I needed to know.

NICK: Well, you know what? I came here to meet a woman I heard a lot of nice things about. Someone I might really like. Maybe even have a future with. I was . . . hopeful.

I didn't come to be a guinea pig.

SARAH: I'm sorry . . . We're not exactly getting along like a house on fire, are we?

NICK: You won't take the veil off?

SARAH: I don't think so.

NICK: Then no, I don't see much future here. I'm sorry, I'm sorry you got hassled. I'm sorry your experiment didn't work out. Goodbye.

SARAH: Don't forget your hat.

(He grabs his hat, leaves. After a moment.)

Shit.

(She takes off the veil. Drinks the rest of his beer. Pause. She puts the veil back on.)

THE END

SMART BRA
Sylvia Reed

Smart Bra was originally produced by Theatre Odyssey, of Longboat Key, Florida, at the Jane B. Cook Theatre, FSU Center for the Performing Arts (The Asolo Repertory Theatre), 5555 N. Tamiami Trail, Sarasota, Florida 34243, on May 1-4, 2014. Directed by Carole Kleinberg. Donna DeFant, Production Stage Manager.

CAST
JANE: Brianna Larson
JOHN: Mitcheal Pearl

CHARACTERS:

JANE: Twenties.

JOHN: Twenties.

TIME:

Now.

PLACE:

A coffee/wine bar. A table and two chairs.

As the lights come up, JOHN is looking at his phone, checking for messages, etc. JANE enters, approaches him cautiously.

JANE: Ummmm . . . Are you . . . ?

JOHN: Jane?

JANE: *I'm* Jane.

JOHN: Of course. I wasn't saying I'm Jane. You're Jane. I'm John.

(They shake hands.)

JANE: Nice to meet you.

JOHN: Yes. Face to face. Please sit down.

JANE: So.

JOHN: Yes.

(Awkward silence, then finally—)

JOHN cont'd: Your voice is different than I thought it would be.

JANE: Really?

JOHN: Yeah.

JANE: Different . . . in a good way?

JOHN: Yeah. I mean, it's not like I thought you'd have a bad voice or anything, but your texts were really, really clever, and I was kind of picturing Tina Fey when I read them and my god, I love her, even though she's older than me, but I love her and the way her voice is—not her doing Sarah Palin—but actually kind of like that because when I see her now all I can think of is Sarah Palin.

JANE: I hate Sarah Palin.

JOHN: Oh. Well . . . I don't really have an opinion of her one way or the other but—JANE: You don't?

JOHN: No.

JANE: I don't think I've ever met anyone who doesn't have an opinion one way or the other about her.

JOHN: She's kind of irrelevant these days so . . .

(The SOUND of a soft buzzing noise.)

JOHN cont'd: What's that?

JANE: It's my bra.

JOHN: Your . . . bra?

JANE: It's sensing something.

JOHN: Like what?

JANE: It's telling me I don't believe you.

JOHN: Believe me? About what?

JANE: About Sarah Palin.

JOHN: What about Sarah Palin?

JANE: It's telling me to be skeptical about your statement you have no opinion of her.

JOHN: Your bra can tell you that?

JANE: I guess my heart started beating a little faster and my heart-rate fell into the category of Proceed With Caution/ Don't Trust What's Happening Around You, and I took this to mean maybe I shouldn't believe what you just said.

JOHN: A bra can do that?

JANE: It's a Smart Bra.

JOHN: Do you . . . want to order something? Coffee? Glass of wine?

(JANE'S bra starts to buzz again.)

JOHN *(cont'd)*: Is that . . . your bra . . . again?

JANE: It's warning me I'm about to eat comfort food.

(speaking to her chest)

You are really clever.

(to JOHN)

This thing knows me. It knew I was about to get a cookie.

JOHN: So it's like a diet thing.

JANE: I guess. I still don't know the extent of what this bra can do because I'm just getting to know it. An Amazon drone dropped it at my front door yesterday.

JOHN: Oh.

JANE: And it came with this link to a website where you program in all this stuff about yourself and you synch it to your bra like what time of day are you most likely to crave junk food and when you crave it do you go for chips or do you go for cookies and cake—salty versus sweet, I guess—'cause maybe the heart beats differently depending on how you like to binge?

(shakes her head as if "this stuff eludes me")

I don't know. Technology.

JOHN: Wow.

JANE: Right? And the manual says you have to be really honest about it or it won't work properly and quite frankly it was kind of hard for me to program in just how much I love wine because I know it's gonna be buzzing like crazy every time I get the idea I want a pinot grigio and that's gonna suck because it's like I've got the Alcohol Police strapped to my chest.

JOHN: Huh. That's . . . wow. Maybe that's why it buzzed then. 'Cause I mentioned wine.

JANE: I was really feeling chocolate chips when it buzzed.

JOHN: I never would have gotten this . . . from your texts.

JANE: I didn't have it when we started texting. And of course I had to program it and that took For. Ev. Er.

JOHN: I suppose if I would have called you we could have had some talks and maybe I would have learned you are a sweet versus salty eater and you like white wine more than red. I could have learned some things about you. Heard your voice.

JANE: That might have been awkward.

JOHN: What?

JANE: Talking? On the phone? Who does that?

JOHN: What about this?

JANE: What?

JOHN: You don't think this is awkward?

JANE: What?

JOHN: You think this is going well?

JANE: What's wrong with it?

JOHN: Well your bra called me a liar for one thing.

JANE: My bra doesn't call people out like that.

JOHN: Yes, it did.

JANE: It simply indicated I might not want to believe you that you have no opinion of Sarah Palin. It was just a . . . red flag. An advisory sort of thing.

(The bra buzzes again.)

JOHN: What's happening now?

JANE: I guess I'm nervous.

JOHN: Because . . .

JANE: Because you're making me feel uncomfortable.

JOHN: Can we start over?

JANE: I guess.

JOHN: I think we should just sit here and be silent for a moment and erase all the stuff that's just gone on, okay?

JANE: Like just sit here and not say anything?

JOHN: Yeah.

JANE: And just look at each other?

JOHN: Or look wherever you want. Just breathe. Just . . . be in the moment.

(They breathe. After a moment, the bra makes a loud noise like a zap.)

JANE: Ouch!

JOHN: What happened?

(JANE gets up. She jogs around the table as she talks to JOHN. He follows her with his eyes round and round.)

JANE: My god that hurts.

JOHN: What did it do?

JANE: It shocked me.

JOHN: The bra?

JANE: Yeah. I need to adjust that setting, holy crap.

JOHN: Are you okay?

JANE: Yeah, I'm okay. It's just when you sit for too long it gives you a jolt and makes you get up and get moving. It actually counts your steps and if it looks like you aren't going to get 10,000 steps in by the end of the day it goes full-on bitch-mode and gives you a jolt.

JOHN: That sounds awful.

*(JANE does some jumping jacks. JOHN watches.
She finally sits back down.)*

JANE: *(practically out of breath)* Okay. . . . I think it's safe
to sit down. . . . I was counting in my head as I jogged
and I got about 25 steps in. And then . . . when I did the
jumping jacks . . . that really helped because it dumps
that activity into a savings account sort of thing that lets
you sit for a little longer. And the bra massaged me like,
Good job, Jane! It's supportive like that.

(to her chest)

    Thanks for the props, Bra.

(to JOHN)

I guess I've appeased it for the time being. So where
were we?

JOHN: I . . . have no idea.

(JOHN looks at his phone.)

JANE: What are you doing?

JOHN: Ummm. Nothing.

JANE: You're checking your phone.

(pause)

Are you with me or are you with your phone?

(The bra buzzes again.)

JANE cont'd: *(looking down at her chest)* I know, I know,
I'm getting it loud and clear you don't have to tell me.

JOHN: What? What are you getting loud and clear?

JANE: I'm getting that your phone is more important to you
than being here with me.

JOHN: You're getting that?

JANE: Yes I am.

JOHN: Well you want to know what I'm getting?

JANE: What are you getting?

(The SOUND of crickets chirping.)

JOHN: *(looks down at his lap)* Nothing.

JANE: What are you looking at?

JOHN: Let's just say they make similar technologies for men.

JANE: Like a Smart . . . ?

JOHN: Yep.

JANE: And you get nothing from me?

JOHN: Crickets.

JANE: Like . . . you don't think I'm attractive?

JOHN: I actually find you attractive. On the surface.

(JANE is very hurt. Her bra buzzes along with the crickets. Then the noises finally stop.)

JANE and JOHN: What just happened?

JANE: It stopped. I don't know what I feel.

If I had to guess, I think I feel like maybe I blew it with you.

JOHN: I think maybe I was a little too harsh.

(pause)

What if we tried something new?

JANE: Like what?

JOHN: What if you took off your bra?

JANE: I suppose I could do that.

(JANE reaches under her shirt and unhooks her bra. She shoots it off like a sling shot.)

JANE: Your turn.

JOHN: Okay.

JANE: I guess you'll need to go to the bathroom.

JOHN: There's an app on my phone.

(JOHN turns off the app. He looks at JANE. After a moment—)

JOHN: *(holds out his hand)* I'm John.

JANE: I'm Jane. Nice to finally meet you.

SMITTEN

Mark Harvey Levine

Smitten was produced in October, 2014 by Ballybridge Players Drama Club, (Ballymacoda/Ladysbridge, County Cork, Ireland).

Directed by Anne Smyth

CAST
AMY: OLIVIA O'ROURKE
BARB: ORLA RIORDAN

AMY: twenties to forties, BARB:'s trusty friend, a little sassy.

BARB: twenties to forties, currently upset, going through a break-up.

SETTING:

Barb's apartment.

TIME:

Afternoon.

BARB: is busy packing all her belongings.
(AMY knocks at the door and BARB lets her in.)
BARB: Oh, AMY:! I'm so glad you're here.
(They hug.)
AMY: What's wrong?
BARB: It's just . . . I'm . . .
AMY: Is it . . . him?
BARB: Yes it's him. Of course it's him.
AMY: Well, how's it going?
BARB: I need you to help me pack.
AMY: That good, huh?
BARB: I've had it with him. I've completely had it. I'm moving out.
AMY: Now Barb, before you do anything crazy . . .
BARB: No, I'm serious. It's over. I'm completely done. I need you to start putting clothes in this.
(She hands amy a duffle bag.)
AMY: Where are you going to go?
BARB: I don't know, I'll get a hotel room until I can sort things out.
AMY: Oh shut up, you know you can stay with me.
BARB: You really don't need to—
AMY: Please! I'm not going to hear another word about it.
BARB: Well, thank you . . . that would be fantastic.
AMY: So what did he do this time?
BARB: Nothing. He didn't do anything.

AMY: So?

BARB: That's the point. He never does anything. He doesn't talk to me. He's never here.

AMY: Oh, come on, how can he never be here?

BARB: He's never here.

AMY: Honey, he's God, he's everywhere.

BARB: I know! I know! That's what everyone says. But do you see him around?

AMY: Well, you can't see him. You knew that when you moved in.

BARB: Yeah, well, if he's everywhere, why is this place falling apart? The disposal's backed up, the a/c is on the fritz and my car broke its timing belt! Why doesn't he fix any of those things?

AMY: You know he doesn't work like that.

BARB: I had a boyfriend in college who was more handy around the house. And he wasn't omnipotent.

AMY: You know he loves you.

BARB: Yes, darling. He loves everyone. I was hoping for something a little more exclusive. Put the kitchen stuff in those boxes over there.

AMY: Honey . . . you can't dump God!

BARB: Why not? Why not? I wouldn't put up with this from any other boyfriend. I talk and talk until I'm blue in the face and you know what he says? Bupkis. Nothing.

BARB: starts putting things from around the living room into boxes.

AMY: But . . . but . . . he's God.

BARB: Yeah, yeah. God is great, God is good. But have you tried living with him? No flowers, no gifts, no miraculous cures, nothing. I give and give and get nothing in return.

AMY: Well, he gave you life . . .

BARB: He gave the same thing to the cockroaches. Which, by the way, I think we have.

AMY: Surely he speaks to you in mysterious ways.

BARB: I don't want mysterious ways! I want face to face! I want to come home and tell him about my day. I want to complain about the idiots in Marketing, meanwhile, he's off bringing a plague down on some poor village halfway around the world. It's very disheartening.

AMY: Well, we warned you.

BARB: I know, I know, never date a deity. I thought it would be different with him. I mean, he's God.

AMY: No, it always turns out badly. There's this girl at work, dated Apollo for a few weeks, got third degree burns all over her body. She went through five bottles of aloe a day. It's just not worth it.

BARB: It was fun at first. He'd take me places.

AMY: Like where?

BARB: Oh, everywhere. No, seriously, everywhere. All at once. It's kind of hard to describe. And he would cook for me. You should see what he can do with a burnt offering.

AMY: Sounds great.

BARB: But then it got a little weird . . .

AMY: Tell me.

BARB: Well, it started shortly after I moved in. Or maybe right before. It's hard to tell, because he exists out of time. It really messes up our TiVo. Anyway . . . he started to ask me to . . . do things.

AMY: Like what?

BARB: Like . . . well . . . worship him.

AMY: No!

BARB: Oh yes. Now, I'm a pretty open-minded girl. I've been around the block once or twice. But I mean. He set up this whole altar thingie. Wanted me to worship him at it.

AMY: Kinky.

BARB: And praise his name!

AMY: Girl! Mmm! No!

BARB: Now there are some things I just won't do. And then he puts this whole list of commandments on the dry-erase board on our fridge.

AMY: For real?

BARB: Honey, you don't know the half of it.

AMY: Well, you're not perfect either.

BARB: Oh I know. Trust me, I know. He makes me feel guilty about every little wrong thing I do.

AMY: Well . . .

BARB: I mean, I steal a couple envelopes from work and suddenly it's a sin.

AMY: So when are you going to tell him that you're leaving?

BARB: I'm not. I can't face him. Not to mention that I'd have to prostrate myself. It's killing my back. I'm just going to leave a note.

AMY: What?

BARB: That's why I need you to help me pack! I have to get out of here fast.

AMY: You can't dump God with just a note!

BARB: It's on a scroll. He likes scrolls . . .

AMY: He's still going to be furious. Wrathful, even.

BARB: I don't care! After this, I'm through with gods.

AMY: That's what you said last time.

BARB: I mean, there is this one guy at work . . .

AMY: Here we go.

BARB: But he's a demi-god. His mother was human. His father was disguised as a swan. I'm sure there's a whopper of a story there.

(There's a burst of lightning and thunder.)

AMY: Oh boy.

BARB: *(looking up)* Go ahead! Be angry! I don't care!

AMY: Honey . . .

BARB: I'm going to run off and be a Satanist! Amy, jump on the internet and see when the next Black Mass is.

AMY: *(panicking)* Oh man. Oh man. What do we do? I never know what to do in these situations.

BARB: *(calling upwards)* Is it too much to ask for a phone call every so often?

AMY: What do we do, build an ark?   Get two of every animal . . . ?!

BARB: You can part oceans, but you can't be home for dinner?

AMY: I know two people who own golden retrievers! That's it!

BARB: I mean, what do you want?! I don't even know what you want out of our relationship.

(More thunder and lightning, louder.)
(Amy and Barb hold each other tight.)

AMY: Barb . . . I think you'd better stop . . .

BARB: I'm supposed to love you. But how? There's no communication! All I get are these conflicting signals from you.
(Thunder.)

AMY: Barb, if you don't knock it off, this is going to be a planet with one girl and a whole lot of golden retrievers.

BARB: How am I supposed to love you?
(Thunder.)

AMY: BARB!

BARB: Huh? How am I supposed to love you? Tell me! Give me a sign!

AMY: Just give it one more try, for me! Just do it for me!

BARB: No. I've had it. He can smite me if he wants.

AMY: Smite?!

BARB: Yeah, he's big with the smiting. You better get out of here. Go on, get out, you don't want to get killed.

AMY: I'm not going anywhere. I'm with you, girl.
(Thunder, even louder. They hold each other tightly.)

BARB: I guess this is the end.

AMY: Man, when you dump someone, you really dump someone.

BARB: I'm so sorry.

AMY: It's okay. What are girlfriends for?
(More thunder.)

AMY: (CONT'D) We're gonna get smited!
(They hold each other tightly, bracing for the end, but the thunder subsides.)

BARB: I think it stopped . . .

AMY: What did you do?

BARB: I didn't do anything . . .

AMY: Well somebody did something . . .

BARB: I think you did . . .

AMY: Me?

BARB: You came over. You helped me pack. You listened to me complain. You were willing to stay and get smited with me.

AMY: *(joking)* I'm a good friend.

BARB: You are a good friend. Y'know . . . having a friend like you somehow . . . makes me feel . . . that somebody up there loves me.

AMY: I think he does. You still leaving?

BARB: *(she isn't)* . . . Oh man. Help me unpack.

AMY: I think you're making the right decision.

BARB: God help me. I'm so glad you came over here.

AMY: I'm so glad you called me.

BARB: *(stopping)* I didn't call you . . .

Lights fade.

ORIGINAL PRODUCTION

18th Annual One-Act Festival - Hot from the Oven: Smörgasbord presented by/at The Fine Arts Association, Willoughby, OH
March 28-April 12, 2014

Directed by Ann Hedger

CAST
A: Maria Lister Lyons
B: Catherine Remick

PRODUCERS
JAMES MANGO, DIRECTOR OF PERFORMING ARTS &
Ann Hedger, Director of the Fine Arts Association's 18th Annual One Act Festival

10 by 10 in the Triangle (13th Annual) presented by ArtsCenter Stage
at The ArtsCenter, Carrboro, NC
July 11-27, 2014

Directed by Jerry Sipp

Cast
A: Jillian Rose Lea
B: Page Purgar

Producer
Jeri Lynn Schulke
Artistic Director, ArtsCenter Stage
The ArtsCenter

CHARACTERS:
> A: A person, any age.
> B: A person, any age.

SETTING:
> This stage.

TIME:
> Now.

> Properties note: The gun can be mimed with a hand.

(A and B are on stage.)

A: This is not a play.

B: It doesn't have a beginning, middle and end.

A: It does begin, "This is not a play."

B: And it does end, "This is the end."

A: And there are lines in between those two lines which are in the middle.

B: But it doesn't have a "beginning, middle and end" beginning, middle and end.

A: It does have a gun.

> *(A displays a gun.)*

B: Now you've done it.

A: What?

B: Chekov's law. If you display a gun in act one, you have to use it in act three.

A: This play doesn't have an act three.

B: I thought you said it wasn't a play.

A: Then it can't have an act three.

B: But you called it a play.

A: This is not a play.

B: Then it doesn't have to obey Chekov's law.

A: That's a relief.

B: I assume it doesn't have a plot.

A: You know what happens when you assume, don't you?

B: No, I don't. What happens when you assume?

Lawrence Harbison

A: You run the risk of making an incorrect conclusion based on insufficient data.

B: So, does it have a plot?

A: Alas, it does not. It does, however, have a MacGuffin.
    (A displays a box.)

B: I want that.

A: You can't have it.

B: Give it to me.

A: No.
    (B attempts to get the box from A. A runs offstage and returns without it. B runs offstage. There might be thrashing about and anguish. B returns.)

B: Where did you hide it?

A: How do you know I hid it?

B: I can't find it.

A: If you could get it, it wouldn't be a MacGuffin.

B: But this is not a play. There's no need for a MacGuffin.

A: But you still want it.

B: Yes. I want it desperately. But you won't tell me where it is.

A: If you didn't want something desperately, it wouldn't be a play.

B: But it isn't a play. And I am not the protagonist.

A: That would make me the protagonist.

B: If it were a play. But it's not.

A: If I were the protagonist, what would I want? Diamonds? Ruby slippers? Big dumb objects?

B: That's your problem! You don't know what you want.

A: It's my tragic flaw.

B: Therapy might help.

A: Too expensive.

B: Brainstorming.

A: No brain.

B: Wizard of Oz!

A: Beg pardon?

B: The tin woodsman in the Wizard of Oz wanted a brain.

A: That was the scarecrow.

B: Oh, right.

A: I never said I wanted a brain. I'm perfectly fine without a brain. I can read, drive, wash dishes, talk on the phone, tweet, all without thinking.

B: If you say so.

A: No, really.

B: Maybe you want a purpose in life.

A: I'm not the protagonist! This is not a play and there's no protagonist.

B: I was only trying to help.

A: You are trying to force an Aristotelian model of storytelling on me.

B: Only with the best of intentions.

A: This is not a play!

B: Alright, alright, let me think.

A: That's it, rub it in. That you have a brain.

B: I wasn't trying to be stuck-up about it.

A: Fat lot of good that does. I'm hurt.

B: I'm sorry.

A: I'm not appeased.

B: Appeased. That's a grand word for someone who doesn't have a brain.

A: I heard it the other day. I liked it and that's why I used it. I was waiting for an opportunity to say it and you presented it to me, wrapped in a package.

B: That's it! I want that package! Now where did you put it?

A: Somewhere safe. I put it in a safe.

B: You weren't offstage long enough to put it in a safe.

A: I didn't say I closed the safe.

B: Did you close the safe?

A: Yes.

B: Excrement!

A: That's not very polite.

B: It's not polite to offer me a package then run away with it.

A: I didn't offer you the package. I merely displayed it to you.

B: To tantalize me!

A: Yes.

B: I demand an apology.

A: There is none to be had.

B: Then I'm not speaking to you.

Lawrence Harbison

A: Fine, I'll speak to the audience.

(To audience)

You might wonder what is going on here. I'm afraid the playwright—well, they can't be a playwright if this is not a play, can they?—the writer of the, um, literary work, is being rather difficult. Annoying even. They set up a—

B: Why are you calling the writer "they"? Writer is singular.

A: I though you weren't speaking to me.

B: I wasn't expecting you to speak in a ludicrous manner.

A: So if I continue being ludicrous you'll continue speaking to me? The moon is made of cheese. Gravity makes cakes rise. The earth is made of porridge.

B: Stop! Just give me the package.

A: What package?

B: The MacGuffin.

A: Silly actor. If I were to give you the MacGuffin, I would be violating thousand-year-old traditions of MacGuffin history.

B: MacGuffins haven't been around that long. And I'm not an actor. I'm a character.

A: You don't even have a name. In the script, it just calls us "A" and "B."

B: Which one am I?

A: "B."

B: I suppose you're "A" then.

A: I might be.

B: You're just being difficult.

A: Maybe I won't speak to you.

B: You will. You need me. Without me you'd be a solo piece.

A: There's nothing wrong with being a solo piece. There are lots of solo pieces. Or I could simply be a monologue. There's a long theatrical tradition of monologues.

B: Fine. Be that way.

A: *(To audience)* I once took a walk upon the banks of the Potomac. The river that runs through our nation's capital has a deep history. The Americ—

B: Talk to me!

A: I thought you told me to be that way.

B: I spoke in anger.

A: Is that supposed to be some kind of apology?

B: The deeply flawed kind.

A: I'm not sure I want to accept that kind of apology.

B: Please, please give me the MacGuffin.

A: It's no longer mine to give. I gave it to an orphan.

B: How is it even relevant that they are an orphan?

A: More sympathy that way.

B: I give up.

A: You can't give up. The whole point of a MacGuffin is that you want it and pursue it.

B: But this is not a play and I am not the protagonist.

A: That's very inconvenient.

B: Why?

A: The playwright was going to submit this to _(Insert name of theatre)._ He was going to write a ten-minute play.

B: It's not ten minutes yet. Maybe we have time to save this.

A: So what do we need to make this a play? Fast. We have two minutes.

B: We need an inciting incident. Where it all begins.

A: _(Insert name of theatre)_announces they are looking for ten-minute plays.

B: Now a point of attack.

A: What's that?

B: The thing that sets the plot in motion. Where the protagonist takes an action but is thwarted in meeting their desire.

A: The playwright starts this play, but my first line announces that this is not a play.

B: Excellent! Then we need rising action. The protagonist keeps trying for their goal and keeps getting thwarted.

A: The playwright keeps writing, but we go back and forth about the MacGuffin.

B: Yes. Now we're almost at the bottom of page nine. The protagonist needs to make one last, desperate try to get their wants met and meet almost overwhelming odds.

A: Wait. It sounds like you're talking about a climax.

B: Exactly.

A: Well, if we put the climax on page nine, then that's a whole page left for the resolution. Boring.

B: Okay, so we'll wait until we get to page ten.

A: We're already on page ten. We can have the climax.

B: We had that exchange just so we could delay the climax?

A: Do you have a problem with that?

B: I feel so used.

A: All characters are merely tools of the playwright.

B: This is not a play!

A: It's nearly a ten-minute play. We're so close.

B: Alright. This is a play. We're almost at the climax.

A: We displayed a gun on page one. We have to use it on page ten. This is page ten.

B: I can't do this any more. It's meaningless. Experimental plays are the worst. I'm going to end this right now.

A: What about the climax?

B: I'll give you a climax!

   (B shoots self. B dies.)

A: Wait! What about the resolution? There's supposed to be a resolution. I'm supposed to be sadder but wiser. No wait, I'm not the protagonist, the playwright is. The playwright is supposed to feel sadder but wiser. The ten pages are up. The play is over. This is the end.

   (End of play.)

WHAT REMAINS OF YOUTH
Erik Gernand

ORIGINAL PRODUCTION

Source Festival, Washington, DC, June 2014

Directed by Jarrod Jabre

CAST
JACOB: Seth Rosenke
SYDNEY: Tori Boutin

CHARACTERS:

> Jacob: nineteen, male, a college student
> Sydney: nineteen, female, a college student

SETTING:

> A college apartment in the present.

Jacob's college apartment. An evening in the present.

SYDNEY: *(back-tracking)* That's not what I think.

JACOB: *(angry)* But it's what you said.

SYDNEY: I'm sorry.

JACOB: How can you even ask that?

SYDNEY: I just felt . . . I don't know.

JACOB: Is that what you do with all of your friends? Go through their things? Their personal property?

SYDNEY: You left it sitting out.

JACOB: IN MY ROOM.

SYDNEY: That's not how I think of you. You're more than my friend.

JACOB: Yet that doesn't feel like something a friend, or possibly more than, would do.

SYDNEY: I know.

JACOB: That's more akin to a violation. To betrayal.

SYDNEY: I said I was sorry.

JACOB: Because that's pretty messed up. Really, really messed up. If that's what you truly think.

SYDNEY: At least you can understand why I asked.

JACOB: No. I'm afraid I don't

SYDNEY: Let's just go eat.

JACOB: I'm not hungry any more.

SYDNEY: I want to take you out for your birthday.

JACOB: It's not my birthday. Not for another three hours at least. I'm not going anywhere. Not now. Not with you. *(Beat.)*

SYDNEY: I already did the reading for tomorrow. I don't know why. It's a waste of time. And you're right, Masterson is a total pompous prick. I think he just wants to torture us. See how long it takes before we all slowly dwindle away into nothing from his vapid ramblings, as you say. If it weren't for the fact that my parents would both separately and completely kill me if I dropped another class, I'd be so out of there. I swear, this is the last time I take a class where the prof wrote the textbook. In theory that sounds like a good idea, like you're taking the class with some kind of genius or something.

JACOB: He's not a genius. The TAs just fawn over him because they don't know any better.

SYDNEY: I took really good notes on the reading. You can have them if you want.

JACOB: I don't need them.

(Beat.)

SYDNEY: Your story was really beautiful.

JACOB: *(annoyed)*

Jesus.

SYDNEY: I mean the language . . . writing and everything.

JACOB: I thought we'd moved on.

SYDNEY: I just want to explain.

JACOB: I don't care.

SYDNEY: It just seemed so intense. Personal. I mean, I think everything people write is personal. But this just seemed . . . it was just different.

JACOB: It's a story.

SYDNEY: It was just so violent.

JACOB: Perhaps I neglected the whimsy of a mass shooting.

SYDNEY: So when I read it, I just . . . it freaked me out. That's all.

JACOB: By this same flawless logic would you accuse Mary Shelley of a sewn-together monster? Or Swift a giant? Was Dr. Seuss planning to steal Christmas?

SYDNEY: I'm not accusing you of anything. I just wanted to talk to you about it.

JACOB: All you do is talk.

SYDNEY: When you hear those stories . . . on the news . . . every time something happens . . . I always think . . . I think . . . why didn't somebody stop it? Didn't somebody know?

JACOB: What do you think you know?

(Slight beat.)

SYDNEY: I know you're not like that. That you wouldn't do that.

JACOB: Is that a statement or a question?

SYDNEY: I know you.

JACOB: Then why are we still having this conversation?

(Slight beat.)

SYDNEY: What do you think your mom's going to send for your birthday?

JACOB: Nothing.

SYDNEY: Yes, she will.

JACOB: She probably doesn't even remember. She has a job. A life. Her own shit to deal with.

SYDNEY: I guarantee there's some package in your mailbox tomorrow when you go out. It might even be there already. You can tell me what it is in class.

JACOB: (dubious) OK.

SYDNEY: Your mom won't forget your birthday. She can't.

JACOB: Uh . . . she can.

SYDNEY: It's not just your day, you know. It's hers, too. The anniversary of this day twenty years ago that she birthed you out of her body. That she groaned, and kicked, and fought, and pushed this beautiful, slime-covered, little boy out into the world.

JACOB: I was a c-section.

SYDNEY: (a joke) That explains a lot.

JACOB: What bullshit does that possibly explain?

SYDNEY: Nothing.

JACOB: Except unfortunately there is no such thing as nothing with you.

SYDNEY: My dad's sister, she has two kids, older than me . . . the younger by c-section . . . and she's not close to that one. Actually, the kid kind of hates her. It's pretty sad. My dad's theory is that it started because they didn't make that connection at birth. Like the guy missed out on that natural transition into life, you know, out of the birth canal, and so ever since they had difficulty bonding.

JACOB: Or your cousin is just an asshole.

SYDNEY: Maybe.

JACOB: Throw that on your list of conspiracies.

(Beat.)

SYDNEY: That professor in your story, the one who gets shot in the face . . . it's Masterson.

JACOB: It's fiction.

SYDNEY: Right. I know. But it's like, based on him.

JACOB: Is something seriously wrong with you?

SYDNEY: Because it seemed like him, I mean I wasn't sure, but . . .

JACOB: How much time have you wasted pondering this?

SYDNEY: Because in the story, when the guy walks into the lecturehall, the TAs are all fawning about some article he wrote . . .

JACOB: Nancy fucking Drew!! It's a goddamn piece of fiction! A story. I made it up. It doesn't mean shit.

SYDNEY: You don't have to yell at me.

JACOB: How would you suggest I respond to stupidity?

SYDNEY: I'm not stupid.

JACOB: I want you to leave.

SYDNEY: But you never answered my question.

JACOB: You've asked about a hundred.

SYDNEY: Are you planning to do it?

JACOB: What do you think?

SYDNEY: I don't know. Every time I try to ask you something you just answer with another question.

JACOB: And why do you suppose I do that?

SYDNEY: I'm serious.

JACOB: What if I don't want to answer your asinine questions?

SYDNEY: I just need to hear you say it.

JACOB: Or what?

SYDNEY: I don't know.

JACOB: Clearly you came here with some agenda. I can see it churning behind your eyes.

SYDNEY: I just want to talk.

JACOB: What if I don't answer?

Lawrence Harbison

SYDNEY: I don't know.

JACOB: What will you do?

SYDNEY: I could turn you in!!

(Beat.)

JACOB: Wow.

SYDNEY: I mean, I'm not going to.

JACOB: You watch too much cable news.

SYDNEY: I just want to talk.

JACOB: That's quite an escalation.

SYDNEY: I haven't told anyone.

JACOB: But you've thought about this?

SYDNEY: I don't know.

JACOB: To whom would you even turn me in? The literary police. That you've discovered a dangerous writer. Because all I did was write a story. A fucking story.

SYDNEY: That's your gun. You own that exact same gun. I know you do. You told me.

I remember because I looked it up after and it was scary looking. You said your dad taught you how to use it.

JACOB: Lots of people have guns. Should we round them all up?

SYDNEY: This is just . . . all of this is just freaking me out. And I hate it. I don't want to think like this. To be like this.

JACOB: Not that it's any of your goddamn business, but I own my guns legally. Even my fucking mom knows that.

SYDNEY: But that's what the guy uses in your story.

JACOB: The fictional guy.

SYDNEY: Please answer my question.

JACOB: Will that help you sleep better tonight?

SYDNEY: Yes.

JACOB: That's idiotic. You know that. That makes no sense. At all. Because if I were really going to do it, I would lie.

SYDNEY: I would know.

(Beat.)

JACOB: I need to shower.

SYDNEY: Don't you want to eat something?

JACOB: I don't want anything to do with you.

SYDNEY: Sometimes I think people, some people, they just

end up in a really dark place. For whatever reason. They don't mean to. They don't want to be there. But they don't know how to get out.

JACOB: Go home.

SYDNEY: Maybe you left that story out on purpose. Maybe you wanted me to read it. To talk to you about it.

JACOB: Goodnight.

(He indicates for her to leave. She doesn't move.)

JACOB (CONT'D): Fine. Enjoy my room. I'll be in the bathroom. Close the door on your way out. And feel free to covertly look for guns under my bed, or bombs in my closet, or whatever else your mind has concocted. Knock yourself out.

(Beat.)

(Jacob starts to exit.)

SYDNEY: In your story the guy does it on his birthday. That's tomorrow.

Long beat.

JACOB: If I were you I'd stay home from class.

(shrugs)

But I can't stand the professor. I skip every chance I get.

He exits.

Alone in the room, Sydney hesitates. She picks up her phone. She ponders making a call, but finally decides against it. She puts the phone away. She exits.

End of play.

WINTER GAMES
Rachel Bonds

ORIGINAL PRODUCTION:

Ars Nova, February 1, 2012.

Directed by Wes Granton

CAST
MARY: Susan Kelechi
JAMIE: Zach Schaffer

SECOND PRODUCTION:

Actors Theatre of Louisville, April 5 2014.

Directed by Pirronne Yousefzadeh

CAST
MARY: Julia Bynum
JAMIE: Jason Huff

CHARACTERS:

MARY: Twenty-eight to Thirty. Defensive, frank, very smart. Her humor/brashness covering up her vulnerability. Claustrophobic in her life, she always has the feeling that the world is going on in some fantastic way—far away and without her.

JAMIE: Twenty-nine to Thirty. Playful and warm. He's resilient and practical; it is not in his nature to brood or worry.

PLACE:

Behind a bakery in a small, somewhat desolate town near Scranton, PA. Winter.

Notes: A / indicates where the next line should begin:

JAMIE: It's freezing /out here.
MARY: I know.
JAMIE: You don't wear coats /anymore?
MARY: Jamie I'm on my break.

*****

(Early, early morning. Mary stands behind the bakery, smoking, her eyes closed. It's quiet and cold out, grey, a little bleak. She doesn't wear a coat.)

(Jamie opens the back door and peers at her.)

JAMIE: You're smoking already?
MARY: I'm tired.
JAMIE: So you're smoking.
MARY: It helps me wake up.
    (He steps outside)
JAMIE: It's freezing /out here.
MARY: I know.
JAMIE: You don't wear coats /anymore?
MARY: Jamie I'm on my break.

JAMIE: We open in like /ten minutes.

MARY: I know I'm taking my break before everyone starts screaming at me about what kind of bran muffin they want.

JAMIE: There's pretty much just the /one kind.

MARY: Jamie I'm on my break.

JAMIE: Okay, sorry.

(He stares at his breath.)

Why're you so tired?

MARY: I was up late.

JAMIE: Ahhhhh okay.

MARY: *(opening her eyes)* Shut up, not like that.

JAMIE: Okay.

MARY: I was watching the Olympics.

JAMIE: Figure skating?

MARY: Yes.

(He cringes.)

It's a sport /, Jamie.

JAMIE: Yeahhh, not really /a sport.

MARY: It's a /sport.

JAMIE: Not really a sport, /Mary.

MARY: Have you seen the legs on those people? Their muscles are like bulging out all over the—they are super-athletes, Jamie.

JAMIE: I don't know if they're *super* /athletes . . .

MARY: Jamie I'M ON MY BREAK.

JAMIE: Okay okay okay okay.

(quiet, almost to himself)

I mean they wear glittery costumes.

MARY: Fuck off.

JAMIE: Whoa!

MARY: Well I'm tired and you're pissing me off!

JAMIE: I'm sorry.

(They both stare at their breath.)

Haven't seen Mr. Belvedere around lately.

MARY: I know. I brought some food out for him and the little grey guy yesterday and usually they greet me at the door, but I didn't see them anywhere. The orange one/ wasn't around either.

JAMIE: John Adams.

MARY: Yeah, John Adams.

Auugghh I'm worried about them in the cold. That little grey guy is so little.

JAMIE: Yeah. You shouldn't worry, though. They're like little ninjas. Did you see Mr. Belvedere scale the fence /that time?

MARY: I'm just worried . . .

JAMIE: You worry about too much stuff.

MARY: Not really.

JAMIE: Yeah, you always have this face like aughhhh I'm really tense and worried about stuff.

MARY: I do /not.

JAMIE: *(twisting his face)* Yeah, since like tenth grade you've had this look, like auuughhhhh /my brain is having a heartattack.

MARY: I don't—

I hope I don't look like that.

JAMIE: No, you—I'm kidding. You look . . . nice.

MARY: *(amused)* Right. How come you're eternally cheerful?

JAMIE: Don't know.

MARY: Like you actually enjoy getting up at 4AM and baking things for people who know every embarrassing thing about you.

JAMIE: I do enjoy it.

MARY: I know. It's weird.

JAMIE: I like that people know who I am and I know who they are.

MARY: You like serving scones to your high school girlfriend and her husband.

JAMIE: I don't know. They're good people.

MARY: Yeah, Melissa's a gem.

(Jamie stares at his breath, quiet.)

MARY: . . . Haven't you ever wanted to get out?

JAMIE: *(shrugging)* I don't know.

MARY: *(peering at him)* You don't ever want to just, like, tear your skin off and run away and be a whole different person?

JAMIE: No.

MARY: *(peering at him)* No . . .

JAMIE: I'm happy here.

MARY: Really?

JAMIE: Yeah.

MARY: *(sighing, staring at her breath)* . . . We are very different people, Jamie Hewitt.

JAMIE: I guess.

What happened on figure skating?

MARY: Nothing.

JAMIE: I'm not fucking with you.

(She peers at him. He stares back at her earnestly.)

MARY: Okay. Okay, well. This was like the final final for the women's single competition, okay?

JAMIE: Yeah.

MARY: And there's this skater from Estonia, right, and she's amazing, her short program was killer, and so everyone's looking to her, you know, because she's like come up from the bottom, like Estonia's never won a medal in this category or even this sport EVER, so she'd be making big-time history.

JAMIE: Whoa.

MARY: Yeah, AND her husband has just died.

JAMIE: Oh God.

MARY: I know. So she's skating *anyway*, despite this horrible thing that's occurred like a few *weeks* before—she just has to nail her long program and she's got the gold. So the music starts, and the entire coliseum is dead quiet. Like the air in the place is so taut, you can just feel it tightening around her. And then, like, bing!, she lifts her head and starts moving. And it's lovely and it's light and just the most graceful but also the most like—full thing you've ever seen, like every single tiny movement is full of this this like incredible energy and presence, and they keep flashing the camera into the stands where her parents are sitting, and her dad's really frail-looking and he's wearing this hat and he's kind of stoic and eastern European but you can tell he's like beaming underneath, and she's going and she's going and it's beautiful, like even the commentators are silent, and she nails the double axel and then she nails the triple axel and then another triple axel her mom has her arms up in the air, like victory, like—*(she demonstrates)*— and then she goes for the last triple axel, with this like incredible force—and she screws up the landing.

JAMIE: *(quiet)* Oh no.

MARYL: She doesn't fall—she just loses her balance for one tiny moment, like she tips forward and has to catch herself with her hand. And the crowd gasps and her dad closes his eyes and time freezes for a second . . . . and then she rights herself and moves on to finish the program. So she throws herself into the final pose . . . and everyone's cheering and her parents are holding each other and her arms are in their pose but you can just—. You can see something break in her—like a little crack running down the side of a teacup, just this terrible sense of failure like running across her skin. And she's thinking, I missed it. I missed it.

JAMIE: Wow.

MARY: Yeah. So. I couldn't sleep at ALL after that so I had to watch Aladdin.

JAMIE: Like a whole new world Aladdin?

MARY: Yeah.

JAMIE: Really?

MARY: I always watch it when I can't sleep.

JAMIE: Why?

MARY: Because everything turns out right in the end.

JAMIE: Not for Jafar. /Or that weird little parrot.

MARY: Yeah, but for the good guys. Why, what do you watch when you can't sleep?

JAMIE: I sleep pretty well.

MARY: Of course you /do.

JAMIE: My head hits the pillow and I'm pretty much out.
(She shakes her head, looking away. He watches her for a moment.)

JAMIE: I built a hotel.

MARY: What?

JAMIE: For the cats. See—*(he points)*—it's over there—I

kind of tucked it into that little space between the dump-
ster and the fence.

MARY: Oh my God.

JAMIE: It's like a double-decker type thing—I lined it with
straw. Which should apparently keep them pretty warm.
I looked up how to build it on feral cat villa dot org.

MARY: Jamie.

JAMIE: I checked on them when I got in this morning. Mr.
Belvedere was asleep on the first floor. John Adams was
up top with the little grey guy.

MARY: /Oh man . . . Jamie . . .

JAMIE: They're so damn cute.

MARY: Yeah.

JAMIE: I was worried about them. It's fucking freezing out
here.

MARY: I know.

JAMIE: So.

Yeahhh.

We're not all that different.

MARY: . . . No.

(They watch their breath.)

JAMIE: Okay. So . . . I'm going to go open the doors for
the angry mob.

MARY: Okay.

JAMIE: You still on break?

MARY: No, no. I'm coming.

*(He opens the door. After a moment she follows him
inside.)*

End of play.

Original Production

Produced as part of the
FIVES New Play Festival
June 26-28, 2014
At the Black Box Theatre

Directed by Nancy Holaday

Producer
Nancy Holaday
(719) 330-1798
nancy@blackboxdrama.com

Stage Manager: Kylie Hartnett

Cast
Ike Stiehl: Gary Nowinski
Ali Akmed: Sol Chavez
Ernie: Andrew Davis
Sandhal: Arwen Fonzen
Soldier: Jonathan Rivera

CHARACTERS:

IKE STIEHL: Owner of a bakery in Bethlehem, PA. Fifties.

ALI AKMED: Owner of a bakery in Baghdad. Fifties.

ERNIE: Ike's son. Late teens.

SANDAHL: Ali's daughter. Mid-twenties.

A SOLDIER: (voice-over)

SETTING:

A pair of bakeries, separated by a distance of 6071 miles.

TIME:

Now.

SCENE 1: *Two separate bakeries. One in small-town Pennsylvania, owned by IKE STIEHL; the other in war-torn Baghdad, owned by ALI AKMED. At first both men talk out loud, oblivious to the other.*

IKE: If there isn't any bread, you're askin' for chaos . . .

ALI: If there is no bread, there is chaos . . .

IKE: I can remember not having enough bread at Thanksgiving one year. Not even enough for mom to stuff our sorry-assed turkey.

ALI: Just yesterday, another bakery in Baghdad was bombed. Suicide. And murder, of course. It is getting to the point where no one wants to work for me anymore.

IKE: Bread fills the gut, so your mind can focus on more important things. Like, for instance, on

Thanksgiving, the football game . . .

ALI: Bread fills the heart. And the insurgents stick daggers in the hearts of every Iraqi! Everyone has to eat.

IKE: Everyone has to eat. My boy, Ernie, just turned 17—eats like there's no tomorrow.

ALI: My daughter, Sandahl, says I am crazy to stay here in Baghdad. But it takes a special kind of discipline in life to achieve in the face of adversity. I pray to Allah for love and security.

IKE: I met Ali through one of those internet websites. Well, didn't actually meet him, but we posted a couple of messages, then started exchanging emails. (unfolds a piece of paper) I still have the first one . . .

ALI: Ike Stiehl is a good American. At least he seems like a good American. Though some days when I look out my front window and see G.I.'s marching by, I wonder what separates a good American from a bad one. (unfolds a piece of paper) But it helps to know there is someone across the globe who also struggles . . .

IKE: Dear Ike . . .

ALI: *(reciting his own letter)*

I read with interest your posting at the website. At my bakery, the bread is somewhat different from yours. Loaves in the shape of diamonds, puffy and doughy inside. The way we consume it probably differs as well—commonly as a sandwich made with cream cheese and over-ripe tomatoes. Bread is as much a part of daily life here as . . . well, water. (pause) Mr. Stiehl responded thusly. Dear Ali . . .

IKE: *(reciting from letter)*

Bread like diamonds? Our loaves here are shaped like . . . well, loaves. Sometimes, when nothing else is around, I use a stale loaf as a paperweight. (laughs) Yeah, sandwiches are nice. We Americans like anything if it's between two slices of bread.

(Ike and Ali turn toward each other.)

ALI: Tell me, my friend, does everyone buy your bread today?

IKE: Everyone? That's a relative term.

ALI: You mean onlty your relatives buy the bread you make?

IKE: I mean "everyone" could mean the whole freakin' population of Bethlehem.

ALI: Bethlehem? I do not follow . . . I thought you said you lived in the United States?

IKE: I do . . . Bethlehem is in Pennsylvania.

ALI: Oh. I worried for your safety for a moment, my friend.

IKE: My safety? That's funny. I don't see anyone wearin' a bomb-vest outside my door.

(Ali sits down.)

IKE: What about you? Did you sell bread to "everyone" today?

ALI: It feels like it. In my arms, my back, even my eyes. The price of electricity continues to rise. So does the cost of cooking fuels. My neighbors can no longer bake for themselves.

(Ike sits down; opens a can of beer.)

ALI: Oh. How are you doing with the drinking, my friend?

(Ike stops drinking in mid-sip.)

IKE: Well, I only drink when I bake now.

ALI: This is good progress, then?

IKE: Maybe for the bread. I've got an awesome sourdough that I make with lager.

ALI: And what about your son?

IKE: Ernie? He's too young to drink.

ALIL: No, I mean what does he think about your drinking?

IKE: Until he knows what it's like to lose a wife—and almost your business—then it shouldn't matter to him.

ALI: But he also lost . . . his mother.

IKE: I know . . . *(he sips his beer)* I know.

ALI: You still haven't told him about the cancer?

IKE: He knows I'm sick—but not how sick. I don't want the poor kid to feel like he's gotta take over the business ten months from now.

ALI: But it could be that soon, right?

IKE: *(gulps his beer)* Could, would, who knows! I mean, you could be hit by an asteroid tomorrow, right?

ALI: Much more likely I'll be hit by something else, but yes, it is—what would you call it—an astronomical possibility. *(pause)* Has it been spreading?

IKE: Like shit on a shingle. But can we not talk about this right now. Ernie is due home—

(ERNIE enters side door, carrying a huge stack of books.)

—any minute now.

IKE *(cont.)*: Hey Ernie!

ERNIE : Can you not call me that right now?

(He smacks the books onto the coffee table.)

IKE : Earnest? Do you like that better?

ERNIE: *(plopping down on the couch next to his dad)* No! Christ, dad, what were you and mom thinking? Why didn't you just name me Snuffleupagus. At least Snuff might have been a cool nickname . . .

IKE: Well, we can still call you Snuff . . .

ERNIE: There is no "we" any more, dad. Mom's been dead for a year, and you still keep saying we.

(Ernie puts his head in his hands. Ike pats his shoulder.)

ALI: It is a tough life for a teenager. But they don't know how much tougher it might get.

IKE: Do you have a big family, Ali?

ALI: Just one daughter. She is the reason I make so much bread.

IKE: You make bread so you can send her bread, huh? Something metaphysical there.

ALI: Or metaphorical. Let me tell you what has happened with my dear Sandahl—

(Ernie suddenly raises his head, shouts)

ERNIE: I think I want to go to college. No, I know I do!

IKE: That's kind of sudden. I thought you didn't like school.

ERNIE: I don't. But it's the only thing I'm good at.

IKE: Oh. Okay. I guess we . . . I mean "I" could look into financial aid.

ERNIE: Christ almighty, dad, didn't mom have any life insurance?

IKE: We own a small bakery. How much extra cash do you think we have floating around?

ALI: What an irony. All that bread in the house, yet no bread.

IKE: And your point is?

ERNIE: My point? Don't most parents try to set aside a few bucks for their kids. You know, for emergencies . . . Spring Break . . . a sports car?

IKE: No, I wasn't talking to you, son. I was talking to . . . I mean, I had just been reading the latest email from Ali, and—

ERNIE: Ali, Ali, Ali! Everything Ali! Maybe if you didn't spend so much time on the net you'd be the White House baker by now!

ALI: A baker for the president's house? Is that a post to which you aspire, my friend?

IKE: No. Not especially. I don't like politics. Hate the two-party system.

ALI: At least you have a system.

IKE: We're trying our damnedest to give you a system!

ALI: Oh, but did we ask you to?

IKE: You shouldn't have to be asked. I mean, who wouldn't want a democracy?

ERNIE: Excuse me. I'm still here. Only way to get rid of me is to cough up some room, board . . . and tuition!

IKE: That would take . . . gee, I don't know, more bread? Which means . . .

ERNIE: I know, I know . . . let me grab a snack and then I'll haul some sacks of flour for ya.

IKE: That's my boy!

ALI: What a boy!

IKE: Speaking of children . . . you were going to tell me something about your daughter?

ALI: Ah, yes, Sandahl. Beauty of my beastly life. Breath of fresh air through the gunpowder. Reason above all reason to live long and prosper.

IKE: I get it, okay. You love her. Could you just try not to sound like Mr. Spock.

ALI: Sorry, I tend to get carried away when I talk about my baby girl. Only she is no baby any more. Got married and moved to Pakistan five years ago. To a very fine young man, but apparently one with a sleep disorder.

IKE: He snores?

ALI: No.

IKE: He walks?

ALI: No.

IKE: He talks?

ALI: As you say in America, bingo! But in a most detrimental way. As my Sandahl explains. Dear baba . . .

(SANDAHL steps from out of the shadows, faces Ali.)

SANDAHL: *(reciting from letter)* It is under much duress that I send this correspondence. Last night, Said's problem got out of control. At 3 a.m., he uttered the word "Talaq" three times—Talaq, Talaq, Talaq!—loudly enough to wake me, but also loudly enough to alert a Mullah walking outside our window. What an Imam is doing out and about at that hour, I do not know, but now that Said has uttered a decree of instant divorce, they intend to separate us! This even though Said continues to pledge his undying devotion to me—and I to him. Tell me, baba, what am I to do? How can we afford to fight this matter with the meager amount of income Said makes teaching here in the village?

ALI: Signed, your devoted Sandahl . . .

IKE: Wow. I thought they banned that instant divorce crap?

ALI: Maybe not in rural Pakistan. So you see my dilemma. If I lose my income, then my Sandahl may lose her husband. And if she loses her husband, then she will be stigmatized for years.

IKE: Hey, at least you got to go to your kid's wedding. That's looking doubtful for me right now.

(Sound of knocking off stage.)

ALI: Excuse me for a moment, there is someone at my door. *(shouting)* We are closed for today. Please come back tomorrow.

SOLDIER (off stage): United States Army. Routine safety check. Open the door, please.

ALI: Here we go again. How is it I should trust opening my door at this hour? I will be sure my firearm is within easy reach before I greet this visitor . . . even though my Sandahl said . . .

(Sandahl enters.)

SANDAHL: Dear baba . . . I know you say you purchased a gun on the local black market. But remember when I

---

was a girl, how you told me that a mind is always a better defense than a bullet? That good hearts trump bad wills? Please turn to violence only as a last resort . . .

(Ali exits)

SOLDIER *(off stage)*: Our battalion is three meters from your door. Don't hesitate to report anything suspicious. Good night!

(Ali re-enters. Sandahl exits.)

ALI: Assistance from a rat? I do not think so.

IKE: So, you're equating the military to rodents?

ALI: No. I am saying my neighborhood at this moment is not unlike a sewer.

IKE: On that note, I think I'm going to turn in for the night . . .

ALI: Fine idea, my friend. Good night to you . . .

(Ernie rises from the couch)

ERNIE: Sorry, pop, for my shitty mood. I guess I'm just tired. You going to bed, too?

IKE: In a few . . .

ERNIE: I'll get up a little early and help get the first batch in the oven, okay?

IKE : That would be nice, son . . . sleep well.

(Ernie goes to bed.)

IKE: Sleep well? *(laughs)* Sleeping at all is a glorious success.
(lights begin to dim; he opens another beer) I propose a toast!
(he raises the bottle; hesitates, opens a 2nd bottle)
To the best damn night of sleep . . .
(he clinks the bottles together, takes a gulp)
. . . this month.

LIGHTS DOWN

(SCENE 2: The next day. Ike and Ali are at their computers.)

ALI: Life is a bitch . . .

IKE: Life is an orphaned bastard . . .

ALI: Dear Ike . . .

(reciting from email)
Yet another bakery was hit last night, near Zayouna. The insurgents, they do not discriminate between richer and poorer, though I am quite certain the victims were all Shiite. *(pauses)* Dear Ali . . .

IKE: *(reciting from email)* I drank myself to sleep last night. No different from any other night, really. But sleep is sleep, I guess. *(pauses)* Any word from your daughter?

ALI: The divorce moves forward. But it has been days without a message. What about your son?

IKE: Very happy mood this morning. Worked an hour before school. He should be home any—
(Ernie comes barging in, out of breath.)

ALI: Like a clock on the mantel, he is.

ERNIE: Dad! Dad! You aren't gonna . . . *(takes breath)* believe this!

IKE: Calm down, Snuff, calm down . . .

ERNIE: Call me anything you want, pop, as long as you put scholarship recipient behind my name.

IKE: What? What are you talking about? What scholarship?
(Ernie pulls out an envelope, plops it down on the couch.)

ERNIE: I won the T. Roccoco Literary Prize, which means I get free tuition. *(pause)* As long as I get good grades, of course. *(excited again)* Free freakin' tuition, just for a silly little poem!

IKE: A poem? You mean you're a . . . poet?

ERNIE: Well, yeah. What do you think I do alone in my room most nights?

IKE: Well, you are a teen-ager . . .

ERNIE: I'm also almost an adult, pop . . . damn, give me some credit.

IKE: I'm . . . happy for you. Honest I am, son. And also a little surprised. So, do we get to hear this little poem of yours?

ERNIE: Well . . . okay. Here goes . . .
(he unfolds a sheet of paper)

Bread
Against the grain
I bake the fake horizon,
I forsake the bleak morning,
I tiptoe and dance round this knead-
ing of my soul, this bleeding of knuckles,
this uncoupling of buckles, from boots
to belt, an apron string fraying at both ends . . .

Against the grain, I seek the warm comfort
I cheek-to-cheek dance with tomorrow's mother,
I sleep more soundly than I ever dreamt

this slice of my heart will rejuvenate like a liver,
and I am a giver to the gaunt faces that haunt me,
I am a giver. I only take the bread I've eaten,
no more.

Belly full,
I sleep more soundly than I have ever dreamt.

(Brief silence. Then Ike jumps to his feet, embraces Ernie.)

IKE: Goddamn beautiful. Your mother would be proud. *(sitting; suddenly sullen)* I'm proud.

ERNIE: I didn't tell you the best part. I'm applying to the community college, pop. They've got a really cool literature prof—a famous published poet. (his father is still silent) Which means, I'm staying home, at least for a couple more years. I wanna help out as long as I can.

IKE *(tearful)*: Beautiful . . . Goddamn beautiful.

ERNIE: Love you, pop. But gotta run. Meeting Sarah at the coffee shop. Wait till she hears!

(Ernie runs off; Ike begins to sob.)

IKE: *(drying his eyes on his sleeve)*I don't deserve this, Ali . . . Not in the least.

ALI: Oh, but you do . . . As much as I deserve happy tidings from my Sandahl. Speaking of which, looks like I've finally got an email.

IKE: Is it from your daughter?

ALI: It is! Dear baba . . .

(Sandahl enters the room, faces Ali.)

SANDAHL: Said can no longer bear the situation here in Pakistan. And I can no longer bear the sacrifice you continue to make for our welfare. I am writing this from the airport, enroute home to Baghdad. We will be a family again very soon . . .

(Sandahl exits)

ALI: Allah be praised!

SANDAHL *(off stage)*: Baba, I have come.

(Sandahl enters.)

ALI: My Sandahl, it is so very good to see you. *(they embrace)* But where is your husband?

SANDAHL: He's outside paying off the driver. We are very hungry. Perhaps a cream cheese and tomato sandwich? But first I better go and help Said with our bags.

(Sandahl exits.)

ALI: It is I who does not deserve this, my friend . . .

(Lights begin to dim.)

IKE: Enjoy it, Ali. Every minute. *(pause)* A sandwich actually sounds good.

ALI: That, my friend, will help you to sleep better than any bottle of beer.

IKE: You mean Ernie is right?

ALI: How so?

IKE: That line from his poem . . . sleep more soundly than I have ever dreamt?

ALI: Yes, bread can help a man sleep better . . .

IKE: Yes. Bread will help a man sleep better.

END OF PLAY

Café d'Automatique
Dave Hanson

Café d'Automatique was originally performed as part of the 2014 Collective: 10 Short Play Festival, produced by The Collective NY, on October 8, 2014 at the Teatro Circulo Theatre in Manhattan.

Directed by Susan Aston

CAST
JIM: Patrick Bonck
ERIN: Victoria Dicce
THE WAITER: Robert Z Grant

Set Design by The Collective NY
Lighting Design by Maria Cristina Fuste
Executive Producers: Mike Houston, Robert Z Grant, Victoria Dicce & Patrick Bonk.

CHARACTERS:

> JIM: Late twenties to early thirties, a nice guy looking for a real relationship, but caught up in the trappings of modern dating.
>
> ERIN: Late twenties to early thirties, a young woman, dealing with the world of modern dating while in search of a man to love.
>
> THE WAITER: A snobby, uptight, French Waiter, complete with accent, tuxedo and smug condescending attitude. A soul trapped in his job.

SETTING:

> A French Restaurant.

Lights up

A French/Parisian restaurant. JIM, dressed nice but casual, sits at a table with two place settings and two menus, waiting for his date to arrive. French Gypsy Jazz, probably by Django Reinhardt, plays quietly. THE WAITER, a snooty French waiter, stops by and drops off a glass of wine for him and leaves. He checks his phone, strumming through emails and texts. Finally ERIN, dressed fashionably for a night out, enters.

ERIN: Jim.

JIM: *(Looking up)* Are you Erin? First contact, an awkward hug.

ERIN: Yes! It's good to meet you.

JIM: Yeah, you too. You look great.

> *(They sit down, JIM pulling the chair out for ERIN before he sits.)*

ERIN: Thank you. I'm so sorry I'm late.

JIM: That's okay. Did you have trouble finding the place?

ERIN: I think you texted me the wrong name.

JIM: Did I really?

> *(JIM checks his phone. Oh, I did. Looks like I tried to send you to Caffeinated Anatomy. I'm sorry. My phone decides to make up my words for me sometimes.)*

ERIN: Mine does that all the time.

JIM: My mom always says, "When you meet the right person, they'll always know what you mean."

ERIN: That's a cute saying from your mom. This place looks great, by the way.

JIM: I thought it would make for a good first date. My mom always says, "Every relationship has a first date."

ERIN: Wow. Another one from your mom.

JIM: Yeah, that's her. Full of overbearing folksy wisdom. God, I really hope I don't end up marrying my mom.

ERIN: Don't think that's legal.

JIM: *(Recovering)* Okay, see, I didn't mean it like that. My mom is great. I'm in love with my mom. No! I love her. I love my mom. But I'm not in love with her. Because I love women, regular women. That I'm not related to. I mean, I'm normal.

ERIN: Okay. On that note, I'm going to order a drink before I say something stupid.

She looks around for a waiter.

ERIN *(CONT'D)*: God, I can't get over how charming this place is. Have you slept with a lot of dates here?

JIM: Wow.

ERIN: That's not what I meant!

JIM: I don't think my mom has a saying that covers that one.

ERIN: No, I was trying to ask if you had been here before! What just happened?

JIM: *(laughing)* The answer is no. First time here. So far, the only person I've slept with is the waiter. Which is probably why he's not coming over here anymore.

ERIN: That's very reassuring. Can we change the subject?

JIM: Yes. What should we talk about?

ERIN: You. What do you do in your free time?

JIM shifts slightly into a well rehearsed date mode.

JIM: Well, I like to stay in shape, so I mountain blow jobs all the time and shit laps in the pool.

ERIN: You what?

(JIM deflates, a total loss for words.)

JIM: Uh, I dont—what about you? Do you like . . . things?

(ERIN becomes overly enthusiastic about the subject.)

ERIN: Oh yeah, I love sports. I go to a lot of accordions. And I like poop teams. The biggest poop.

(JIM stares at her. ERIN becomes very uncomfortable.)

Erin *(CONT'D)*: I-I'm not that into sports. I just said that because I thought guys prefer girls who like sports.

JIM: Yeah, we do. But it's not a deal breaker.

(THE WAITER approaches. He speaks with a thick snobby French accent.)

WAITER: Bienvenue, madame. Welcome to Cafe d'Automatique. Would you like a glass of wine with your unbrushed hair and that dress with the regretful stain on it?

(ERIN and JIM stare back at THE WAITER, who shows no signs of realizing he said something strange.)

ERIN: Yes, I'll have some wine. Thank you.

WAITER: Wonderful.

(THE WAITER exits.)

ERIN: Was that a french thing?

JIM: Must have been. So, what do you do for a living?

ERIN: Oh, I have a great job. I work at a pigwarts school for delinquent boy privates.

JIM: What is that?

ERIN: I, uh, mean, I'm a tater tot. Tamale tits. TEACHER! I'm a teacher and I hate it. (Beat) You?

JIM: I'm in law school and work part time at a bar. I don't love it but it pays the bills.

ERIN: Okay.

(Beat. JIM strikes his dating pose.)

JIM: I like the way your groupon looks.

ERIN: I don't know what—

JIM: I'm sorry. I think you look absinth sniffy. Like your potty pitcher! Profile! Picture! You're not fat! I'm happy!

ERIN: Thank you. I think.

(THE WAITER comes back with a glass of wine and sets it down.)

WAITER: Eh, are you ready to order, awkward young couple

who will undoubtedly get pregnant by accident?

JIM: Do you have any recommendations?

WAITER: Honesty. I always recommend honesty. Tonight's special is a sad salmon with capers and a failed fruit salad. *(THE WAITER leaves.)*

JIM: Listen, I apologize. I'm usually really good at making love dragons.

ERIN: What does that mean?

JIM: Sucking ray guns!
(with shouted effort)
Dates! I am better at dates than this!

ERIN: Oh, do you see a lot of people?

JIM: No! I've had only a few snails in my Nyquil! NOO/ Yes! I internet date a lot! Women are easier to sleep with after you email them!
(JIM sits back, hands over mouth, shocked at his honesty.)

ERIN: *(Disappointed)* Oh.

JIM: I'm sorry. Is that bad?

ERIN: It's fine. Who am I to judge? We're both elderberries and I've been gravy ganged. Oh my God—Yes, it's bad! You're possible husband material but a small part of my heart died when you said you sleep around!

JIM: But I don't Slop Bucket! Slip dicks! Ah, Jesus Chaps!

THE WAITER returns, stopping the conversation.

WAITER: Are you ready?

ERIN: Yes! I'll have the sex with the mash on the branch!

WAITER: One salad. And for Monsieur?

JIM: The puck, the special puck with . . . Dongs!

WAITER: My favorite.
(THE WAITER exits, taking the menus with him.)

JIM: I don't know what I just ordered!

ERIN: What's happening to us?!

JIM: Lets try to relax and menstruate for a second.

ERIN: You mean masturbate?

JIM: I mean meditate!

ERIN: Isn't that what I said?!

JIM: *(Calm)* So, Erin, when was your last relationship?

(ERIN keeps her mouth closed, knowing the wrong words are coming. She struggles.)

ERIN: *(yelling)* Slut Bon Jovi!

(JIM and ERIN are now standing up, shouting at each other, over annunciating, walking/running back and forth across the restaurant, trying to get their words right. Their chairs have been knocked down, or pushed out of the way. JIM gulps down his wine in between lines.)

JIM: Snickerdoodled sunsets!

ERIN: Dry Roasted Penis!

JIM: Fondu my life! Dog walking death star!

ERIN: Penis-penis-penis!

JIM: It's like we're being auto-cocked! God Dildo!

ERIN: Peeeeeeeeeeeeeeenis!

JIM: Auto! Corrected! But it's only auto correcting the bullshit we're saying.

ERIN: That's ridiculous! I've been nothing but fartfull with you!

(THE WAITER brings bread to the table and offers a suspicious and disappointed glance at JIM and ERIN who are still standing across the now messy restaurant.)

JIM: Lets try something. Oh, Waiter!

WAITER: Oui, Monsieur?

JIM: Do you think I'm a handsome man?

WAITER: If handsome means an unfortunate collection of genetic mistakes, then Oui.

(JIM gives ERIN an "I told you so" look.)

ERIN: That doesn't prove anything. *(To THE WAITER)* Hey! I think you're a bad waiter!

WAITER: *(ruffled)* What?! How dare you! I have ne'er been so insulated in all my life! I am ze best water closet! Wookie cookie! C'est-a-dire! I AM ZE BEST WIND BREAKER IN ZE CITY!

(THE WAITER thinks about what he just said.)

WAITER *(CONT'D)*: Very well! I am a terrible waiter! Is zat what you wanted to 'ear?!

(Single Spot Light on THE WAITER. In the distance

an according starts to play. THE WAITER smokes an invisible cigarette.)

WAITER *(CONT'D)*: Years ago, on ze busy streets of Paris! A young, orphaned, buss boy dreamed of some day moving to America and becoming ze greatest waiter ze world has ever known. And I was, for a while. But success does not last forever! For time is an unforgiving straight line and if you do not let go and live, not for ze image of yourself, but for ze truth of each other, you will become as I have. A hilarious caricature of my very self!

(THE WAITER leaves, defeated, putting out his imaginary cigarette. The according music ends. JIM turns back to ERIN.)

JIM: Say something. Anything. As long as it's honest.

(They look frightened and miserable at the task at hand. ERIN takes a deep breath and struggles.)

ERIN: I . . . ass blasted peas on my plate! Oh, I give up!

JIM: Don't give up on us, Erin!

ERIN: I wanted to order a steak but I was afraid you'd think I eat too much!

JIM: I wanted to take you to a sports bar. But I didn't think you'd sleep with me if we did that!

ERIN: I probably would have because I have pretty low self-esteem!

(They look at each other and begin shouting truths from across the room.)

JIM: I have twelve toes!

ERIN: What?

JIM: I have twelve toes say something honest!

ERIN: Last night I drunk dialed my ex-husband! Oh, I have an ex-husband!

JIM: Really?

ERIN: Go!

JIM: The first thing I notice about a woman is her kneecaps! It's not sexual!

ERIN: I'm suddenly feeling insecure about my kneecaps!

JIM: You have great kneecaps!

ERIN: That's the nicest thing anyone has ever said to me!

JIM: That makes me feel sad inside! Keep going! This is great!

ERIN: My legs get gorilla hairy!

JIM: Every sound that comes out of my body reminds me of my Dad!

ERIN: I'm an uncomfortable sexual being!

JIM: I'm a terrible listener!

ERIN: I want to have a home birth!

JIM: I'm sorry did you say something? See!

(JIM and ERIN come to each other CENTER STAGE.)

Jim *(CONT'D)*: When I saw you, I thought you were the perfect height for slow dancing.

ERIN: When I saw you, I saw our wedding day. Your mother never approves of me.

JIM: I saw our first home. It was way below our middle class standards.

ERIN: I saw our first child. A boy. He'll have a lot of promise but . . .

JIM: Our first family vacation will be a regrettable road trip to Disney Land.

ERIN: We'll try to adopt a Chinese baby, but then realize we're just not those people.

JIM: We'll retire with just enough savings for one really great trip. And we'll look back—

ERIN: On our life together—

JIM: And smile.

(JIM holds ERIN in his arms, dipping her slightly, looking into her eyes, a SINGLE SPOT LIGHT circles them.)

Jim (CONT'D): I'm in love you.

ERIN: I'm in love you.

JIM and ERIN kiss, as if in an old movie.

ERIN: I wasn't late getting here. I stayed in my car to fart.

JIM: I just did.

(The lights fade to black with a single spot slowly closing around them. Only Django Reinhardt is heard.)

END OF PLAY

CAKE

Sherry Kramer

ORIGINAL PRODUCTION

Source Theatre Festival, Washington, DC
June, 2013

Directed by Maureen Monterubio

CAST
PACO: Chris Aldrich
SCOTT: Frank Turner
LILY: Amie Cazel
SAMSARA: Mia Branco

Costumes, Props: Joni Martin
Sound: Elisheba Itoop
Light: Sean Forsythe
Production Stage Manager: Patrick Magill

CHARACTERS:

>PACO: A long hair Chihuahua.
>SAMSARA: A long hair Chihuahua/miniature Italian greyhound mix.
>LILY: A woman in her late forties.
>SCOTT: A man in his late forties.

SETTING:

>The second floor porch of Lily and Scott's house. It's twilight. The light is soft and magical, and slightly dramatic. The sound of crickets—a perfect summer evening.

>*(Scott is sitting in an oversized rattan chair with his feet up on a matching, huge comfy rattan ottoman. Paco is sitting on the ottoman at his feet. Lily is standing. Paco often speaks to the Audience.)*

PACO: Hello. My name is Paco. And I was made for love.

SCOTT: They're my dogs, I can give them to who ever I want.

PACO: Of all the dogs in the world, only one breed was bred for love.

LILY: What are you talking about, they're my dogs too.

PACO: The Chihuahua.

SCOTT: Nope. I brought them to the marriage, so they're mine.

PACO: *(Samsara, half Chihuahua, half miniature Italian Greyhound, all trouble, walks onto the porch. She is gorgeous and she knows it.)* It is true that Samsara is only half Chihuahua—her father was a dyspeptic miniature Italian greyhound named Peppi—that's who she got her long, exquisite legs and her short temper from, but still. The breeding for love is deeply etched in her blood and bones.

SAMSARA: And there isn't a damn thing I can do about it.

PACO: Darling—don't talk like that.

>*(Samsara walks past Paco and preens for a bit.)*

SAMSARA: I'd rather be made for retrieving. Or sheep herding.

PACO: You hate sheep.

SAMSARA: So? That would probably make me better at it. All I'm saying is—I wish I'd been bred for something productive. Something honest. Something I could be proud of doing, at the end of the day. What do I do? I smell the smell of love 24/7. And when I am not busy smelling love, I smell like love. That's something to be proud of? I wish I'd been bred for anything other than love.

(She walks around the ottoman and back into the house. Paco looks at her long legs with admiration. He sighs.)

PACO: Being bred for love is less convenient that you might imagine.

SCOTT: I'm giving them to my sister. You won't sacrifice enough for them.

LILY: I don't need to sacrifice anything for them, Scott. I love them! When you love someone you don't have to measure what you gave up.

PACO: How is it inconvenient, you ask? Let me count the ways.

LILY: You don't have to measure how much it hurts to prove you love them!

PACO: First, there is no ultimate measure of love. And then there is the way love smells. Which—surprise? Is not always so sweet.

(Sniffs loudly.)

Smell that? Love, when you measure it, stinks. But I have no choice.

LILY: You know I love them as much as you do.

PACO: If love is anywhere, no matter how badly it smells, I must smell it.

(Paco puts his paws over his nose to try to keep from smelling.)

LILY: I might even love them more.

(The smell almost overpowers Paco. He pinches his nose tightly and bravely goes on.)

PACO: Does she or doesn't she love us more, you ask?

(Shrugs).

It's a stupid question. There is no more or less, no as much or as not. It either smells like love, or it doesn't.

LILY: And unlike you, I love them all the time!

SCOTT: I love Paco all the time.

LILY: No you don't, you love him maybe 87 percent of the time.

PACO: *(Paco lets go of his nose.)* Sacrilege! Outrage! Not true! His love for me is eternal, like the stars!

LILY: On a good day, you love him, but when he's bad? When he pees on the oriental?

SAMSARA (o.s.): PACO! NOT AGAIN! Not the oriental.

SCOTT: That's different. That carpet was my grandmother's.

SAMSARA (o.s.): Paco, you promised!

PACO: You know I can't help it! The oriental is lush and dark and unless they catch me at it they can't tell for sure—but he still loves me when I pee on it! Even when he catches me he loves me! I can smell it! I can always smell love.

SAMSARA: *(She walks onto the porch and gets up on the ottoman with Paco.)* And they can smell when you pee on the oriental.

PACO: No, they can't! I have proven that time and time again.

SAMSARA: They try to smell it. They walk on it barefoot to check for wet spots, they crawl on their hands and knees sniffing—

PACO: But the oriental is a true friend. It absorbs everything like a sponge. After all, it's not as if I am a great Dane. I am a Chihuahua—we are talking a delicate rain, not a monsoon. And as for the smell—well, I have a theory—it is something I have given much thought to. It is my theory that they don't smell it because my pee smells like love!

SAMSARA: You have got to be kidding me.

PACO: But how else can you explain it!

SAMSARA: The degree of self delusion here—

PACO: You never give my theories a chance! You just shoot them down! You never once—

SAMSARA: Please! You're just lucky they love you so much. No matter how strong the smell of your pee, their love for you smells stronger. It blocks the pee-smell out.

PACO: That is the conventional wisdom when it comes to peeing in the house. But in my opinion—

SAMSARA: It's the conventional wisdom because in house after house, with dog after dog, all over the world, it has been proven to be the truth.

PACO: You reject the possibility that my pee smells like love.

SAMSARA: Your pee smells like pee. Their love is stronger. End of discussion.

SCOTT: Don't you get tired of him peeing on the oriental all the time?

LILY: Tired, yes.

SCOTT: See!

LILY: Tired is not the same as not loving.

SAMSARA: Don't you ever get tired of it? Of smelling all their love?

PACO: We were made for one thing only—to attach to them and never to be unattached! Stop asking me to betray my DNA!

SCOTT: It's not a crime to hate him when he pees on the oriental! Who wouldn't.

LILY: I don't.

SCOTT: Well, that's because it's not your grandmother's priceless rug.

LILY: I'm the one who has to clean it up, aren't I? And I still don't hate him.

SCOTT: Then why do you hate me?

LILY: I don't hate you.

SCOTT: You do, you hate me. You hate me every time you have to clean up after me. Don't deny it.

LILY: Sweetheart, you're upset about this morning, well don't be, I didn't even notice that—

SCOTT: I'm not talking about that, I'm talking about cleaning up things like—the thing with the IRS.

LILY: Oh. Well, that was hard. When they seized the business for back taxes.

SCOTT: The three times I let my health insurance lapse and didn't tell you.

(Samsara puts her paw over Paco's nose, and he puts his paw over hers.)

LILY: Oh, God, Scott, don't remind me about that. That was bad. Really bad.

PACO: *(But Samsara and Paco are in agony from the smells.)* Hold your breath, my darling, these things never last long.

(They hold their breath.)

SCOTT: The stock tip I gave your mother that—

LILY: Scott, please. My mother—is fine. She didn't need that big house. It really was too much for her. I didn't hate you for any of those things. The only time I hated you—

SCOTT: Ah ha! I knew you hated me!

LILY: —was the time with the cake.

PACO: *(Gasping for air.)* Oh, no, not the cake. Why does she bring up the cake!

(He tries to stuff tissue, anything into his nose to keep from smelling it.)

I can't stand the smell of the story of that cake.

SCOTT: I'm sorry about the cake, Lily. I don't know why I did that.

SAMSARA: Oh, no, Paco. Not this time. This time, it's time to grow up.

(They struggle, but she removes whatever he has managed to stuff up his nose.)

You must take the bitter with the sweet! You insist on loving him, on smelling his love—so wake up and smell the cake story, buster. Even though, in my opinion, it is not possible to love a man who has done a thing like this!

PACO: That is the greyhound in you talking! A full blooded Chihuahua would know! I must love him! It is not possible to do anything else.

LILY: Valentines Day. You told me to go pick it up at the bakery. You said you'd ordered it special to say "LILY, I LOVE YOU MORE THAN LIFE ITSELF." And then when I got it home and opened the box—

SCOTT: I'm sorry! I've said I'm sorry. You know I'm sorry.

LILY: It said nothing. Nothing at all. It was a blank cake. And you let me call the bakery and scream at them, you stood there and listened to me scream at the counter girl and then you listened to me pry the owner's number out of her and call him and scream at him. Because my cake did not say "Lily, I love you more than life itself", my cake said nothing, and my last Valentines Day had been ruined and by God I was going to make sure that somebody paid! But you'd never ordered it. You'd ordered a plain cake and told me to pick it up. You ordered a cake that did not say I love you and then you told me that it did. I hated you for that. And I still do.

(Paco goes over to Scott, and licks his cheek.)

Oh, Paco, how could he do that?

SAMSARA: Yes, I want to that know too. How could he!

PACO: I don't know. It is not in my blood to know. But the sorrow I feel for him that he can do such a thing?

(Paco licks Scott's other cheek, Scott holds him.)

Makes me love him even more.

SAMSARA: Oh, Paco. And that's why I love you.

(She goes over to Paco, and nuzzles him.)

PACO: You see, Samsara? You don't want to love me for it, but you have no choice. Love. It is hardwired in us both.

SAMSARA: Then why can't he say it? If he loves her—and I admit it, Paco, I can smell it too, he does love her! So why can't he say I love you to her? Why can't he put it on a cake?

PACO: He tried. He tried so hard. He was on the phone to the girl at the bakery and she asked him if he wanted the cake to say something. One minute the words I LOVE YOU LILY MORE THAN LIFE ITSELF were coming out of his mouth. And the next moment—the thought of putting them on a cake made him afraid. And the moment after that he knew that either the cake would say that, or nothing. He could say nothing less. So he said nothing at all. But Samsara, in the end the cake did say I love you more than life itself.

SAMSARA: No, it didn't—

PACO: It did. Just not in words. I could smell it then. You can smell it now. He loves her.

SCOTT: Lily?

LILY: Yes.

SCOTT: Of course you get the dogs. You think I'd give them to my sister? The first time Paco peed on her bed, she'd have him put down. She'd make Samsara wear little doggie dresses. No way is she getting the dogs.

(Lily goes to them, they all hold each other. A little buzzer goes off. Lily kisses Scott, then gets a pill box, hands Scott some pills and a glass of water. Paco and Samsara carefully watch him take his pills. There are lots of them.)

SAMSARA: How long?

PACO: *(Sniffs the air carefully.)* A week or two. Maybe three.

SAMSARA: You're sure? When I try to smell it—

(She sniffs.)

It seems a hundred years away. It smells—

(She sniff again.)

As if he isn't sick at all.

(She sniffs.)

It smells—

PACO: You're downwind of her, darling, that's all. The smell of her love is stronger than the truth.

SAMSARA: *(She moves around so she is on Scott's other side. Sniffs. Sadly.)* Oh. Yes. You're right. *(She leans tenderly into Scott's side.)*

I admit it, Paco. I act like I'm tired of it, like I don't need it, but the truth is I'll miss it.

PACO: When he isn't here to love us?

SAMSARA: No, when he isn't here for us to love him.

PACO: Ah. Yes. That is the hardest thing, I know.

SAMSARA: When he dies, where will the smell of all our love for him go?

PACO: Didn't your mother teach you this?

SAMSARA: No, I looked too much like my father, and she held it against me.

PACO: My darling. It is the one convenient thing about being bred for love. The smell of love doesn't go anywhere.

(Scott finishes taking his pills. The two dogs and Scott

and Lily take deep breaths, inhaling as if trying to
take in the scent of the entire world.)
It never goes away.

(Blackout.)

ORIGINAL PRODUCTION

Call Me was produced April 25—26, 2014 at Roxbury Repertory Theatre, 1234 Columbus Ave., Boston, MA 02120, in Six Playwrights in Search of a Stage.

DIRECTED BY THOMAS KEE

CAST
BLANCHE: Meredith Saran
KATE:　　Kimberly Mae Waller
JIM:　　　Tim Kimani

CHARACTERS

BLANCHE: A 16-18 year old high school student. She is nerdy, casually dressed and has an iPhone.
KATE: A 16-18 year old high school student. She is very pretty, casually dressed and has an iPhone.
JIM: A 16-18 year old high school student, somewhat geeky. He has an iPhone.

SCENE:

The basement of Blanche's parents' house.

TIME:

The present

SETTING: The basement of Blanche's parents' house, which consists of an old couch and a chair.

AT RISE: It is afternoon. Kate and JIM are seated on the couch, Blanche on the chair nearby. All three of them are texting on their iPhones. Occasionally one of them laughs.

BLANCHE: Do you follow Yellowbird?
KATE: No.
BLANCHE: Hilarious.
JIM: Oh, hilarious. Did you read her review on—
KATE: Oh my God, too funny.
BLANCHE: What?
KATE: Kim just posted a picture of Barb passed out under the carport.
JIM: No way. Let me see.
(Kate passes Jim her iPhone.)

JIM: Oh my God.

(Jim laughs)

BLANCHE: Let me see!

(Blanche grabs iPhone away from Jim)

Oh my God. She is such a wreck.

KATE: Excuse me.

(Kate reaches for her iPhone)

BLANCHE: What a mess.

KATE: Could I have my phone back, please? Jeez.

(Blanche and Jim stare)

BLANCHE: You don't have to get all thing about it.

JIM: Really.

KATE: People could be trying to get hold of me.

BLANCHE: Relax.

JIM: Chillax.

KATE: Easy for you to say. You don't have as many friends.

JIM: *(Snorts derisively)*

(Kate, Blanche and Jim all text and laugh periodically, not speaking to one another)

BLANCHE: Crap.

(Blanche puts down her iPhone. Kate and Jim continue to text and laugh)

JIM: Kate.

(Jim snaps a photo of his foot with his iPhone. Jim e-mails it)

KATE: What the—

(Kate turns to Jim)

Did you take that?

JIM: Just now!

KATE: I am so posting this!

JIM: Go 'head!

KATE: *(Turning to Blanche)* Did you see this?

JIM: Check my Facebook page!

BLANCHE: *(Halfheartedly checks page)* Yup.

KATE: Jim, that's hilarious.

JIM: I know, right?

(Blanche does not react. Jim and Kate stare at Blanche.)

BLANCHE: Yup.

(Jim and Kate continue to text and laugh, while Blanche sits glumly. Gradually Jim and Kate slow down until they stop)

KATE: What's up with you?

JIM: Yeah? It's like you're not even here.

BLANCHE: I'm sorry.

KATE: I haven't heard from you in like—what? Five minutes.

JIM: You didn't even comment on my foot picture.

BLANCHE: What foot picture?

JIM: Check your screen again!

BLANCHE: *(looks at iPhone and laughs)* That's funny.

JIM: So why don't you say something?

BLANCHE: I can't.

KATE and JIM: Why not?

BLANCHE: Guys—I just got some bad news and, um, I can't post anything.

(Blanche puts down the iPhone)

KATE: Whoa.

JIM: This is serious.

KATE: What happened?

(Kate and Jim lower their iPhones reluctantly)

BLANCHE: Betsy's boyfriend was in a car accident and he's in the hospital.

KATE: Oh, that's terrible.

JIM: Wait—which one is Betsy?

KATE: You know—magenta hair, kind of a big girl—

BLANCHE: My roommate at Camp Wampatuck.

JIM: Oh—her. Okay. I think I remember—

BLANCHE: She's freaking out.

KATE: Of course she is. Wouldn't you be?

JIM: Can you send her a Starbucks card?

BLANCHE: It's worse than that.

KATE: He's not—

(Kate and Jim look at Blanche with horror)

BLANCHE: No. He's alive.

KATE: Then what is it?

BLANCHE: She wants me to call her.

JIM: Seriously?

KATE: Just say you didn't get the message.

BLANCHE: How can I say that? She messaged me—it's right here.

(Blanche shows Jim and Kate the message)

KATE: Oh my God. She even put the phone number.

JIM: That's brutal.

BLANCHE: I know.

KATE: What are you going to do?

BLANCHE: I can't call her.

JIM: No kidding. Like, what is she, your mother's age?

BLANCHE: We're not even that close. I mean, we're Facebook friends.

KATE: She gave you her phone number.

BLANCHE: I just don't think I can deal with it right now.

JIM: I hear you.

BLANCHE: I mean, come on. It's been years. Why is she reaching out to me?

JIM: You got me.

(Jim checks his screen)

Did you guys remember to like the kid with cancer?

KATE: What kid with cancer?

JIM: You know – if she gets 500 million likes, it'll raise enough awareness for her cure.

KATE: Oh yeah. Done.

BLANCHE: You just did it now? What is wrong with you?

KATE: Sorry.

BLANCHE: My God. The kid was probably one like away from being cured.

KATE: Sorry!

JIM: So you're not gonna call Betsy?

BLANCHE: I can't! I just can't.

JIM: Okay.

(Jim and Kate text and laugh)

KATE: Oh my God.

JIM: What?

KATE: First 100 likes gets a special invite to the new froyo shop opening in the West Village.

(Kate likes)

JIM: *(Likes)* Done!

(Jim and Kate look at Blanche, who shakes her head glumly)

JIM: Maybe I can press like twice?

KATE: That won't work.

JIM: You're right.

> *(Jim looks at his screen)*
>
> I'm in!

KATE: Me too!

BLANCHE: Have fun without me.

KATE: *(Puts down iPhone)* Blanche, you can't just sit here all day doing nothing. My God, you've already missed free froyo.

JIM: It's like—you don't even exist.

BLANCHE: Shutup!

KATE: Just call her.

JIM: I'm with you—I don't think you should have to call anybody. I mean, when was the last time you heard from her before this?

BLANCHE: You know, that's a good question.

KATE: Just—

BLANCHE: I haven't heard from her in like, three years!

KATE:—call her.

JIM: You don't owe her anything.

KATE: What's a phone call?

BLANCHE: I should just get back online—

JIM: Pretend nothing happened.

BLANCHE: Exactly.

KATE: Don't do it.

BLANCHE: Why? What is your problem?

KATE: You're gonna go back online after she told you to call her?

JIM: I don't see why she shouldn't.

BLANCHE: Yeah. What's the big deal?

KATE: What if what's—her name—

BLANCHE: Betsy.

KATE: Betsy—tells everybody what a jerk you are?

BLANCHE: What, for not calling?

KATE: Yes, for not calling! Her boyfriend's in the hospital!

JIM: You have a point.

BLANCHE: Can't I just text her?

KATE: And say what? "My phone is broken?"

BLANCHE: Nooooo……

JIM: You could say there was a thunderstorm and the lines are down!

KATE: How could she text if the lines were down?

JIM: That's true.

BLANCHE: Oh, I know!

(Jim and Kate drift back to texting, ignoring Blanche)

I said, I know!

JIM: Good.

KATE: That's great.

BLANCHE: Guys, I know what to do!

KATE: Spill it already.

JIM: What?

KATE: I'll say I have laryngitis!

JIM: Oh my God, you're a genius.

KATE: That should work.

BLANCHE: Awesome.

(Blanche starts to text)

Do you think it's too late to get in on that froyo thing? Hey, how do you spell "laryngitis"?

JIM: L-a-y-no, that's not right-l-a-r-lar. Rin-it's the rin part that always gets me—

BLANCHE: L-a-r-y-n-g-i-t-i-s. Laryngitis. Awesome.

(Blanche presses send. Her iPhone rings)

Hello? Hello? Who? Betsy? Uh, I was just going to call you—

(Blanche looks horrified as Kate and Jim exit.
LIGHTS FADE)

END OF PLAY

THE DAY TOWER PIZZA STOOD STILL

Darrah Cloud

ORIGINAL PRODUCTION
Originally produced by The Half Moon Theatre, Poughkeepsie, NY in its 2014
10-Minute Play Festival; Molly Katz, Kristy Grimes, Patty Wineapple, Producers

CAST
DORNEICE: Barbara Nolan
JEFF: Sam Rebelein
SUE: Charlotte Katz
CRAIG THOMAS, EXTERMINATOR: Phil Douglas

JEFF: A thirty-something Pizza Parlor owner and chef, stressed.

DORNEICE: A homesick Giant Alien Cockroach, whose son has moved her recently from her beloved planet to the town where he lives, so that he can care for her; seventies.

SUE: Waitress, late teens, Dorneice's granddaughter.

CRAIG THOMAS: A professional exterminator, thirties to sixties.

LOCATION:

A Pizza Parlor in Pine Plains, a very small town in upstate New York, a place where everybody knows everybody.

DORNEICE sits at a table in the restaurant. Dressedup. Purse is on her lap. JEFF comes out of the kitchen and halts in surprise.

JEFF: Dorneice!

DORNEICE: Hello, Jeff.

JEFF: Whatcha doin' here?

DORNEICE: I'm leaving. I came to say good-bye.

JEFF: Well, I—I'm sorry to hear that. Where ya goin'?

DORNEICE: Home. Finally. The ship will be here any minute to pick me up.

JEFF: *(Knowing this can't be right)* Oh. Too bad. I thought you were here to stay.

DORNEICE: I'm sorry. It's a nice town, Jeff. But it's just not home.

JEFF: Well. It's been nice gettin' to know ya.

DORNEICE: It's been nice getting to know you too.

JEFF: What's it like, your home?

DORNEICE: The sky is pink, not blue. The flowers bloom all year. And every window looks out on stars. All my things are there. I wasn't allowed to bring any of my things with me when I came here.

JEFF: Yeah. A person's stuff is sacred.

DORNEICE: You won't call my son, will you?

JEFF: Gee, Dorneice—

DORNEICE: Please?

JEFF: OK, sure. . . . Can I get ya somethin' while ya . . . wait?

DORNEICE: I am hungry.

(She drools a sticky substance. He tries not to gag.)

JEFF: How about a slice?

DORNEICE: Whatever is fast. They're supposed to be here now.

JEFF: I got a new waitress. Lemme get her. Sue! You got a customer!

(SUE runs in, stops short in dread, seeing DOR-NEICE.)

JEFF: You can do this, Sue. Just go slow.

SUE slowly comes forward and sets a glass of water down.

SUE: Hi.

DORNEICE: Hello, Sue.

SUE: *(Hopefully)* You know me today?

DORNEICE: Your name is on your tag!

SUE: *(Disappointed)* Oh. Right. The thing is, I'm—. . . your waitress. Anything to drink besides water?

DORNEICE: I don't really drink dear. It comes out all my ends.

SUE: Oh.

SUE turns away and gags.

DORNEICE: You alright dear?

SUE: *(No)* Sure! Want . . . Want me to take this away then?

DORNEICE: No, leave it. It's always good to appear normal in a small town. How is my hair?

SUE: Your . . . hair?

DORNEICE: Is it alright? Do I have anything in my teeth?

SUE: Do I have to look?

DORNEICE: Always dress nicely when you travel. People treat you better.

SUE: Your teeth are good.

DORNEICE: Say, aren't you one of the Remsberger twins?

SUE: *(Warily)* Yes . . . Yes! I am!

DORNEICE: I saw you in the high school musical this year.

SUE: That was me! Yes! I can't believe you remember me!

DORNEICE: You sang, HEY BIG SPENDER. It was incredible!

SUE: Really? You thought so? My Dad walked out at intermission.

DORNEICE: He missed the best part!

SUE: The part where I go back to the gutter!

DORNEICE: Yes!

SUE: I thought so too!

DORNEICE: Well, those who are offended by anything miss everything.

SUE: He can be very judgmental. Especially when he wakes up from napping . . .

DORNEICE: You really you sold it.

SUE: It was the greatest experience of my life.

DORNEICE: You should major in theatre in college.

SUE: Oh, I'm not going to college.

DORNEICE: A talented girl like you?

SUE: Too expensive. I'd be paying for it for the rest of my life.

DORNEICE: You're worth it.

SUE: I wasn't that good.

DORNEICE: You can be anything if you set your mind to it.

SUE: Sorry, but that's just propaganda transmitted by the ruling species on this planet.
Your slice is up.
(She goes as CRAIG THOMAS walks in. Takes a seat at the counter. Does not see DORNEICE. He wears a jacket with a picture of a dead cockroach on his back.)

CRAIG: Hey Jeff!

JEFF: *(Nervously)* Uhhhhh Craig! How's it goin'?

CRAIG: I'm working on a major infestation down the street. ThoughtI'd stop in for a chicken wrap.

JEFF: To go? Want it to go?

CRAIG: No, I'll eat it here.

JEFF: Comin' right up. *(To SUE)* Keep him busy. Don't let him turn around.

SUE: Oh. Right. *(To CRAIG)* You know, you could eat in

our new garden!

CRAIG: Is there some kind of problem here?

DORNEICE: Craig Thomas?

CRAIG: Yes? *(He turns; finally sees DORNEICE; does a double take in fear)* Yaahhh!

DORNEICE: You're Craig Thomas? The Exterminator?

CRAIG: Yes . . .

DORNEICE: Yes, ma'am.

CRAIG: Yes ma'am!

DORNEICE: I have wanted to meet you for a very long time.

CRAIG: What can I do for you? I've got a real bad infestation down the street I should get back there—Hey Jeff, I'll take that wrap to go!

JEFF: I'm wrapping your wrap up now!

DORNEICE: The mother ship is coming any minute to take me finally back home.

And my only regret was unfinished business. And here you are . . .

CRAIG: I'm sorry! I'm sorry! Please, lady! I have a wife and kids—

DORNEICE: I wish you no harm.

CRAIG: What? Really?

DORNEICE: Insects gave you a life.

CRAIG: I love insects! Love them! I sent four kids to college on them!

DORNEICE: You smile when you exterminate us.

CRAIG: I'm doing my job. Bugs make people itchy! Bugs make them sick and afraid!

DORNEICE: But you, you are not afraid.

CRAIG: No ma'am.

DORNEICE: You understand us.

CRAIG: Yes! I do! I do understand you. I worship you! There, I said it! I confess! I have loved your species with all my heart since I was a little boy. Why didn't I become a biologist and dedicate my life to saving you? Instead, I went in this direction. What happened to me? Secretly, I've always wished . . . that I too were a cockroach. Oh to live a long life with a hard shell on my back, out partying all night, sleeping by day with all of my pals and never lonely.

DORNEICE: I forgive you.

CRAIG: You . . . you do?

DORNEICE: I am nearing the send of my time. I want to make peace.

CRAIG: I can give you peace. But, hey . . . you look great. Really. I don't think your time is close at all—

(SUE brings the slice.)

SUE: Here's your slice.

DORNEICE: I can't eat.

CRAIG: You have to keep up your strength.

JEFF: How is it, Dorneice?

SUE: It took too long.

JEFF: It was up in 5!

SUE: Well she doesn't want it anymore!

DORNEICE: I'm sorry. The food here is just delightful.

SUE: She won't eat!

JEFF: I still have to charge you.

CRAIG: I'll get the check.

DORNEICE: Why how chivalrous.

CRAIG: My pleasure. It's not every day you meet someone from Space.

DORNEICE: Really, we're everywhere. You just don't see us. Too busy with your lives thinking you're going some-where. While I am at then end of mine and still have so much to offer.

CRAIG: No! Don't say that!

DORNEICE: When it's my time, I want you to do it.

CRAIG: What?

SUE: No!

DORNEICE: Please. Tell me you will help me. I . . . I don't want to stay past my usefulness.

CRAIG: I, uh, I, uh, I, uh . . .

JEFF: *(Thinking fast)* Does that mean you're stayin' then, Dorneice? Cause, you know, Craig can't go back home with you . . . on the ship? He can't survive the atmosphere.

DORNEICE: Well, to tell you the truth, the food back home on my planet isn't very good. They let a McDonald's franchise open up.

CRAIG: Yeah, I work a lot in those . . .

SUE: Jeff went to the Culinary Institute of America, y'know. He did his internship with Mario Batali.

CRAIG: Hey! So did I!

(He and JEFF high five.)

DORNEICE: Pizza is the only human food that doesn't make me gassy.

SUE: *(Aside to men)* The slice is gone. She didn't eat it and it's gone. Did you see her eat it?

(They shake their heads, eyes wide.)

SUE: How are the beds back home?

DORNEICE: Hard. Lumpy.

JEFF: Hmm . . . On Earth we have tempurpedic.

CRAIG: Bedbug resistant.

SUE: I have one. The dog won't get off it.

JEFF: Is there anyone waiting for you on your . . . planet?

DORNEICE: No, everyone's gone now. No one even remembers me anymore.

CRAIG: A sense of purpose is everything, ma'am. Owing to your species, I have found that in my life.

SUE: You?

CRAIG: What would this town do without me?

SUE: That settles it! I'm going to college! No matter what it costs!

CRAIG: Well, then. I better get back to work. Good-bye, ma'am. Nice to meet you. And thank you. Thank you for your forgiveness.

DORNEICE: You didn't answer me before: Will you come, will you come someday, when I finally call?

CRAIG: I'll always be here for you, 24 hours a day.

(He takes her pincer. It breaks off in his hands. He screams.)

DORNEICE: It's alright. Another one will grow back soon. Though not as quickly as they used to . . . Keep it.

(He looks down at it in surprise.)

CRAIG: Always. I will keep it always. You have changed my life. Thank you. Thank you.

(He holds it to his heart. Leaves.)

JEFF: Ready to stay here then, Dorneice?

DORNEICE: Yes. Yes I believe I am. I feel much better now.

JEFF: Good. Want me to call your son to pick you up?

DORNEICE: I don't like him very much I'm afraid . . .

JEFF: Is there somebody else?

DORNEICE: No . . . Thank you, Morwon.

JEFF: I'm . . . Jeff.

(JEFF exits to make the call.)

SUE: What did you do with the slice? Tell me what you did with the slice!

(DORNEICE regurgitates it into her hand. SUE gags.)

(DORNEICE pops it back into her proboscis.)

DORNEICE: I'll just wait outside for my son. Don't want to get in the way . . .

(She's gone. SUE sighs.)

SUE: *(Sadly)* Bye, grandma.

DOCTORS AND LAWYERS
(1ST EDITION RULES)
David Strauss

ORIGINAL PRODUCTION

Doctors and Lawyers (1st Edition Rules) originally premiered at the Lowndes Shakespeare Center in Orlando, Florida on January 9-18, 2015 as a part of an evening of short plays entitled "Launch 2015." It was directed by Charles R. Dent and produced by Playwrights' Round Table.

CAST
XANDOR: Anthony Marando
ARALDAN: PJ Metz
MIRIEN: Chelsea Scheid
CADY: Hayes Lasseter

3004 Delaney Street
Orlando, FL 32806
407-230-3401
December 26, 2014
dstrauss@gmail.com

Production rights can be obtained by contacting the playwright at the above email address.

CHARACTERS:

> XANDOR: The host and leader of the group. A little nerdy, but excitable.
> ARALDAN: A warrior. Loud, boisterous, and full of himself.
> MIRIEN: A wizard. Snarky, smart, and ready for anything the guys can throw at her.
> CADY: A thief. Confused by this new adventure but quickly adapts. Think of the cool girl perplexed by the interests of her geeky friends.

> Note on ages: Generally, it's better if the characters are all twenties to thirties, although older teens could play them as well.

SYNOPSIS:

> Xandor the Stout invites his adventuring friends to join him on a quest, the latest adventure in the fantasy world of "Doctors and Lawyers," a fantasy game taking place in "our" world.

SETTING:

> Xandor's dwelling, a sparse location with table and stools/chairs.

TIME:

> Undetermined.

> *LIGHTS UP on a table with four chairs or stools around it. We see one man, XANDOR the STOUT, in D&D type robes, carrying a large book. He walks over and puts it down on the table, then looks around the room, pleased.*

XANDOR: Ah yes, today is a day for a fabulous quest! When my compatriots arrive, we shall truly undertake a journey that will be spoken of. Nay, sung about, for generations to come!

(Xandor exits, and as he does there is a pounding at the door, as if a mighty force has arrived at this location. This is ARALDAN THE BRAVE, and he is a warrior. Everything he does shouts that this is not a man to be trifled with.)

ARALDAN: (O.S.) Xandor the Stout, it is I, Araldan the Brave! I have come to join in your quest! Allow me to enter or I shall tear the door from its hinges!

(Xandor reenters, this time carrying a plate of snacks and places them on the table as he speaks.)

XANDOR: Alright, Araldan! Hold your stallions! I am coming. My door was just repaired from the last time you joined me on a Quest, I don't want to have my—

(Araldan enters, carrying a sword [and perhaps a doorknob with broken wood around it]. He cuts off Xandor before he can finish.)

ARALDAN: It is I, Araldan the Brave!

XANDOR: Yes, yes, I know. You were, you know, banging on my door.

ARALDAN: I have come to join you on your quest! Are we ready to begin?

XANDOR: Not yet, not yet. We're still waiting on two others.

ARALDAN: Who will be joining us?

XANDOR: Mirien the Wizard will be bringing her magicks to our party.

ARALDAN: Mirien?

XANDOR: Yes.

ARALDAN: This . . . is not good news.

XANDOR: I assure, you, she has come a long way since the demon fiasco of Seraconis.

ARALDAN: I should hope so. I still chafe on hot days.

XANDOR: Yes, she will be a valued member of our group.

ARALDAN: And who is the fourth?

XANDOR: Mirien brings a new adventurer to our quest, a cunning thief named Caderrakath-Ulilannon.

ARALDAN: Who?

XANDOR: Caderrakath-Ulilannon.

ARALDAN: I shall not be repeating that.

XANDOR: Understood.

(Suddenly the lights blink on and off, and then go to black for a few seconds. When they come back on, standing right near Xandor and Araldan are MIRIEN THE WIZARD with her staff, and CADERRAKATH-ULILANNON THE THIEF, aka CADY.)

MIRIEN: Behold, it is I, Mirien the Wizard!

ARALDAN: Must you always make such an entrance?

MIRIEN: Ah, Araldan, my old friend! How's that chafing these days?

(Araldan readies to draw his sword, Mirien prepares her staff, but Xandor stops them both. Caderrakath sneaks around the group, well, sneakily.)

XANDOR: Enough! We have come here for a Quest! Mirien, please introduce your friend, Cader—Cadd—Cad . . .

MIRIEN: This is Caderrakath-Ulilannon the Thief, Darcaryn Swordhand. Also known as Darcaryn the Rogue, Lady Darcaryn, Lady Swordhand, Lady Darcaryn Swordhand the Rogue, Lady Darcaryn Swordhand Much-Smiling, Darcaryn Swordhand the Fence, and also Cady.

ARALDAN: Cady?

CADY: Saves time when I have left my griffin with the valet.

XANDOR: Are we all ready? We are ready to begin our quest?

(The other three all indicate they are, and for a second, look ready to charge out the door into action, when Xandor opens his book and shows them all, and the audience, what looks to be a guide book for Dungeons & Dragons, but instead of a fantasy-inspired cover, it shows some generic corporate clip art and displays the words "t.")

XANDOR: Then, welcome! For tonight, we will be playing . . . DOCTORS AND LAWYERS! First edition rules, of course.

(Cady is confused. The others sit around the table. Xandor pulls out his dungeon master documents as he speaks.)

MIRIEN: Ooh, a new quest!

XANDOR: Tonight, we will be visiting a fantastical imaginary world populated by such creatures as insurance adjustors, malpractice lawyers, corporate headhunters, HR specialists, and dental hygenists.

CADY: What is a . . . "law-yer?"

ARALDAN: Oh, my new friend, you will find out. Nobody forgets their first battle with a "lawyer."

XANDOR: Tonight we will be playing this adventure, "The 14th Floor Human Resources Department."

ARALDAN AND MIRIEN: Oooooohhhh . . .

XANDOR: Now, Cady, since you are new, you will need to create a character. We all have characters we play in Doctors and Lawyers.

CADY: What's yours?

XANDOR: I am your guide for this evening's quest, my character is "Leroy Jenkins, 17th level VP of Sales."

CADY: How do I do that?

(Xandor hands her a character sheet and some D20 dice.)

XANDOR: You will need to roll dice to figure out who your character is. I will help you. First, you need a character name.

CADY: I can name them anything I want?

XANDOR: Well, this is a fantasy world. So you wouldn't want to give them an everyday name like Umania or Silillan.

CADY: I don't know what to call them.

MIRIEN: Oh, I have a blank character sheet you could use as a starter. Her name is "Mildred Smith."

(Note: If the director wants to insert the name of someone in the audience, or famous in local theatre, or even a celebrity, go for it.)

CADY: "Mildred Smith." I like it. It's so . . . exotic.

XANDOR: Okay, Mildred Smith. Let's find out more about your character. Roll the die.

CADY: *(After rolling.)* Thirteen.

XANDOR: Oh, okay, your credit rating is 712.

CADY: Is that good?

XANDOR: Depends on if you're looking to rent or own.

ARALDAN: I recommend renting at first. You don't need to build up equity at your level.

XANDOR: Now, let's find out your current salary. *(Cady roles.)* Oh, that would be 32,000. Now roll again for debt. *(Cady rolls.)* Oh, that's an unlucky roll, looks like you have 88,000 in student loans. Shouldn't have gone to Rollins. *(Note: Replace with a local expensive private college, somewhere where the privileged kids go.)*

MIRIEN: Oh, that liberal arts degree isn't going to help.

XANDOR: Okay, now roll for charisma. *(Cady rolls.)* Oh, look at that, you have your own podcast and 1700 followers on Twitter.

ARALDAN: I recommend you start a Tumblr, they will really help you if we ever enter a Starbucks during a quest.

XANDOR: Roll for hit points. Oh, look at that, you have high blood pressure. Watch your cholesterol.

MIRIEN: I will remind you to stay away from the Cinnabons.

XANDOR: Now, a costume.

CADY: I always wear plate mail.

XANDOR: No, no, in our fantasy world, you must wear a suit. *(Cady grabs the DM's character sheet and looks at it.)*

CADY: What's this? I want one of these, an Arr-mahn-ee.

ARALDAN: An Armani on 32k a year, not likely my friend.

CADY: Thirty two k what? What is a k?

ARALDAN: Thirty two thousand dollars.

CADY: What is a dollar, like a gold piece?

MIRIEN: Sort of, although every time we play they're worth less.

XANDOR: And finally, your skill.

CADY: *(Consulting sheet.)* I will be . . . an actuary.

ARALDAN: Oh, excellent choice. If you are going to kill us of boredom.

CADY: Fine, an *(consulting sheet again)* accountant. What do you have?

ARALDAN: I am Mark the Needlessly Flatulent, a

fifteenth level commercial realtor.

XANDOR: Mirien, which character were you playing with this time?

MIRIEN: I will be playing my level 17 executive assistant, Elaine the Liar, daughter of Herbert, The Not Relevant. And I'll be playing this time using my +4 Android instead of the +1 iPhone 4. I grow tired of the battery dying every time we play, and the +3 smugness of my iPhone never seems to help.

XANDOR: Okay, then our party is complete. Welcome, all, I am Leroy Jenkins, VP of Sales. You are all standing on a crowded sidewalk outside the offices of our company, Wickets Incorporated. Other employees pass by you into the front entrance of the company offices, a twenty story tower of glass and steel in front of you. Up at the top, the office of the CEO, Wilson the Arrogant, awaits. But nobody under the level of Senior VP has ever entered it. Legend has it that the boss—

CADY: Is he a dark sorcerer?

XANDOR: No, a Protestant. Legend has it he has in his office an all-powerful set of documents that will . . . approve any vacation request.

MIRIEN: Oh my Goddess.

ARALDAN: Wow.

XANDOR: You have all decided that you want next Friday off to attend the Nickelback concert in a nearby city. As a team, your goal is to get to the top floor, find the boss' office, sneak in, get the vacation requests, and then submit them to the HR department.

ARALDAN: Alright, let's do this!

XANDOR: As the three of you stand by the entrance, a young woman with red hair approaches you and asks for ten dollars. Cady, as our newest team member, you go first. What do you do?

CADY: I don't know. How do I play? *(pointing at Araldan)* Do I kill him and use his blood to summon a Hosgarth demon? *(She takes out her knife and makes a move to cut his throat)*

XANDOR: No, you tell me what you want to do and I roll dice.

CADY: Oh, okay. *(To Mirien)* Should I kill this woman?

MIRIEN: No!

CADY: I don't understand this stupid game.

XANDOR: The woman says that she is asking for donations to help the homeless. She says ten dollars would help feed and house someone for a day.

ARALDAN: Inventory.

XANDOR: You are carrying your wallet. The wallet has two dollars, 10 cents, and an unused condom. The woman again asks for a donation.

ARALDAN: I convince her that I can offer her a great place to build a homeless shelter. I use my +4 voice of arrogance.

XANDOR: The woman is terrified as you begin talking, then slowly backs away and retreats to the other side of the sidewalk.

ARALDAN: That's why I'm a 15th level commercial realtor. Booyah.

XANDOR: Mirien, your move?

MIRIEN: I lead us all into the lobby.

XANDOR: You enter the lobby. It is twenty five feet tall and full of glass artwork and framed paintings of former company CEOs on the wall. The security guard stands next to his desk between you and the elevators to the upper floors.

MIRIEN: I walk towards the elevators.

XANDOR: He stops you and demands to see your employee ID.

MIRIEN: Inventory.

XANDOR: You are carrying a ludicrously hot cup of Starbucks coffee, and your purse. Your purse has 17 dollars, three credit cards, two debit cards, a key that you have no remembrance of, two cards to Hilton hotel rooms, four business cards from the vegan recipes meetup you attended the night before, a driver's license, nine receipts that you have not yet submitted for reimbursement, a phone charger, jump drive, memory card reader, earbud headphones, penlight, container of mace, bottles of Advil, Aleve, Midol, and Tums, wet wipes, Kleenex, a small hairbrush, hair ties, breath mints, dental floss, lipstick, lip gloss, lip balm, two packs of gum, one sugarless, face powder, hand lotion, bobby pins, a day planner. *(deep breath)* And your employee ID.

CADY: I thought there was no magic in this world?

XANDOR: There is none.

CADY: There's no way she could fit all that in a, what did you say, "purse"?

XANDOR: She's also a 9th level mom. They have . . . special abilities.

MIRIEN: I take out the employee ID and show it to the guard.

XANDOR: He waves you by. Cady?

CADY: I also try and pass the security guard.

XANDOR: Barring you from passing, he says, "I don't recognize you, you must be new."

CADY: I distract the guard.

XANDOR: How?

CADY: I have breasts, don't I?

XANDOR: Oh yes, very well. *(He rolls.)* You have successfully distracted the security guard with your breasts and he lets you pass.

ARALDAN: Hey!

MIRIEN: This game is so sexist. Ugh, pillaging culture.

CADY: Ain't no thang.

ARALDAN: I don't have my ID, do I?

XANDOR: You left it at Mirien's after the Adventure of the Too Many Tequilas.

ARALDAN: I attempt to sneak past the security guard.

XANDOR: *(Rolls.)* Oh, a 3. That's not good. The guard whacks you in the wrist with his night stick. *(Rolls.)* He does 7 damage plus 3 since he's been, you know, working out. Your wrist is rapidly turning a shade of purple. He approaches you and is about to hit you again.

CADY: I use my breasts again!

XANDOR: *(Rolls.)* You have successfully used your breasts to distract the guard.

CADY: *(To Mirien)* Quick, get him into the elevators!

MIRIEN: I grab Mark and shove him into the elevator.

XANDOR: *(Rolls.)* You get him into the elevator without further injury.

CADY: Can I join them?

XANDOR: The security guard slips you his number and tells you he gets off at 5. *(Rolls.)* You run and get into the elevator just as it closes. Your offices are all on the 3rd floor. But just as you push the button, you notice an unpleasant aroma in the elevator car.

(All three look at Araldan.)

MIRIEN: Mark!

CADY: The needlessly flatulent?

ARALDAN: I'm sorry, my character does that when he's stressed!

XANDOR: You all get off on the third floor. The company health office is down the hall. Your wrist is severely bruised, Mark.

CADY: Mirien, I mean, Elaine, use a spell of healing!

MIRIEN: I can't do that, remember? No magic.

CADY: This game is stupid.

ARALDAN: I need to go to the . . . um, what is it called, doctor! The health office.

XANDOR: *(Rolls.)* Oh, unfortunately, your HMO won't cover it.

MIRIEN: I told you to upgrade your deductible!

ARALDAN: Dammit!

MIRIEN: Don't I have some . . . ummm . . . Aleve in my purse? I give Mark some Aleve.

XANDOR: *(Rolls.)* The swelling starts to go down a little.

MIRIEN: We need to get up to the top floor. Does Mildred have any special skills?

XANDOR: She has—

(They are interrupted by the voice of hell. Or at least one seriously scary sounding demon, deep and powerful and the stuff that nightmares are made of. It should not sound even remotely female.)

DEMON VOICE: XANDOR!

(Xandor is noticeably upset and hesitant to answer back. The others look him with shame. Finally, after a few seconds.)

XANDOR: Yes?

DEMON VOICE: I TOLD YOU TO TAKE OUT THE GARBAGE AND TAKE YOUR LITTLE SISTER TO THE PIT OF ULTIMATE DESPAIR BEFORE YOUR LITTLE FRIENDS CAME OVER. IF YOU CAN'T ACT LIKE A GROWN UP I WON'T LET YOU PLAY THAT STUPID GAME.

XANDOR: *(Mortified.)* Yesssss, mom!

DEMON VOICE: DON'T YES MOM ME! NOW TAKE OUT THE GARBAGE NOW OR I'LL ASK YOUR FRIENDS TO LEAVE!

XANDOR: Um, sorry guys, we have to take a break.

ARALDAN: No problem.

MIRIEN: Yeah, I probably have to go soon. My mom will destroy the whole Kingdom if I don't have my homework done by the time she gets home from the hell dimension of Askanoth.

CADY: I should probably get going too. My dad is making my favorite meal, spaghetti with lots of Halfling.

ARALDAN: Oh, Mirien, you just wanna quit because you know your Level 17 Executive Assistant totally wants to go on a date with my Level 15 commercial realtor.

MIRIEN: Oh my Goddess, she so does not.

ARALDAN: She totally does.

(They all start to exit.)

MIRIEN: Does not!

ARALDAN: Does too!

MIRIEN: You're such a barbarian tool.

ARALDAN: Take that back!

XANDOR: C'mon, if I don't take my sister to the Pits I'll be grounded for a week. We can pick the game up tomorrow, I should be getting in the new expansion pack, "The Staplers of Accounting." I hear it's really amazing. Seriously! Guys, I mean it!

(LIGHTS DOWN.)

FILM APPRECIATION

David Susman

ORIGINAL PRODUCTION

Film Appreciation was first produced by Mill 6 Collaborative as part of the Boston Theater Marathon XVI (Kate Snodgrass, Artistic Director) on May 11, 2014.

Directed by Barlow Adamson

CAST
TRISHA: Bridgette Hayes
BRIAN: Daniel Berger-Jones
KEVIN: Brett Milanowski
GEORGE: Bob Mussett
ARTHUR: Barlow Adamson

CHARACTERS:

> TRISHA: In her mid or late twenties; also seen in flashback at different ages, as young as eighteen.
> BRIAN: Same age as Trisha; also seen in flashback at different ages, as young as eighteen.
> KEVIN: In his mid or late twenties.
> GEORGE: In his mid or late twenties.
> ARTHUR: In his mid or late twenties.

SETTING:

> Various locations, all represented minimally.

TIME:

> The present.

SETTING:

> Minimal set: Two chairs should be available, as well as a makeshift wall.

> *At Rise: Trisha sits alone, in one of two side-by-side chairs facing the audience. She addresses us directly.*

TRISHA: I met Brian when I was young. I was in college. We met at a movie house, as you might expect.
(As the lights darken slightly, BRIAN enters and sits beside TRISHA. He carries a box of movie-house popcorn. He stares straight ahead, rapt, as if looking at a movie screen.)
It was a Fellini film, and he was the only one who seemed to know when to laugh.

BRIAN: *(Eyes still on the "screen.")* Ha, ha, ha . . . Oh, God . . . Ha, ha, ha . . . That's genius . . .

TRISHA: *(Joining in awkwardly, obviously unsure.)* Ha, ha, ha . . . yes . . . ha, ha, ha. *(To audience.)* It was hard not to be intrigued by that. The lights come up again. The film has ended.

BRIAN: *(To no one in particular.)* That was remarkable! That was absolute genius. Fellini is a complete and total genius.

(Turning unexpectedly to TRISHA.)
Did you like it?

TRISHA: I'm sorry?

BRIAN: Did you like the film?

TRISHA: Me? Um . . . I think so. I'm not sure I fully got it.

BRIAN: Fellini takes time. Are you a film buff?

TRISHA: Well, I like films. I'm trying to get into them more. You know, as an art form. But I like them. You seem . . . pretty into them.

BRIAN: I breathe them. I inhale them. As far as I'm concerned, film is the most relevant of all media. And it's the busiest. Image, music, language, movement, theatricality—it's everything. It's all other art forms combined. *(Beat.)* Don't you think?

TRISHA: *(To audience.)* I mean, seriously. That's the kind of passion you look for. He just vibrated like a molecule whenever he talked about film. And he talked about film a lot. *(To BRIAN.)* What's your name? I'm Trisha.

BRIAN: *(Imperiously.)* They call me Mister Tibbs!

TRISHA: Um . . . okay.

BRIAN: No, no, it's from In the Heat of the Night. Sidney Poitier. You've never seen it?

TRISHA: Oh. No.

BRIAN: It's good. Ahead of its time in its honest portrayal of race relations in the U.S. (Beat.) I'm Brian.
(TRISHA leans toward BRIAN, smiles warmly, takes a handful of his popcorn.)

TRISHA: Well, Brian, maybe you can take me to see it. *(To audience.)* You can understand the appeal, right? He was attractive, smart, interesting. The thing is, film was his life. He didn't just talk about film, either. He talked film. *(BRIAN has produced two glasses of wine. He hands one to TRISHA. They're now at an imaginary dinner table.)*

BRIAN: *(As they clink glasses.)* Louie, I think this is the beginning of a beautiful friendship.

TRISHA: *(To audience.)* It was quirky but sweet. You knew that whatever he said, he meant. Even if the words weren't exactly his.

BRIAN: *(Leaning in intimately.)* You had me at "hello."

TRISHA: *(Smitten.)* Really?

BRIAN: Really.

(They kiss. It's slow, romantic.)

Mrs. Robinson, you're trying to seduce me.

TRISHA: *(Gazing into his eyes, mesmerized.)* I was. I mean, I am. *(To audience.)* I was. I was totally into him. And we were good together. His "movie talk" took some getting used to, but I kind of liked it. It was different.

(TRISHA stands while BRIAN remains seated. She takes the wine glasses from him; she's clearing the imaginary dinner table.)

(To BRIAN.) How was dinner? Did you get enough?

BRIAN: Are you kidding? I'm stuffed. As God is my witness, I'll never be hungry again.

TRISHA: *(To audience.)* And he was kind. He was a genuinely nice guy. When my cat, Rosebud, got hit by the truck . . . *(She starts to tear up.)* . . . I just . . . I'm sorry . . . it was just so sad . . . and I . . . Oh, God . . .

BRIAN comes to her, holds her.

BRIAN: *(Gently.)* Hey. It's okay. Shh. There's no crying in baseball.

TRISHA: *(To audience; regaining her composure.)* What else could you want in a man? Intelligence, compassion. A good listener. *(BRIAN, still holding her, has begun to kiss her neck.)* And also, he was . . . *(She's becoming aroused.)* Did I mention he was also . . . I mean, that is to say, we had a good . . . *(To BRIAN.)* What are you doing?

BRIAN: *(Continuing to nuzzle her.)* I'm making you an offer you can't refuse.

TRISHA: *(To audience.)* Excuse us for just a minute.

They retreat behind the makeshift wall. Sounds of lovemaking begin.

TRISHA: (O.S.) Oh, Brian . . .

BRIAN: (O.S.) Trisha . . .

TRISHA: (O.S.; escalating.) Oh, God . . . Mmm . . . Oh, God . . . Yes . . .

BRIAN: (O.S.; escalating.) Trisha . . . Jesus . . .

TRISHA: *(O.S.; rising to climax.)* Oh, God . . . Yes . . . Brian . . . Yes, yes, yes . . . !

BRIAN: *(O.S.; rising to climax.)* Trisha . . . Jesus . . . Oh, God . . . I'll have what she's having!)

(TRISHA emerges from behind the wall.

TRISHA: *(To audience.)* Okay, so it could be a little weird. And it didn't stop. Day in, day out, this was how he communicated.

(BRIAN enters, briefcase in hand. He crosses the stage briskly.)

BRIAN: I'm off to work. Hasta la vista, baby.

(He kisses TRISHA, then exits.)

TRISHA: And yes, it started to bother me. All these other voices coming between us. You begin to ask yourself what it means. You know, whether it's about distance. Like he can't just talk to me as himself. Like there's this gap we can't bridge. It's obviously not the healthiest way to have a relationship. Also, it just plain got on my nerves.

(BRIAN enters, puts down his suitcase.)

BRIAN: Ah. There's no place like home.

TRISHA: *(To BRIAN.)* Okay, look. Can you just give it a rest?

BRIAN: Houston, do we have a problem?

TRISHA: I'm just saying, it's getting old, the constant film references. It's not normal. It's not how a normal relationship works.

BRIAN: So you're mad as hell, and you're not going to take this anymore.

TRISHA: Will you quit it?! It's not funny anymore, Brian. It's not funny and it's not charming. It's just annoying and stupid, and it makes me not want to be with you. *(Beat.)* I don't want to be with you, Brian. I guess I didn't realize that until now. I'm leaving you.

BRIAN: Don't.

TRISHA: Why not?

BRIAN: Because I'm scared, Trish. Don't you see that? I'm scared of everything. I'm scared of who I am. I'm scared of the way I act. But most of all, I'm scared of you walk-

---

ing out of this room, and me never feeling the rest of my life the way I feel when I'm with you.

TRISHA: *(Moved.)* Oh, Brian. I just . . . *(Beat. She stiffens.)* Wait a minute. Is that from Dirty Dancing?

(BRIAN nods sheepishly.)

TRISHA, CONT'D: Jesus Christ. It's over. Get out.

BRIAN: Seriously?

TRISHA: Yes, seriously. How else do you want me to say it, Brian?

We're done. The end. Roll the credits. It's a wrap. No sequel, no additional footage. We're packing up the set and the crew is off the clock and the studio lot is closed. It's finished. We're finished. Goodbye, Brian.

(Silence.)

BRIAN: *(Softly.)* I know it was you, Fredo, You broke my heart.

He exits.

TRISHA: *(To audience.)* So that was that. I moved on. I gave up everything that reminded me of Brian. I stopped going to the movies. I wouldn't so much as look at a Raisinet. I sold off all my Fellini DVDs on eBay, which was tricky—I still didn't know whether to call them comedies or dramas.

(As she talks, KEVIN enters and sits in one of the two vacant chairs.)

TRISHA, CONT'D: And then eventually, I started dating again. My "rebound" date was with Kevin.

(She takes a seat beside KEVIN and turns to face him.)

TRISHA: So, Natalie tells me you're a musician. That must be interesting.

KEVIN: *(Speaking, not singing.)* Well, it's nice work if you can get it.

TRISHA: That's cute. Do you have other interests?

KEVIN: I like New York in June. How about you?

TRISHA: *(To audience.)* That's when the alarm bells went off. Or should I say, the clarinets.

KEVIN: And of course, I like a Gershwin tune. How about

you?

TRISHA: *(To audience.)* You guessed it. Kevin was into jazz standards. Totally into jazz standards. I suppose I should have found it romantic.

KEVIN: Look, I'm just going to put myself on the line here. I mean, everybody loves somebody sometime, right? So the thing is, Trisha, I adore you. You're the top. I've got you under my skin.

TRISHA: *(To audience.)* But when you think about it, those songs are actually a little pervy.

KEVIN: *(With rising passion.)* Embrace me, my sweet embraceable you! Let's live devil-may-care! Let's misbehave!

TRISHA: Let's not.

(KEVIN exits. GEORGE enters and takes his place in the chair.)

TRISHA, CONT'D: *(To audience.)* Next was George. He was all about Shakespeare.

GEORGE: Sure, I'm not the handsomest guy on the planet. I don't have rock-hard abs. But then, love looks not with the eyes, but with the mind. And therefore is winged Cupid painted blind. Am I right?

TRISHA: *(To audience.)* Definitely not my type.

GEORGE: Ah, the lady doth protest too much, methinks.

TRISHA: *(To GEORGE.)* Just doth give me some space, okay?

(GEORGE exits. ARTHUR enters and takes his place.)

TRISHA, CONT'D: *(To audience.)* Arthur was into philosophy.

ARTHUR: I'm willing to come to a relationship tabula rasa. After all, when you get right down to it, love is a categorical imperative. So I'm ready to give up my solipsistic leanings and engage in, well, let's just say a dialectic that focuses on romance.

TRISHA: *(To audience.)* I'm sure I would have found him completely annoying if I'd understood anything he said.

ARTHUR: *(Mumbling as he exits.)* She's probably a logical

Lawrence Harbison

positivist anyway . . . .

TRISHA: I started thinking about Brian again. I missed him. I missed his stupid film references. I don't know. Maybe all men are weird, and the trick is to find the weirdo who fits. Or maybe weird has nothing to do with it. Maybe the weird stuff is actually the good stuff, once you understand it.

(As she speaks, BRIAN enters and stands at some distance from TRISHA.)

TRISHA, CONT'D: (To audience.) Or maybe it's simpler than all that. Maybe you just miss what you miss. But I missed him. *(Turning to BRIAN.)* I miss you. I want us to be back like we were.

BRIAN: *(coldly)* You talkin' to me?

TRISHA: Come on, Brian. We were good together. You know we were. It was stupid to break up.

BRIAN: Stupid is as stupid does.

TRISHA: *(With great earnestness.)* Brian, listen. I love you. You complete me. You're the stuff that dreams are made of. I wish I knew how to quit you, but I can't. Look, I know the problems of two little people don't amount to a hill of beans in this crazy world. But right now I'm just a girl, standing in front of a boy, asking him to love her. And maybe I wasn't ready before. Maybe I was the one who was afraid. But I'm ready now. Mr. DeMille, I'm ready for my close-up. Surely that means something.

BRIAN: *(With utter passion.)* I love you, too—and don't call me Shirley!

They kiss—a long, dramatic movie kiss. BRIAN returns to the chairs and sits. TRISHA remains standing.

TRISHA: *(To audience.)* And that was it. We got back together, and we stayed. A happy ending, just like the movies. It's funny, everyone always says life isn't like the movies. But I don't know. Maybe life is exactly like the movies. Or maybe it's just mine. Anyway, everyone has their thing, right? Everyone has their way of making sense of it all. As long as you've got something.

(She returns to the vacant chair next to BRIAN. They smile warmly at each other and nestle. BRIAN produces a TV remote control.)

BRIAN: Should we pop in a film?

TRISHA takes the remote.

TRISHA: Nah. Let's just watch TV.

(She points the remote directly at the audience and clicks. Instant blackout.)

End of Play

HAPPENSTANCE
Craig Pospisil

ORIGINAL PRODUCTION

Happenstance had its World Premiere at the Purple Rose Theatre Company (Jeff Daniels, Founder; Guy Sanville, Artistic Director; Katie Doral, Managing Director) as part of the "Spring Comedy Festival: Lovers, Liars and Lunatics" on April 11, 2014. It was directed by Guy Sanville, and the stage manager was Stephanie Buck. The cast was as follows:

CAST
CASSIDY: Rhiannon Ragland
MARTIN: Rusty Mewha
ABE: Michael Brian Ogden
SERENA: Lauren Knox

CHARACTERS:

> CASSIDY: thirties to forties, a somewhat high-strung woman.
>
> MARTIN: thirties to forties, her accommodating husband.
>
> ABE: thirties to forties, Cassidy's ex-boyfriend, who broke her heart.
>
> SERENA: twenties, Abe's chic and beautiful girlfriend.

SETTING:

> A coffee house.

TIME:

> The present, but with a twist.

Lights come up on a blank space, with only a small café table with two chairs.
CASSIDY, thirties, enters arm-in-arm with her husband MARTIN, who is in his forties, a newspaper in one hand.

CASSIDY: Oh, there's a free table.

MARTIN: You grab it, I'll get the coffee. What do you want?

CASSIDY: Grande iced white chocolate mochacino, half caf, half decaf, half skim, half soy, with just a little whipped cream and a dash of cinnamon on top?

MARTIN: It would be faster if you just said "the usual."

CASSIDY: Thank you, Martin.

> *(Martin smiles, shakes his head, and heads off to get the coffees. Cassidy turns to the audience, very animated, and probably not in need of coffee.)*

CASSIDY: Okay, before we go on, it's really important for you to know that I'm not crazy.

> *(slight pause)*

I know what you're thinking. "If the first thing she has to say is that she's not crazy, you know the chick is nuts." And normally, I would totally be with you on that. But, see, not this time.

(slight pause)

The meds I'm on are mild. Very mild. And I just take them for some . . . low level depression. Really. I'm not, like, suicidal or anything. It's just a, a . . . soupcon of depression. And anxiety. But I'm good, and the pills I'm on now work really well. I don't have those days when the mind races all over the place into these weird . . .

CASSIDY (CONT.): *(slight pause)* Well, okay, you don't need all the details. The point is it's just normal stuff. And, please, today? Who isn't anxious and depressed, right? I do wish the pills didn't make me crave sugar so much . . . Not that I'm hung up my weight. No body issues here. I am good with who I am, how I am and all the rest. *(pause)*

What was I talking about? Oh! Crazy. Right. I'm not crazy. I just wanted to make that clear.
(pause)

I really messed that up, didn't I? We should probably . . . you know, keep going.

(With her index finger extended, she makes twirls her hand in a circle, a "let's get this going" gesture, and then sits down in one of the chairs at the café table. Martin enters a moment later with their coffees. He sets one down in front of her and then seats himself.)

MARTIN: Here you go. One grande iced . . . the usual.

CASSIDY: Thanks.

MARTIN: Of course. I love you.

CASSIDY: I love you too. *(to the audience)* Actually, Martin is the thing that keeps me sane. He's just great, so calming. He makes everything better.

(Martin starts to read his newspaper. Cassidy takes a big drink of her coffee and leans back contentedly in her chair. Until she bubbles over.)

CASSIDY: I am so relaxed!

MARTIN: Really?

CASSIDY: Yeah. I'm so at peace.

MARTIN: Good. Me too.

(He goes back to the paper. Cassidy drinks more cof-

fee. Abe enters, coffee cup in hand, looking around the café for an empty seat or table. Cassidy see him and reacts with a start. She clearly knows him, probably hasn't seen him for a while and wishes it had been longer.)

CASSIDY: Oh my god.

MARTIN: What?

CASSIDY: Nothing.

MARTIN: Okay.

(He goes back to the paper, and Cassidy openly stares at Abe, who scans the room for a place to sit. He glances at Cassidy, keeps scanning the room, then stops, realizing who he just saw. Cassidy sees him stop. She looks down at her coffee cup, then over to Martin, but he's engrossed with the newspaper, and then finally she finds something very interesting to look at on the floor behind her chair.

Abe turns and looks at the back of Cassidy's head. A moment.)

ABE: Cassidy?

CASSIDY: *(pretends not to hear him)*

ABE: *(knows she's ignoring him)* Cassidy.

CASSIDY: *(turning back)* Yes? Oh . . . Abe?

ABE: Yeah.

CASSIDY: Wow. Abe. I can't believe it.

ABE: How are you?

CASSIDY: I'm good, I'm good. I'm great. This is my husband . . .

MARTIN: Martin.

CASSIDY: I know.

MARTIN: *(holding a hand out to Abe)* Hi.

ABE: Hi. *(shaking Abe's hand)* I used to screw your wife.

MARTIN: I know, she's told me all about it. I'm jealous of your hot animal passion.

CASSIDY: *(to us)* He didn't say that. No one said that. *(to them)* Do it again.

(Cassidy makes twirls her hand in the 'let's get going' motion for them to try the scene again.)

MARTIN: *(holding a hand out to Abe)* Hi.

ABE: *(shaking Abe's hand)* Hi. Nice to meet you.

CASSIDY: So . . . did I hear you're in San Francisco now?

ABE: Yeah, I've been there a few years.

MARTIN: You in the tech industry?

ABE: No, doing time in Alcatraz for murder.

CASSIDY: *(to them and the audience)* No.

MARTIN: You in the tech industry?

ABE: Sort of. Internet porn.

CASSIDY: *(to the audience)* I'm sorry.

> *(She makes the twirling sign to re-do things again.)*

MARTIN: You in the tech industry?

ABE: No, I'm a journalist.

MARTIN: Really? Do you write for the Chronicle or—

CASSIDY: *(interrupting)* You know what, I just realized I'm starving. Honey, would you get me a sugar-free bran muffin? Or no, a salad. But no dressing. Oh, screw it, I want a brownie.

MARTIN: To go with the white chocolate mocha usual? Sure.

> *(Martin smiles and exits.)*

ABE: He seems nice.

CASSIDY: He's very calm. I mean, he's great. We're really good together.

ABE: That's great.

CASSIDY: I love him.

ABE: I'd hope you do.

CASSIDY: What does that mean?

ABE: He's your husband, I would think you love him.

CASSIDY: I do.

ABE: Great. *(slight pause)* How's the sex? Is it anything close to the steamy, hot love we use to make?

CASSIDY: Our sex life is great, thanks.

ABE: Which one of you gets tied up?

CASSIDY: No, no, no.

> *(She makes the twirling gesture to re-do the scene.)*

ABE: He seems nice.

CASSIDY: He's wonderful. We compliment each other really well.

ABE: How long have you been married?

CASSIDY: Just three months.

ABE: Newlyweds. Congratulations.

CASSIDY: Thanks. It was all pretty fast. We just met at the start of last year.

ABE: Did it take you all this time to finally get over me?

CASSIDY: Excuse me?!

ABE: And then you rushed into . . . this?

CASSIDY: When you know it's right, you don't have to drag your feet for years.

ABE: Please. You didn't want to marry me either.

(Martin returns with a brownie on a plate.)

MARTIN: Here's your brownie, Cass.

CASSIDY: Not yet.

(Cassidy points offstage, and Martin turns and leaves. She twirls her hand, and Abe starts over.)

ABE: Newlyweds. Congratulations.

CASSIDY: Thanks.

ABE: I'm married too.

CASSIDY: You are?

ABE: Yeah, a couple years now. Actually, I think you'd really like her.

CASSIDY: Well then, I'd love to meet her. Did she come to town with you?

ABE: No, she's home with the baby *(Cassidy twirls her hand)* No, she's home with a sick dog. *(Cassidy twirls her hand)* No, she's home with terrible menstrual cramps.

CASSIDY: Oh, that's too bad.

ABE: I'm kidding. There she is. Serena!

(SERENA, a beautiful, thin young woman, probably ten years younger than Cassidy, struts into the café in high heels and a strapless dress. She goes straight to Abe, and they make out for a long time. Cassidy watches, fuming.)

CASSIDY: Okay, enough.

(They stop making out.)

CASSIDY: Lose some of that.

(Serena kicks off her high heels, then takes a pair of

flats from her chic bag and puts them on.)
CASSIDY: Keep going.
*(Serena takes a T-shirt out of her bag and pulls it on
to cover up. Then she pulls her hair back in a simple
pony tail and puts on a pair of ugly glasses.)*
SERENA: Okay?
CASSIDY: Much better.
(Martin steps back in.)
MARTIN: Brownie?
CASSIDY: Give it to her.
SERENA: Thank god. I'm starving.
*(Serena wolfs down the brownie, getting crumbs on
her face in the process. Abe gently brushes some of
the crumbs off her cheeks.)*
ABE: Isn't she something?
CASSIDY: Have you cheated on her yet?
ABE: *(quietly)* No.
CASSIDY: Did you cheat on your previous girlfriend with her?
ABE: No.
CASSIDY: Then I hate her.
SERENA: Can I have another brownie?
CASSIDY: Aren't you worried about getting fat?
SERENA: No, I pretty much eat whatever I want. But I do
yoga. Sometimes.
CASSIDY: Martin, go buy her some more.
MARTIN: Okay.
CASSIDY: At least ten. Or fifteen.
SERENA: Awesome.
*(Martin and Serena exit. Cassidy turns back to Abe
and makes the twirling gesture.)*
CASSIDY: What brings you back then?
ABE: I came back for you.
CASSIDY: You can't have me.
ABE: Can't I?
CASSIDY: No.
ABE: Should I believe you?
CASSIDY: I'm happily married.
(Serena and Martin re-enter. She carries a plate

*piled high with brownies, and she has more smeared
around her mouth.)*

MARTIN: We're back.

CASSIDY: I'm not ready for you yet.

SERENA: Hey, am I going to get anything else to do here?

CASSIDY: *(thinks)* I don't think so, no.

SERENA: Are you kidding? You know, I turned down other
work for this. I need a new agent. This sucks.

MARTIN: Can I have one of the brownies?

SERENA: Knock yourself out.

*(Serena hands him the plate and stalks off the stage.
Martin follows, nibbling on a brownie. Cassidy turns
back to Abe, who starts over.)*

ABE: Should I believe you?

CASSIDY: I'm very happily married.

*(Abe breaks down melodramatically and goes on an
anguished rant.)*

ABE: Damn, my foolish pride! Damn the terrible choices
I made and my faithless ways! I am naught but a evil
cad! Damn my ever hungering—
(dropping the act)
Don't you think this is a bit much?

CASSIDY: No, I like it.

ABE: Damn my ever hungering penis and the vile paths it
took me down, leading my astray and away from the one
to whom I never should have been untrue. All my hopes
are now dashed. My life is a meaningless shambles. If
I were not so evil I would join the priesthood. I might as
well strip to the waist and simply wade out into the rolling
surf of the ocean, never to be seen again. Or use my life
savings to pay for the gender reassignment surgery that
I've always secretly wanted. For a life without you . . .
is too terrifying to contemplate.

*(By now Abe has collapsed and lies prostrate on
the floor.)*

CASSIDY: It hurts, doesn't it.

ABE: It burns.

CASSIDY: It burns for years.

ABE: I'm sorry for what I did to you.

CASSIDY: Are you?

ABE: I wish I'd died before cheating on you and leaving the way I did.

CASSIDY: Thank you. But don't worry. I got over you.

(Abe drops his act, picking himself up off the ground with a new found purpose.)

ABE: Have you?

CASSIDY: Of course.

ABE: Have you?

CASSIDY: For a long time now.

ABE: Have you?

CASSIDY: Yes.

ABE: Have you?

CASSIDY: *(twirling her hand)* That's enough.

(Abe falls back into his original, easy going personality.)

ABE: It's good to see you. You look great.

CASSIDY: You too.

(He kisses her cheek, and turns away. Cassidy watches him go and then returns to her seat. Martin re-enters with two cups of coffee as he originally did. He puts her cup down in front of her and sits.)

MARTIN: Here you go. One grande iced . . . the usual.

CASSIDY: Thanks.

MARTIN: Of course. I love you.

(Cassidy smiles at him.)

CASSIDY: I love you too, Abe.

(Cassidy freezes in panic. Martin is confused, stunned. He looks across the table at her. She can't return his gaze.)

CASSIDY: Thanks for the coffee. Did I say that?

(She glances at him, flashing a weak smile. The lights fade out.)

End of play.

How I Met the Sopranos
Irene L. Pynn

Original Production

Playwrights' Round Table in July, 2014, in Orlando, Florida

Directed by Jim Cundiff

Cast
Anchor: Bob Brandenburg
Man: Alexander Mrazek
Woman: Maria Ragen

CHARACTERS:
(ONE WOMAN, ONE MAN, ONE FLEXIBLE)

ANCHOR: Male or female. Any adult age. Charismatic news anchor.

MAN: Male, any adult age. Plays all male characters, including the following:

DAVID: A television show creator who has recently come under fire for his series finale.

BARNEY: A low-rent protester who is furious about the ending of *How I Met the Sopranos*.

WHISTLEBLOWER: The person who leaked an important clip of the final episode months before it was due to air.

TONY: Businessman who loves *How I Met the Sopranos*.

TED: A reporter looking for the best scoop.

WOMAN: Female, any adult age. Plays all female characters, including the following:

CATRINA: A nervous, green reporter, probably on her first job.

ROBIN: A confident reporter.

PRESIDENT: The President of the United States.

CARMELLA: A loud mom who loves TV and supports the ending of *How I Met the Sopranos*.

PROPS LIST:
News microphone
Several costume pieces to denote different characters
Bottle and a rag

(News desk where ANCHOR sits alone.)

ANCHOR: We are now entering the 49th hour of riots all over the world, from Asia to Australia, and the death toll continues to climb. Civilians are urged to stay indoors as most areas of the United States and other countries are currently under various forms of martial law. With us via satellite is

David Thomas, creator of television smash hit *How I Met the Sopranos*. David, what can you tell us about the riots?

DAVID: *(DAVID enters and stands at one side of the stage. He visibly distraught)* I have no words. I really just . . . *(can't continue)*

ANCHOR: Did you have any idea this would happen?

DAVID: Murder and explosions? Vandals? Looting?

ANCHOR: There have been reports of suicides, as well.

DAVID: I don't understand how this could happen.

ANCHOR: Do you consider the ending of your series to be a "cheat," as so many have called it?

DAVID: No! We filmed the ending the same day we filmed the first episode. Every single part of the story has been leading to—*(hears something offstage)* Did you hear that?

ANCHOR: Let me read this excerpt, if I may, from a recent review. "David Thomas' *How I Met the Sopranos* was a much-beloved series that turned out to be a massive troll. Thomas demonstrated that he has no respect whatsoever for his fans who have been so devoted for the past eight years." What do you say to that?

DAVID: Of course I care about the fans. I wasn't trolling. This was the end. This was—*(hears another sound)* oh, my God.

ANCHOR: It never occurred to you in the past seasons that fans might have grown too attached to the story? You didn't consider changing your ending?

DAVID: Did it occur to me that the entire world would *riot* because of my finale?

ANCHOR: David, we're going to cut to our reporter in Boston for a moment. Please stay on the line, if you can.

DAVID: Wait! Can you send help? I think they're outside my hotel room—

ANCHOR: David, we'll come back to you in just a moment. *(to the audience)* Now we're switching to Catrina Chase, who is live with a protester now. Catrina?

CATRINA: *(CANTRINA enters on the other side of the stage carrying a microphone. DAVID leaves his position, changes a costume piece, and goes to CATRINA to play BARNEY. Loud sounds of sirens blare in the background, and CATRINA appears nervous)* Yes, I'm here with—what was your name, again?

BARNEY: *(appears to be lighting a Molotov cocktail)* Barney.

CATRINA: And what can you tell me about the state of things here?

BARNEY: Well, we're *(censored sound)* rioting, aren't we?

CATRINA: Because of a television show?

BARNEY: Look, lady. It's not *just* a television show. *HIMTS* was my life. For most of us here, it was all our lives. It gave us hope. *(tosses the bomb offstage, and there is a sound of a distant explosion. CATRINA jumps, but BARNEY does not)*

CATRINA: Did you just—was that a bomb?

BARNEY: Bastards been saying the show had a proper ending. Proper ending my *(censored sound) (another censored sound)*! I'll show you a proper ending – *(begins pulling down his pants, but CATRINA stops him)*

CATRINA: You realize this is a live broadcast? The whole world just saw you blow up a gas station.

BARNEY: Good! Book me a reality show, baby. I'll show you all kinds of explosions, and I'll never let you down!

CATRINA: What about the ending of *How I Met the Sopranos* was so problematic?

BARNEY: Are you *(censored sound)* with me?

CATRINA: *(afraid)* No . . .

BARNEY: You give us a show like that for eight years. Eight *(censored sound)* years. I never missed a single one. It defined me. It told me I could be someone, and I became someone. *(gets in her face)* Because of that lying son of a *(several censored sounds)* false hopes I got a job and a house and a wife and a kid—and then this? What am I supposed to make of this?

CATRINA: *(terrified, meekly)* What?

BARNEY: A *dream*? A bloody *dream*? You had better be *(censored sound)* joking us, Thomas, because we're coming for you, and when we find you, you'll write something better, I swear to *(censored sounds over and over)*!

CATRINA: *(speaks over the censoring)* Back to you! *(exits in terror while BARNEY runs off to riot)*

ANCHOR: Thanks, Catrina. Stay safe out there. It seems we've lost connection with David Thomas. Perhaps he'll call back in later on. In the meantime we'd like to share with you an exclusive interview we had this morning with the so-called Whistleblower. Here's a clip.

WHISTLEBLOWER: *(WHISTLEBLOWER enters and sits in an area with the least light possible—his voice is modulated)* I leaked the final episode on YouTube because I thought it wasn't right. It wasn't right what David Thomas was doing to his fans after all this time. To take all those years and then say it was just a dream ... I knew it would break their hearts. So I released the clip early. I didn't want fans wasting another minute of their lives—another

WHISTLEBLOWER (cont.): piece of their hearts—on this despicable troll. Because that's what this was. It was a big troll, and David Thomas knows it. I couldn't be part of that anymore.

ANCHOR: That was recorded this morning in an undisclosed location for the safety of the Whistleblower who released the now infamous "Dream" clip of the *How I Met the Sopranos* series finale. Minutes after the clip went live, it reached over a million views, crashed YouTube, and has been blamed for thousands of violent acts worldwide. Let's go now to reporter Robin Bays, who has located a viewer without knowledge of the finale. Robin?

ROBIN: *(ROBIN enters dressed differently and addresses the audience)* I'm here with Tony, a longtime fan of *How I Met the Sopranos* who has miraculously not heard a spoiler for the series finale. We're meeting outside, on the roof of his skyscraper office. Usually this spot offers a picturesque view of the city horizon, but today we're treated to the smell of smoke and the sound of fighting hundreds of feet below. *(to TONY)* Tony, tell me what this show means to you.

TONY: It's amazing. Honestly. I've never been so captivated by a show. My whole family and I love it.

ROBIN: How have you avoided hearing about the finale?

TONY: Well, I've heard about the riots, of course. You can look down there and see it. I've had to sleep in my office the past two nights because it's not safe in the streets.

ROBIN: Are you deliberately avoiding spoilers?

TONY: Not really. I mean, I generally watch my shows in order, and we still have, what? Seven episodes to go before the finale's due? But I don't see how this makes any sense. Eight years in, and not a single bad episode. I trust David Thomas. He'll make it work.

ROBIN: It was all a dream.

TONY: *(beat)* I'm sorry. What?

ROBIN: That's the end. The show finale.

TONY: A dream?

ROBIN: Yes.

TONY: You're serious?

ROBIN: Yes.

TONY: *(beat)* You're . . . it was a dream . . . the whole show?

ROBIN: Yes. Do you have any thoughts about that?

TONY: *(beat, then walks offstage—ROBIN reacts as if he's walking off the top of the building)*

ROBIN: Oh, my God! *(looks down and watches him fall, then turns to audience)* Back to you . . . .

ANCHOR: Thank you. We're going now to an emergency update from the President of the United States, who is addressing the nation from inside Air Force One. Let's listen in.

PRESIDENT: *(barely manages to change her appearance in time to become the PRESIDENT)* My fellow Americans, I reach out to you today with a heavy heart and a desperate plea for peace. It is true that our nation—indeed, our entire world—has been heinously played for fools by the television show creator David Thomas. I, too, felt the pang of a broken heart when I saw the leaked clip online, but that does not mean we must fall prey to this writer's trickery! We are a strong people, and we will send a message to the entire world that we will not forget who we are. We will not dissolve into madness and violence. We will stand up, hand in hand, and reaffirm that we are a peaceful, entertainment-loving nation of—

ANCHOR: We're going to cut away now to go now to reporter Ted Dante, who has an exclusive interview with a viewer who says she supports David Thomas' decision to end the show as a dream. Ted?

TED: *(TED arrives to interview CARMELLA, who has just barely changed into Mom clothes)* I'm here with Carmella Marshall, a mother of two who says she loves the series finale. Carmella?

CARMELLA: Hi!

TED: Tell me a little about why you feel this way. You actually don't mind that it was all a dream?

CARMELLA: Ted, I think it's genius. Here we are, eight years in, and none of this really happened? I mean, it's such a—what's the word . . . it's like one of those metaphors!

TED: A metaphor?

CARMELLA: Sure. You know how everything we see on TV is fake?

TED: Everything?

CARMELLA: Reality TV—fake. Sitcoms—fake. News—fake.

TED: The news?

CARMELLA: Trust me on this one. *(referring to herself, still partially dressed as the PRESIDENT—TED gives a sign that he sees her point)* And so this David Thomas guy, he writes us a show where we're all believing in ourselves and having a good time, and it's all nice and stuff until Boom! *It's just a dream. (beat as if to let this sink in)* There you go. A clear reminder of what's important in life.

TED: And what is that?

CARMELLA: Life. Not TV. Not that fake stuff. The real

stuff. It's all a dream. Don't you get it?

TED: I see . . . *(he doesn't get it)*

CARMELLA: Look at them over there. *(gestures offstage to an unseen group of rioters)* They think it's some kind of practical joke the TV studio played on them. They're addicted.

TED: You don't like TV?

CARMELLA: Oh, sure. I love it. We watch it every day. But I know what's real and what's not. *(to the unseen group)* Hey! Idiots! Get it into your skulls! It's all a dream! *(meaningfully)* It's *ALL* a dream! *(a shot is fired, and CARMELLA falls down, fatally injured)*

TED: What! Someone call 911! Carmella? Carmella, say something!

CARMELLA: Tell my son . . .

TED: *(dramatically puts the microphone to her mouth)* What? Tell your son what?

CARMELLA: Tell him . . .

TED: Hang in there. What should we tell your son?

CARMELLA: . . . to set the DVR. *(dies)*

TED: *(beat, then to audience)* Back to you.

ANCHOR: Fascinating report, Ted. This just in: the cities of New York, Tokyo, and London have gone dark. We cannot access our staff in these areas, and satellites no longer display images of the cities at all. Each one is under heavy smoke. Whether they have deliberately cut off their connections, or they are in a state of serious distress is unknown at this time. That's all we have for the hour. We'd love to stay with you longer, but it's time now for the much-awaited fifth season premiere of *Lost in the Dallas X-Vampire Slaying Files*! Be safe.

(Blackout.)
THE END

THE JOKE ABOUT THE SMALL BIRD
Luc Reid

ORIGINAL PRODUCTION

Valley Players Theater, Waitsfield, Vermont
August 14-17, 2014

Directed by Monica Callan

CAST
HALIÁDY: Sachiko Parker
CHIRYA: Jasna Brown
VESZUNÁDY: Jeffrey Parry

Produced by Kim Ward for Vermont Playwrights'
Circle, TenFest 2014
vtplaywrightscircle@gmail.com

HALIÁDY: The respected and influential leader of a national democracy movement. Well-educated and often reserved, but down-to-earth. Either gender, fifties to seventies.

CHIRYA: Haliády's friend and most trusted advisor. Chirya has been through some harrowing times and is a bit worse for wear, but remains fiercely devoted to the cause. Either gender, thirties to seventies.

VESZUNÁDY: A member of the movement. Either gender, twenties to sixties.

SETTING

The poorly-furnished office belonging to the leader of a barely-tolerated democratic political movement in an Eastern European country in the present day. At one end of the room is a writing desk. At the other, near the door, two chairs sit by a small rug.

A NOTE ON PRONUNCIATION

Names may be pronounced in whatever way best suits the production. Here is one set of suggested pronunciations.

Haliády: hall-ee-AH-dee
Chirya: CHIHR-ya
Veszunády: veh-soo-NAH-dee
Ugrész: OO-gress

A NOTE ON REWINDING

Between each section, characters reverse to the beginning of the following scene by walking backwards, putting things down that they picked up, etc., as though a video is being played in reverse. This is done in an efficient and sedate way. Dialog is not rewound (unless the director chooses to do so with a sound effect cue of some kind). Lights may be dimmed or other effects used to help clarify when time is going backwards.

It's not intuitive, but every time we rewind, we actually rewind through two sections, not just one. This is because we're at the end of a section that the audience has just seen and have to rewind that, then also rewind through the "next" scene (that is, the next scene in terms of viewing order, but the previous moment in time), which the audience is about to see.

The exception to rewinding two sections back is the very beginning of the play. Since the audience hasn't seen anything yet, we're starting at the end of the "final" scene and rewinding just through its beginning.

An easier way to think about this might be to simply say that we're rewinding from what we just barely saw all the way to the beginning of what we're about to see.

Rewind sections are indicated in the script with the word BACKWARDS. They can be done with a detailed reversal of the corresponding forward actions or in a simplified form, at the director's discretion.

When we return to forward-moving time, the script will indicate this with the word FORWARDS.

SCENE ONE

(AT RISE: HALIÁDY sprawls dead on the rug. A gun with a suppressor "silencer" lies on the floor a few feet away. VESZUNÁDY kneels beside the body, devastated.)

(THE DIRECTOR (or other person not in the cast) walks onto the stage and addresses the audience.)

DIRECTOR: The following will be presented in reverse order.

(DIRECTOR exits.)

(BACKWARDS: VESZUNÁDY stands and backs out of the room, picking up a sheaf of clipped-together papers on the way. CHIRYA backs into the room and sits at the desk, laying a note on it. Chirya lifts hand to mouth, then moves the hand away, holding something.)

(FORWARDS: CHIRYA, deeply upset, stares rigidly ahead, trying to master difficult emotions before taking a pill from one hand and holding it up to look at. CHIRYA abruptly takes it, swallowing without water, which causes a brief coughing fit. Once the pill is properly settled, CHIRYA looks at the note on the desk, gradually becoming calmer until it appears as though nothing is wrong at all. CHIRYA seems to see the note there for the first time, picks it up, reads it, and laughs uncontrollably.)

CHIRYA: *(finally getting breath back)*

Oh my God . . . and the bird just . . .

(Bursts out in laughter again. Eventually, the laughter subsides.)

Oh, God!

(wipes away tears)

I'll have to remember that one.

(CHIRYA gets up and walks out, taking the note, not looking around or behind the entire time.

VESZUNÁDY walks in with a sheaf of papers clipped together, sees HALIÁDY's corpse, and drops the papers in dismay and alarm.)

VESZUNÁDY: *(dropping to knees)* Help! Someone help!

Haliády's been shot!

(BACKWARDS: VESZUNÁDY stands and backs out of the room, picking up the papers again en route. CHIRYA backs into the room, sits, leaves the note on the desk, lifts hand to mouth, pockets the pill, gets up, backs away to within a few feet of HALIÁDY—picking the gun up along the way—and turns around.

FORWARDS: CHIRYA stands, devastated, and lets the arm with the gun drop limply. Turning away, CHIRYA takes out a handkerchief and carefully wipes the gun before laying it on the floor and proceeding to the desk to sit.)

(BACKWARDS: CHIRYA turns back around and picks up the gun. HALIÁDY sits up, does a reversed version of a gesture warning someone away, then stands and takes the gun from CHIRYA in both hands. FORWARDS.)

HALIÁDY: I thought I could depend on you, Chirya . . . you of all people.

(CHIRYA grabs the gun from HALIÁDY and points it at HALIÁDY's heart before shooting, twice. With the suppressed barrel, the gun only makes a muted snapping noise with each shot.

HALIÁDY looks down, hands clasped to chest, and sinks to the floor. CHIRYA takes a step forward, but HALIÁDY makes a "stay back" motion.)

HALIÁDY: Don't, please. You'll get blood on your clothes.

(BACKWARDS: HALIÁDY gets back up, backs up to the desk, and puts the gun in the drawer. CHIRYA backs up to the other side of HALIÁDY and turns to stand face to face.

FORWARDS.)

CHIRYA: At least we should wait for tomorrow. We can see how the people react. There are other options!

HALIÁDY: No! It must be this, and it must be now. Please, Chirya, my friend: I can't do this without your help. Don't let democracy die. Only the people can bring down this terrible regime, and if the regime destroys me, the people will lose faith, and everything will go back to what it once was—or worse. President Ugrész will act in the morning; you can save me tonight.

CHIRYA: The others will be back within the hour. We should—

HALIÁDY: It's because the others will be back soon that we have to begin now. Just a moment. I'll write the note.

(HALIÁDY walks to the desk and begins writing a note on the paper CHIRYA backed in with.)

HALIÁDY: *(turning to CHIRYA for a moment)* Oh, I heard a wonderful joke, about a small bird! Listen: there was a bucket—

CHIRYA: I don't want to hear a joke!

HALIÁDY: But it's very good! I really think you'll appreciate it. Oh: I'll just add it to the note.

(continues writing)

CHIRYA: What? No, please don't!

HALIÁDY: I'm sorry, it's already there. Believe me, you'll have need of a joke by the time you read this. Laughter lifts us out of our sorrows. It makes us forget the things that tie us down.

CHIRYA: Sometimes the things that tie us down are the most important.

HALIÁDY: And sometimes it's important to forget them.

(HALIÁDY picks up the gun and returns to CHIRYA with it in one hand, the other hand extended, offering the pill. HALIÁDY's momentary cheerfulness fades.)

HALIÁDY: I'm so very sorry to do this to you, Chirya, but since I must, please: accept the pill.

(CHIRYA reluctantly takes the pill in hand, then pockets it. HALIÁDY holds the gun in both hands and looks down at it, lost in thought.

BACKWARDS: HALIÁDY backs up to the desk, puts the gun in a drawer, then backs up to face CHIRYA again, placing one hand on CHIRYA's shoulder. FORWARDS.)

CHIRYA: But that would destroy the movement. We wouldn't survive such a disaster!

HALIÁDY: Imagine what the movement would be without me, if I were dead. What brings the people together? Is it better for the people to be distracted by scandal or for them to wake up and hear that I've been killed? They're stronger than you think. We must trust them.

CHIRYA: Even if what you say is true, I can't do what you're asking! How can you bring me such a choice?

HALIÁDY: With a heavy heart. I know it's a horrible task, but you must bear it, just as I will, just for a little while. If you don't, how many people will die? How many will disappear, be imprisoned, just as they did before we began, and for decades before that? I beg you to do this. You are the only one who can. You can save our broken country, but there is no one else.

(Pauses, saddened.)

A friend of our group obtained a gun for me. It can't be traced to us: it's a government weapon, and it has a suppressor that will quiet the sound. If I were to fire it, even a person in the next room might not hear.

CHIRYA: You told me, years ago, that we'd never have need for guns.

HALIÁDY: Yes. Yes, I did. How different the world is from what I hoped for!

(Laughs sadly)

I do aspire never to be mistaken, but I've never quite gotten the trick of it.

CHIRYA: What if you were right then, and wrong now? Please reconsider, if not because of the act itself, then because there's too much that can go wrong.

(For a moment CHIRYA is lost in thought, trying to come up with an example.)

What about the pill? I know it's meant to keep me from revealing what we've done, but what if, after taking it but before our secret is safe, my weakened mind betrays us?

HALIÁDY: *(distressed)* You're right! I thank God we have you to think of such things.

(considers briefly, pacing)

Oh, it's simple: I'll write a note! You'll know my hand-writing, and I'll begin the note by reminding you to do exactly what I say and not deviate, and not to turn around. It will tell you to simply go home, just at the right time, looking only ahead of you as you leave and taking the note along to burn.

CHIRYA: So there won't be any evidence to point to either of us.

HALIÁDY: *(Steps closer, lays a hand on CHIRYA's shoulder)* You understand why it's important that neither of us be under any suspicion? God, I wish I were wrong! This is a cruel way to end our friendship.

(BACKWARDS: HALIÁDY removes the hand from CHIRYA's shoulder, paces backwards several times, then backs up to sit on a chair by the door.)
(FORWARDS.)

HALIÁDY: I heard the same news only a little while ago.

CHIRYA: Did you also hear that Ugrész will make an announce-ment tomorrow morning? His timing is fiendish! But the people won't believe such a disgusting lie. The elections—

HALIÁDY: It isn't a lie.

CHIRYA: Of course it's a lie!

HALIÁDY: *(shakes head, pained by having to make this confession)* I was ten. My parents both worked, and during the days they left me in charge of my little sister, Naszia. She was three years old.

I was very bored, very impatient. One day I convinced myself Naszia would be all right by herself for a little while—she was sleeping just then—and that I could go out to play with my friends. I forgot all about her. I ran and played ball and made jokes with my friends for hours, never giving her a thought, until I heard someone scream. I ran to see what happened, and there she was, lying crumpled in the street, dead. She'd run out in front of a truck. I hadn't even known she could open the door herself.

CHIRYA: That's terrible. I'm so sorry ... my friend, that's awful!

HALIÁDY: There was a moment . . . we had just heard the

scream, and one of my friends told some joke—I don't remember what it was. We ran to see what the commotion was . . . I didn't think whatever it was had anything to do with me . . . so we were still laughing when I saw her. Her body was crushed in the middle, quite flat. She was soaked in blood, covered in dirt, lifeless . . . how I'd love to forget that moment! I've spent my whole life trying to make up for that single, stupid day, but it hasn't been enough. Not yet, anyway. My sins have come back for me.

CHIRYA: You can't be held responsible for that. You were a child! You weren't even there when she died.

HALIÁDY: *(Harshly)*

That's why I'm responsible!

(Haliády calms somewhat.)

One might ask: how can a person who can't take care of a small child take care of a country? It's a reasonable question, Chirya. The people will ask that question, and they're not wrong to do it.

CHIRYA: But with elections so soon . . . if you're disgraced, the entire movement will falter! What can we do? Can you confess before he makes his announcement?

HALIÁDY: It would be too little a response, and we can't reach the people any earlier than he will. We have to consider a more radical path.

CHIRYA: You have a plan!

HALIÁDY: I do. You must kill me.

CHIRYA: What? This is not the time to pay for your crime, Haliády! Our people need you!

HALIÁDY: If I'm dead, then anything the regime may say will fall on deaf ears. It will appear to be only a desperate attempt to discredit a martyr.

CHIRYA: *(furious)* You're not making any sense! You, dead? I, kill you?

HALIÁDY: You will never be suspected. I will die a martyr, killed by an unknown hand, and democracy will strengthen, and the old regime will crumble.

CHIRYA: Please, Haliády! I need you to think with me! Stop talking this way!

Lawrence Harbison

HALIÁDY: You must shoot me—here, tonight. Then you will take the pill—

CHIRYA: The pill be damned!

HALIÁDY: —and then you will return home, and it will be as though it never happened. Yet there I'll lie, dead . . . and uncompromised.

CHIRYA: I can't believe what you're telling me. You've planned this . . . in detail . . . ?

HALIÁDY: I knew this day might come. It seemed important to prepare.

(BACKWARDS: HALIÁDY stands, turns to face the chair, backs up to the desk to sit there, then opens the drawer with the gun. At the same time, CHIRYA backs out the door.)

(FORWARDS.)

CHIRYA: *(from offstage, urgently)*
Haliády? Are you in there?

(HALIÁDY closes the drawer quickly, turns toward the door, and stands.)

HALIÁDY: Here!

(CHIRYA enters.)

Close the door, please. I need to speak with you, privately.

CHIRYA: I have news. Not good news.

HALIÁDY: If the news were ever good, there'd be no need for a new government. Sit down! I want to tell you about a pill. It's a new invention, from America. Technically, it's still an experiment, I suppose.

CHIRYA: I think my news is more urgent. You should sit down.

HALIÁDY: President Ugrész again? Let me tell you about the pill first.

CHIRYA: Forget the pill. Of course it's President Ugrész. A friend in the People's Palace has information that he's trying to discredit you. He plans to claim that you killed a child! You! He seems to think people will believe it.

HALIÁDY: Please, I want to tell you about the pill. Really, it will only take a moment.

CHIRYA: But Ugrész—!

HALIÁDY: Only a moment. This pill, it interferes in form-
ing memories. Taking it, a person forgets every recent
thought and action as soon as it's done—everything is
lost. The effect lasts for more than an hour.
(reflects for a moment)
Each memory . . . it's like a small bird.
(cups hands around an imaginary songbird)
One moment it's with you, but then . . .
*(gently throws hands into the air, releasing the
imaginary bird)*
. . . it flies away, and it's as though it was never there.
(reflects a moment longer)
It's like a child, who runs away to play.
CHIRYA: But children come back.
HALIÁDY: Not always.
CHIRYA: *(impatient, shaking off the spell of HALIÁDY's
speech)*
So that's it: a date rape drug?
HALIÁDY: Nothing like that! It simply erases a short period
of time from your mind.
CHIRYA: But merely a drug. Why does it matter? Is it
something the regime is using, some new form of abuse?
HALIÁDY: No! It's exactly what we need most. It's almost
a kind of magic.
CHIRYA: Forgive me, but I don't see how this has any
importance.
HALIÁDY: It's important to me. After all, sometimes we do
things it's better to forget.
CHIRYA: You're worrying me, Haliády. But now that you've
told me about this magical drug, will you please speak
to the problem at hand? Why are you acting as though
this means nothing?
HALIÁDY: Forgive me. My mind is . . . distracted.
*(BACKWARDS: CHIRYA backs out the door as
HALIÁDY backs up to the desk. HALIÁDY sits, opens
the drawer, takes the gun out, wraps it in a piece of
cloth, puts it away.)*
(FORWARDS: HALIÁDY unhurriedly opens the

drawer, takes out something wrapped in cloth, and sets it on the desk. HALIÁDY opens the cloth fold by fold, and when the gun is revealed, contemplates it. Finally HALIÁDY puts the cloth in the drawer and then the gun. While looking into the drawer, HALIÁDY seems suddenly distracted, remembering something, then bursts out laughing.)

HALIÁDY: And the bird just . . .

(HALIÁDY can't suppress more laughter for several moments, but eventually stops and wipes away tears.)

I'll have to remember that one.

CURTAIN

ORIGINAL PRODUCTION

Kiss a Squid was first produced at Lee Street Theatre in Salisbury, NC on May 8, 2014, with the following company:

Director: Tony Moore

CAST
TESS: Sue McHugh
BESS: Natasha Decker
CLARICE: Addison Bevis

Stage Manager: Lisa Perone
Light, Set and Sound Design: Chris Speer
Costume Design: Lisa Perone
Sound and Light Board Operator: Jake Shue
Props Design: Jamison Middlemiss
Managing Artistic Director: Justin Dionne

CHARACTERS:
> TESS: Twenties to forties. Comfortable with routine, afraid of change. A little acerbic and sharp.
> BESS: Twenties to forties. A bit sensitive, afraid.
> CLARICE: Twenties to forties. Usually a "yes" girl, today something happened to make her want to not be that corporate, trapped person anymore.

SETTING:
> Three desks are equally spread across the stage, facing the audience. (These should be no more than just tables with keyboards on them. The actors will sit behind the 'desks' facing the audience and look as though they are looking at the monitor on the computer.)

TIME:
> Present.

At Rise: "Waiting for My Real Life to Begin" by Colin Hay begins to play in the darkness. After about 30-45 secs of the song, lights come up on BESS and TESS at the outside two desks like bookends. They type rhythmically, identically, and without nuance or life. This happens for about 5 beats, then CLARICE enters in a flurry. She goes immediately to her computer, settles in quickly, and assumes the routine of the other two, albeit with a flush in her cheeks and some different hint at energy. Her entrance causes a slight fluctuation of rhythm in the typing, but then BESS and TESS return to their routine. They are all now in typing rhythm, although because of the late arrival of CLARICE, all of the characters' eyes are darting and uncertain. Typing happens continually unless indicated otherwise.

CLARICE: Hitler is dead.
(Pause. Only the sound of typing.)
CLARICE: Did you hear me? I said Hitler is dead.

(Pause. All we hear is typing for 2-3 beats.)

CLARICE: Don't you care? Are you listening?

BESS: *(whispers)* We're not supposed to talk until the break.

TESS: Shhhhh!!!

(Typing again. Eyes shifting, etc. CLARICE is trying to play the typing game but not fully succeeding.)

CLARICE: *(stage whisper, explosion)* Hitler is dead.

BESS: I thought he died decades ago . . .

TESS: Shhhhhhhh!!!

CLARICE: *(as an immediate retort to TESS)* Shhhhh!!! *(to BESS)* Hitler's my ferret, you idiot!

(Pause. More typing.)

BESS: That was hurtful.

CLARICE: *(overlapping)* I'm sorry.

(Typing. Pause.)

CLARICE: I put him in my lunchbox.

(Typing slows down as TESS and BESS process this information.)

CLARICE: He's on ice.

There is renewed and more obvious eye movement.

CLARICE: I couldn't just leave him where he was.

(Typing. Pause.)

CLARICE: I didn't have time to bury him, I was already late as it was.

(Typing. Pause.)

BESS: Hitler's in your lunchbox?

CLARICE: Yes, but . . .

TESS: Shhhhhh!!!!

(Typing. Pause. There is a bell indicating break time. When this bell rings, the three all launch into simultaneous rants. This should be immediate and a stark contrast in sound and action, so big gestures, hit words hard, and fly!! We should be able to catch glimpses of words here and there.)

CLARICE: You guys have to understand that this changes everything, don't you see? Hitler meant something to me and I wake up this morning and he's just not here anymore and that's huge and I don't think what I'm do-

---

ing here, or anywhere for that matter, really makes sense anymore. So, I'm already confused about what to do with him—I mean you can't just flush him like a fish. He's a mammal! And I thought he probably wouldn't go down anyway. I fed him well. But anyway he's gone and I'm alone now and it just . . . it just . . .

BESS: Hitler, your dead ferret, is in your lunchbox at this very moment? Do you understand how disgusting and unsanitary that is? You must have some kind of mental issue to be carrying around the carcass of a dead rodent right next to foodstuffs that will end up in your mouth! So I presume that you've never heard of germs or food-borne illnesses? Ridiculous. And, by the way, I do NOT forgive you for calling me an idiot! Where do you get off calling ME the idiot when you're the one toting a rodent corpse for lunch! This is UNBELIEVABLE!!

TESS: You are going to get us fired, do you understand that? You know we're not supposed to talk until break and you just sit here talking one sentence after another and it's ridiculous for you to think that we'd remember who your stupid ferret was anyway! I try to help you keep your job here but instead you're going to cost us our jobs, too, and I need this job because I have bills to pay. I don't know if you understand the concept of bills and jobs and money, but you must because you do work here and all, but God almighty, do you not get that you need to SHUT UP!??!

CLARICE: Stop!!!!!!!!!!!!!!!!

(All dialogue ceases and they all just look at each other.)

TESS: I need some coffee.

(TESS exits.)

BESS: You need to get rid of that thing.

CLARICE: This is my lunch!

BESS: That thing in your lunch! You need to get rid of it NOW!!

CLARICE: *(goes to her desk to get lunchbox)*

I won't! He deserves a decent burial. Hitler didn't do anything wrong!

(TESS re-enters as CLARICE finishes this line.)

TESS: Hitler didn't do anything wrong? I think gassing 6 million Jews goes on Santa's naughty list.

BESS: Did you hear what you just said? You mixed Jews and Christmas. That's weird.

TESS: You're weird.

BESS: That was hurtful.

CLARICE: MY Hitler, not THE Hitler. MY Hitler didn't do anything wrong.

TESS: How would a ferret do something wrong?

BESS: You ask the strangest questions.

TESS: You wear the strangest clothes.

BESS: That was hurtful.

TESS: Why did you name your ferret Hitler anyway?

CLARICE: He had a moustache like Hitler's.

TESS: Ferrets have mustaches?

BESS: What are we even talking about here?

CLARICE: Nothing! We're talking about nothing here! We never talk about anything here! We never do anything here! We type and we word process and we excel document and we sit and we type and we type and we type and it all doesn't mean anything! A 5-minute break every hour where we compare relative protein grams in our breakfast bars. We shove 5 minutes of nothing between 55 minutes of even more nothing and we've accomplished nothing! We're sitting and wasting, and dying! We're wasting time here! We're wasting our lives here! I need someone to understand me.

(TESS takes a sip of her coffee. A loud, deliberate slurp. She and BESS just stare at CLARICE.)

BESS: Clarice, are you okay?

(CLARICE stares at BESS as though she were a Picasso with 3-year-old Sharpie scrawled on it.)

CLARICE: What does that question mean, Bess? Why would you ask me that? I only have about three more minutes until our break is over to get something through to the two of you and it just isn't enough time. You won't get it. No. I'm not okay. I don't think I've ever been okay,

---

but today I'm the least okay I've ever been!! Let me try to explain . . . Hitler died. Just like the real Hitler died. And after that people could live. I mean live more. More living and not dying anymore. Ahh! I don't know how to tell you this. I'm not okay. But neither are you. Do you get it? Will you get it before our five minutes is up?

TESS: We get another break in another hour.

CLARICE: But we might not, don't you get it?? *(holds up lunchbox)* Hitler is dead!

TESS: I still think that name was a mistake.

CLARICE: I don't care!! I don't care!! Hitler, Martin Luther King, George Washington, Katherine Hepburn, Betty White, JFK—they're all dead!

BESS: Betty White is still alive, actually . . .

CLARICE: Not for long! Not for long, girls, and that is my point exactly! Do you see?? All those innocent people died at the hands of the real Hitler. He dies, and people can be free. Right? And now MY Hitler dies and I have to live . . . and be free, too . . .

TESS: Your ferret stopped you from living?

CLARICE: No, no, no . . . that's not what . . . I can't . . .

BESS: I think I understand, Clarice. The Jews died. Her ferret died. And we have to live.

TESS: Her ferret dying is not the same as people dying. It's ridiculous.

BESS: That was hurtful.

CLARICE: How do you know? How do you know it's not the same thing, Miss High-and-Mighty?! Suddenly you have a direct line to the afterworld and you know what the universal rules are for living and dying?

TESS: It's a ferret.

CLARICE: He was MY ferret. I think his dying may actually mean something. Maybe it was serendipitous I named him that. I don't know!!! Damn it, don't you get it?? We have to stop this. We have to stop this bus and get off.

BESS: We have to stop what?

CLARICE: Follow my metaphor, Bess! This meaningless, dead-end job is killing us! Maybe not today, maybe not tomorrow, but it will kill us eventually.

TESS: Everything kills you eventually.

CLARICE: But we don't have to go quietly. We don't have to click, click, click our way to the grave. Does this place inspire you? Does this job fulfill you? Are you happy? Excited about living? Contributing to society? Living life to the fullest? Are you????

BESS: I . . .

CLARICE: You hesitate to answer because you're not. You're not happy because this isn't YOU. My God, ladies, we only get one spin around on this crazy planet and I can't spend it on this ride. I'm breaking out of here, ladies. Are you with me?

BESS: Breaking out of here?

CLARICE: I'm blazing a new path!! Raising a new flag!!! Hitler died and that must lead to something good.

TESS: I think Hitler dying lead to a lot of good, historically speaking.

CLARICE: MY Hitler! MY Hitler! But who the hell cares! MY Hitler, THE Hitler . . . Rise up!! RISE UP, I say, and LIVE the life you have been chosen to live! We deserve more than this! We need more than this! We were called to more than this!!

BESS: I'm frightened . . .

TESS: I'm nauseous . . .

CLARICE: That's right, Mrs. Skeptic-with-an-acid tongue. Your lips say you're about to throw up, but your eyes say you are with every word I'm saying. Your eyes don't lie. You don't want this any more than I do. Do you? *(TESS falters)* Do you??! You don't!!!!!! Come on, ladies. This is our moment. The whole world is out there, waiting for us to just take it by the horns and milk it for everything it's worth.

TESS: I . . . I think you're mixing metaphors there.

CLARICE: I don't care!! I'm mixing success with courage and getting the best damn life smoothie there ever was! And when that life smoothie has been drunken . . . drunk . . . drinken . . . . has been consumed, God will smile

---

and wipe his lips and say, "That was damn good." Are
you with me?

TESS: You're really bad at metaphors.

CLARICE: But I'm good at living! I'm going to be GREAT
at living!! From now on, I'm going to be AWESOME at
LIVING!!! Hitler is dead but I am alive! Are you with
me?? Are you with me?!?!?!?!? What have you always
wanted to do, Tess? Bess?? Name one crazy thing you've
always wanted to do!

BESS: Ride in a hot air balloon?

TESS: Really?

CLARICE: *(admonishing)* Tess!! *(then inviting to answer)*
Tess??

TESS: Find the Secret Grove of the Titan trees.

CLARICE: I have no idea what that is, but let's do it. Damn
it, let's DO IT!!!!!

BESS: I'm with you!

CLARICE: Come on, ladies! Tilt at some windmills, hop on
your horse and conquer this enemy called death! Let's
go ascend to the Heavens in a hot air balloon! Find the
giant trees! Kiss a squid!

BESS/TESS: Kiss a squid???

CLARICE: Kiss a squid!!!!! Dream the impossible dream!!
*(CLARICE starts to sing 'The Impossible Dream'
from Man of LaMancha. CLARICE holds up her
lunchbox like it's a sacred item on a platform above
her head. BESS and TESS join about the time she's
singing "This is my quest, to follow that star . . . ")
(Just as they actually head to the door, the bell rings
again. (ideally, the bell rings when they are singing
"To be willing to march into Hell for a Heavenly
cause." It stops them in their tracks. There is a
moment or two, then BESS heads back to her desk.
She begins typing again, looking resolutely in front of
her. After another few beats, TESS goes to her desk as
well, definitely not making eye contact with anyone.
CLARICE is left with the lunchbox aloft, alone near
the door, frozen. She looks to the door, looks back,*

looks back to the door. She walks slowly back to her desk, sits, and deliberately places the lunchbox in front of her keyboard, gives it a moment of reverence, and begins typing. After a few beats of only typing, we hear CLARICE begin humming 'The Impossible Dream' quietly. As she hums this, she sneaks looks at her co-workers, who do all they can to keep their eyes on the screen. They are successful in not looking at her. It looks as though CLARICE is going to give up the humming when BESS takes up the humming, quietly at first, then stronger. When TESS hears this, she does, too, and then all three of them are. The beginning theme of 'Waiting for My Real Life to Begin' fades up and takes over the scene.)

The lights fade to BLACK OUT.

MAID SERVICE
David Fleisher

ORIGINAL PRODUCTION

Maid Service was produced May 2, 2014, during "Celebration of the Arts" at the Wold Performing Arts Center at Lynn University, Boca Raton, FL.

Directed by Carrie Simpson

CAST
ALEXANDER HADLEY: John Pickering
A.J. BARCLAY: Adam Simpson
ELAINE: Marcheta Wright
LAVERNE: N'Quavah Velasquez

This play is an extension of an original work by Shelley Berman, entitled "Little Soaps," which is included in his book, *A Hotel is a Funny Place* (Price, Stern, Sloan. Copyright 1972, 1985).

CHARACTERS:
> ALEXANDER HADLEY: Hotel Manager; efficient and courteous, twenty-five to forty.
> A.J. BARCLAY: Successful businessman; single-minded and decisive, middle-aged
> ELAINE: Barclay's wife; protective of her husband and a bit haughty, middle-aged
> LAVERNE: Housekeeper; a hard worker and conscientious, twenty-five to forty.

SETTING:
> A hotel.

TIME:
> The Present.

AT RISE: A.J. BARCLAY and his wife, ELAINE, are S.L.LAVERNE, a maid, is S.R. ALEXANDER HADLEY, hotel manager, is C.S. ALL are facing the audience.

BARCLAY: Dear Maid,
> Please do not leave any more of those little bars of soap in my bathroom. I have brought my own bath-sized Dial. Remove the six unopened little bars from the shelf under the medicine chest and also the three in the shower soap dish. They are in my way.

> Thank you, A.J. Barclay

LAVERNE: Dear Room 535,
> I took the three hotel soaps out of the shower soap dish. You know the six bars under the medicine chest? Well, I put them on top of the Kleenex box just in case you

change your mind. That leaves only three bars I left today. My boss wants me to leave three soaps every day. Is this okay?

Your Maid, Laverne

BARCLAY: Dear Maid,

No, this is not okay. Apparently, you did not read carefully my note concerning the little bars of soap. When I got back to my room this evening, I found you had added three little Camays to the shelf under my medicine cabinet. I don't want them. They are in my way when shaving, brushing teeth, etc.

A.J. Barclay

LAVERNE: Dear Room 535,

I had the day off yesterday. My Relief Maid - her name's Rosita - she didn't see your note. Sorry about that. Anyway, I took the six little hotel soaps that were bothering you and put them in the soap dish where your Dial was. I put the Dial in the medicine cabinet. I didn't remove the three soaps inside the medicine cabinet because we have to put three soaps in there for all new check-ins. Is this okay?

Your Maid, Laverne

HADLEY: Dear Mr. Barclay,

I was informed this morning that you are unhappy with your maid service. Please accept my apologies. In the future, contact me directly so I can give it my personal attention. Feel free to call extension 913 between 8 A.M. and 5 P.M. Thank you.

Alexander Hadley, Manager

BARCLAY: Dear Mr. Hadley,

It is impossible to contact you directly since I leave the

---

hotel on business at 7:45 A.M and don't get back before 6 P.M. The maid—I don't recall her name—must think I'm a new check-in. She left another three bars of hotel soap in my medicine cabinet, plus three bars on the bathroom shelf. In just five days here, Mr. Hadley, I have accumulated twenty-four little bars of soap. Why are you doing this to me?

A.J. Barclay

HADLEY: Dear Mr. Barclay,
Your maid, Laverne, has been instructed to stop delivering soap to your room. If I can be of further assistance, please don't hesitate for a moment to contact me at extension 913 between 8 A.M. and 5 P.M.

Alexander Hadley, Manager

ELAINE: Dear Mr. Hadley,
My husband's bath-sized Dial soap is missing. In fact, we have no soap at all. I had to call the bellhop last night to bring us four little Cashmere Bouquets.

Elaine Barclay, Room 535

HADLEY: Dear Mrs. Barclay,
I have taken measures to rectify your soap situation. Your maid, Laverne, has been severely reprimanded, plus her bonus for being "Maid of the Month" has been revoked. I hope you accept my sincerest apologies. If you should experience any further problems, please call me at extension 913 between 8 A.M. and 5 P.M.

Alexander Hadley, Manager

BARCLAY: Dear Mr. Hadley,
Who the hell left fifty-four little bars of Camay in my room? I came in last night and found fifty-four little

bars of soap. I don't want fifty-four little bars of soap. Do you realize I have fifty-four bars of soap in here?! All I want is my bath-sized Dial. Please give me back my bath-sized Dial.

A.J. Barclay

ELAINE: Dear Mr. Hadley,

It is incumbent upon you to have my husband's bath-sized Dial returned to the room at once. Please understand: we have a situation here in Room 535.

Elaine Barclay

P.S. If I appear edgy and rude, it is only because my husband has not had a shower in six days.

HADLEY: Dear Mr and Mrs. Barclay,

I'm sorry if you were under the impression this hotel issues bath-sized Dial. I was able to locate some bath-sized Ivory which I left in your medicine cabinet. The hotel has important foreign heads of state arriving today. But, please, don't let that deter you from contacting me for assistance at extension 913 between 8 A.M. and 5 P.M.

Alexander Hadley, Manager

LAVERNE: Dear Mr. Hadley,

I'm married with three children. Please give me back my "Maid of the Month" bonus. I'm trying real hard in Room 535, but the people in there complain about everything. You know me, Mr. Hadley, and you know how hard I work. Now I know you got a lot on your mind, but so do I. My husband left me this week. Please, Mr. Hadley, give me back my bonus.

Sincerely, Laverne

ELAINE: Dear Maid,

Do you have a screw loose? How many times do we have to tell you we want only one bar of soap in this room! The name of the soap is Dial. Got it? Dial! My husband is a very busy man. He doesn't have time for this nonsense. I will be returning from Saks Fifth Avenue at 3 P.M. today, and I expect to see one bar of bath-sized Dial in the soap dish.

Elaine Barclay, Room 535

P.S: I just want you to know my husband has ulcers, and you are making them worse.

BARCLAY: Dear Mr. Hadley,

Just a short note to bring you up to date on my latest soap inventory. As of today, I possess the following: eighteen Camay on the shelf under the medicine cabinet. Eleven Camay on the Kleenex dispenser. Three Cashmere Bouquet and four bath-sized Ivory on the bedroom dresser. Six Camay, very moist, in the shower soap dish. One Cashmere Bouquet, slightly used, on the northeast corner of the bathtub. And six more Camay on the northwest corner of the bathtub.

A.J. Barclay

LAVERNE: Dear Mrs. Barclay,

If you and your husband don't stop complaining about me, my boss is gonna fire me. Mam, I'm doing the best job I can. I'll do anything you want. Just stop saying bad things about me to Mr. Hadley. Please, mam!

Your Maid, Laverne

(LAVERNE EXITS)

ELAINE: Dear Mr. Hadley,
   The maid—I think her name's Lydia - is threatening
   my husband and me. Once more, let me say it plainly:
   my husband and I already have soap. Dial. We don't
   like your soap. We don't want your soap. We don't
   need your soap. Thank you very much. And may I say
   in closing you might consider firing Lydia. Your hotel
   deserves better.

   Elaine Barclay, Room 535

HADLEY: Dear Mrs. Barclay,
   It goes without saying this hotel is quite proud of its
   five-star rating. And we intend to keep it—by any
   means necessary. I have let the maid, Laverne, go.
   Quite frankly, it was not an easy thing for me to do.
   She was quite upset. But it is vitally important to all
   of us here at the hotel that you and Mr. Barclay feel
   comfortable during your stay.

   Alexander Hadley, Manager

ELAINE: Dear Mr. Hadley,
   Thank you for taking the necessary steps to correct the
   problem. I intend to write a letter to your supervisor
   praising you for a job well done.

   Mrs. Barclay, Room 535

   (ELAINE EXITS)

HADLEY: Dear Mr. Barclay,
   I understand you will be with us another two days. I
   would like to inform you about a development that occurred this morning. No reason to be alarmed—I just feel
   you and Mrs. Barclay should be aware of this. Laverne,
   a former employee of this hotel who had been servicing
   your room, shot and killed three guests. Security has

informed me Laverne may still be on the premises.

Warm Regards, Alexander Hadley. P.S. Enjoy your remaining two days with us.

BARCLAY: Dear Mr. Hadley,
I hope you don't plan on charging me for all the extra soap your incompetent maid brought to this room. I refuse to pay for it. If you insist on charging me for soap I never wanted in the first place, you leave me no choice but to take legal action.

A. J. Barclay

HADLEY: Dear Mr. Barclay,
I can't put into words how sorry I am about the recent loss of your lovely wife. Please accept my sincerest con-dolences. If it's any consolation, Laverne was captured in the parking garage not long after she scrubbed your wife to death with a bar of Dial. And now for some good news: as manager of this hotel, I would like to personally invite you to be our guest for another week - all expenses paid, including three meals a day in our fine dining room. Once again, my deepest sympathy over the loss of your wife. If I can assist in any way with funeral arrangements, don't hesitate to call me at extension 913 between 8 A.M. and 5 P.M.

Alexander Hadley, Manager

BARCLAY: Dear Mr. Hadley,
I would be delighted to stay in your hotel for another week. My wife's death has caused me to fall behind in my business, and I will need to stay in town a few more days. Considering my bath-sized Dial is no longer of any use to me, I have reluctantly decided to use your little hotel soap on a trial basis. In the event this new soap arrange-ment doesn't work out, please stash a bar of bath-sized

Dial in the hotel vault. This will save me from having to go to the grocery store and buy another bar. Surely you understand, Mr. Hadley, I am a very busy man.

A most pleasant goodnight, A.J. Barclay
(LIGHTS FADE)
END OF PLAY

MAKE JOHN PATRICK SHANLEY GO HOME
was developed with the EATING Theatre Series at
CRANKY'S in Long Island City, NY June 30, 2012,
producers Erica Silberman and Abigail Zealey Bess.

CAST
MARIE: Marissa Matrone
REGINA: Alexandra Rhodie
IZZY: Ilana Gabrielle

MAKE JOHN PATRICK SHANLEY GO HOME
World Premiere with CITY Theater's Summer Shorts
Festival at the Adrienne Arsht Center, Carnival Studio
Theater, on the Susan Westfall Playwrights Stage, in
Miami Florida, June 2014. Producer, City Theatre,
Susan Westfall, Literary Director and Artistic Director,
John Manzelli. Directed by Margaret M. Ledford with
production design by Jodi Dellaventura, costume design
by Ellis Tillman, lighting design by Preston Bircher.

CAST
MARIE: Irene Adjan
REGINA: Elizabeth Dimon
IZZY: Niki Fridh

CHARACTERS:

REGINA: Italian-American, Long Island Girl. Accent. The oldest of the sisters. She and Marie have the same mannerisms and look like sisters.
MARIE: the middle sister. Same as Regina.
IZZY: the baby of the family. Looks nothing like her sisters.
SHANLEY: playwright. Tall *(This character does not need to be on stage but suggested.)*

SET:

Four top table with setting for dinner. Chairs. Something that says "Bar" near table and chairs.

TIME:

Present.

PLACE:

Restaurant in New York City. Nothing about it is Italian.

(Three sisters step into a restaurant. They stand in the doorway checking out the room. Two older. One younger. The older are very New York. The younger worked to get rid of any regional sounds or ways.)

REGINA: Is there a waiter?
MARIE: Someone to seat us?
IZZY: We seat ourselves.
MARIE: Oh.
REGINA: I see.
IZZY: *(pointing to a table)*There's one.
(They move to the open table. REGINA and MARIE go to seats opposite one another. Look at the seat and then each other and realize, "yes we want to switch." So they do a little dosey doe around the table. IZZY watches and then signals she is headed for the bathroom.)

IZZY: I'm gonna go to the . . .
MARIE: REGINA:
Yes.   Good. Go.

(IZZY exits to the bathroom. REGINA and MARIE sit. Get situated.)

REGINA: *(Looking on the table)* There's no bread.

MARIE: What?

REGINA: No bread.

MARIE: Oh.

REGINA: What kind of restaurant has no bread?

MARIE: Maybe they're bringing it.

REGINA: Don't you think it should already be here?

(MARIE is looking through the menu.)

MARIE: It's not that kind of restaurant.

REGINA: It's not?

MARIE: No.

(REGINA looks at the other tables.)

REGINA: They have bread. And they have some and they have—Jesus what is that?

(MARIE looks at table REGINA is referring to.)

MARIE: What? That? Jesus. I don't know, but lets make sure not to order it.

REGINA: What kind of restaurant is this?

MARIE: I don't know. I didn't pick it.

REGINA: You didn't pick it?

MARIE: Izzy did.

REGINA: Izzy?

MARIE: Uh huh. So you want an appetizer?

REGINA: Order the calamari.

MARIE: They don't have calamari.

REGINA: What? Marie! What kind of place is this?!

MARIE: It's not that kind of place!

REGINA: Okay, okay! You pick the appetizer. We have the same taste.

MARIE: We do.

REGINA: In everything.

MARIE: Everything.

(REGINA and MARIE look at their menus. IZZY is rushing to her sisters. She is upset.)

IZZY: Go go go go go go go go go go . . .
 (IZZY grabs her bag.)
IZZY: Come on. Let's go.
REGINA: Go?
MARIE: What do you mean go?
IZZY: We have to go. Now. Let's go.
MARIE: Did you clog the toilet?
REGINA: You clogged the toilet?
IZZY: No, I didn't clog the toilet. Can we please go?
MARIE: Good lord Izzy we just got here.
REGINA: Yeah we just got here.
MARIE: We're here to eat.
REGINA: We're eating.
 (MARIE looks around and sees everyone is looking at them.)
MARIE: And you should sit down. People are staring.
 (All three look around and yes everyone is staring at them.)
REGINA: Oh Jesus! They are. I am not comfortable with this.
MARIE: No one is.
REGINA: I do not like to be stared at.
MARIE: No one does.
 (IZZY sits.)
IZZY: Alright. I'm sitting. Now can we please get our stuff and go?
MARIE: We can't go until you tell us what happened?
REGINA: Yeah. What happened.
IZZY: I walked out of the bathroom and saw—there at the bar. John Patrick Shanley.
REGINA: Who?
MARIE: Is this some guy you dated?
IZZY: He's a playwright.
MARIE: Oh.
REGINA: One of those.
IZZY: And a screenwriter.
REGINA: Oh good for him.
IZZY: He wrote—please don't freak out—please. He wrote "Moonstruck."

(Neither MARIE or REGINA freak out. They sit in absolute silence. They have no idea.)

MARIE: Moonstruck?

IZZY: With Cher.

(No response.)

IZZY: And Nicholas Cage.

MARIE: On my god! The one where she kicks the can.

REGINA: She kicks a can?

MARIE: Yeah. You know she kicks it.

(MARIE gets up and does the action of Cher kicking the can in Moonstruck.)

REGINA: Oh yeah! The can! She kicks it.

MARIE: And she slaps Nicholas Cage.

REGINA: And she says . . .

REGINA/MARIE: "Snap out of it!"

IZZY: Yes. That's the movie. Now can we go.

MARIE: Don't you like him? His movies?

IZZY: Marie, it's not . . . He was one of the speakers at the writing thing I went to. And I had my play read there and he heard it and later he said that it was more poetry then theatre. Then he ate his nuts.

MARIE: His nuts?

IZZY: He had a bag of nuts that he kept eating. He'd make a comment then eat nuts, make another comment and eat more nuts. It was an endless bag of nuts.

REGINA: So you're saying he was picking on you?

IZZY: Yeah.

REGINA: He was being a bully.

IZZY: Kind of.

REGINA: Do you want me to yell, "bully?"

IZZY: What? No. Why would you do that?

REGINA: I could stand up and yell "bully."

MARIE: You yell "bully?"

REGINA: In the playground when I see a bully. I yell "bully" and I point. It usually makes the bully leave.

MARIE: I should think so.

REGINA: I'm good at spotting bullies.

MARIE: You gotta be.

REGINA: Some one has to take care of the children. Of our children. And bullies are like sharks they don't like being spotted.

MARIE: If they're spotted than they can't attack.

REGINA: Right.

IZZY: Oh my god.

REGINA: When little Joey and I go to the park, the Bank Street Park, it's on a peninsula. You've got cars and kids. All right there. Charging honking screaming yelling. It's fucking chaos. So you have to keep your eyes open. You gotta have a wide peripheral range. So I am always the first to spot the bully and when I see him I yell. "Bully! NO! No no no!" Like that! With my finger pointing. So today this kid, I mean he hadn't done anything—yet! But I knew any minute now—so I start pointing and yelling he starts crying. Total ploy for sympathy. I was not affected by it. Seen it before. But some of the other parents well . . . One of them yells at me.

(Some father. Yelling.) "You're the adult!" I hate that. "You're the adult." So what! So big fucking what! And the ones yelling, "you're the adult," are usually jumping up and down and turning red and I want to say, "Do you think THIS behavior is adult like?" But I don't.

MARIE: Because you're bigger than that.

REGINA: That's right.

IZZY: Can we please go before he recognizes me?

MARIE: Honey it couldn't have been that bad.

IZZY: He told me that the hand in my play should be severed.

MARIE: *(Has no idea.)*

Uh huh . . .

IZZY: I said, that sounds like something from a John Patrick Shanley play, and he said he'd never written anything like, and I said, MOONSTRUCK? And he said oh that. Then I said do you have a thing against hands and he just stared and ate his nuts.

MARIE: Oh I see.

(She doesn't.)

REGINA: Which one is he?

IZZY: The one at end.

(REGINA and MARIE both look.)

IZZY: Could you be a little more discreet.

MARIE: Oh God. He's like sex on a stick.

REGINA: He is. He's like sex on a stick.

IZZY: He is not like sex on a stick.

REGINA: I may be married, but I'm not dead. That is sex on a stick.

MARIE: You know just forget about him and have dinner? He probably doesn't even remember you.

IZZY: On the elevator I tried to get the doors to close before he could get on, but he stuck his hand in the door and they opened, and he got on and held his hand up and said, "Huh, not severed."

MARIE: Oh, yeah.

IZZY: And then he said, "Didn't you hear me call—Hold the door!" and I said, "I don't hear well in elevators."

MARIE: What? What does that mean?

REGINA: I've never heard of such a thing.

IZZY: That's because there is no such thing. It was just something I said, and he knew it.

MARIE: Oh yeah. He might remember you.

IZZY: After that he didn't say anything else. He just ate his nuts.

REGINA: Well that's good, right?

IZZY : I wanted him to say, maybe say, you know, you're an okay writer, you have potential, you don't suck, but no nothing.

MARIE: You have got to stop being like this. Who cares what he thinks? Or what anybody thinks. He's just some guy. Just some writer sex on a stick guy and there are tons of those. This is New York for God's sake.

REGINA: Absolutely.

MARIE: You gotta stomp your feet. Put them down and say I am here and I do not care what anyone thinks.

REGINA: Yeah. Stomp 'em.

MARIE: Stomp em'.

(MARIE stomps her foot.)

REGINA: Stomp.

(REGINA stomps her foot. REGINA and MARIE stomp their feet several times.)

MARIE/REGINA: Stomp stomp stomp stomp . . .

MARIE: You gotta make some noise.

REGINA: Noise.

MARIE: Like us.

REGINA: Yeah of course.

(REGINA and MARIE look at each other and smile.)

MARIE/REGINA: It's us. We're identical.

MARIE: Right down to our choice of underwear.

REGINA: God it's true.

MARIE: So true.

IZZY: What're you talking about?

MARIE: It's twin talk. You wouldn't understand.

REGINA: Yeah. Twin talk.

IZZY: You're not twins.

MARIE: We're Irish twins.

IZZY: Then you would've to have been born in the same year.

MARIE: Close enough.

IZZY: You're three years apart.

MARIE: Who's counting?

REGINA: Yeah? Who's counting?

IZZY: For the love of god can we go?!

MARIE: I think he should go. Stomp. Stomp.

REGINA: I agree. Bully playwright should go. Stomp. Stomp.

(REGINA and MARIE stomp.)

REGINA/MARIE: Stomp, stomp stomp . . .

IZZY: He's not a bully. He's just intimidating and oh god—Its not his fault. Let him stay. I'll drink. I'll drink and look forward to the day when I get to be the one sitting at the end of the bar intimidating everybody. To the day when my life, my apt, my cat, my hair, my—when all of it will be good and then maybe Jeff will come back.

REGINA: What!

MARIE: Where's Jeff?

IZZY: Last night we, you know, we . . .

REGINA: Had sex?

MARIE: Sex?

IZZY: Yes sex! And I don't know why but after, something made me look under the bed. And there under our bed is this dead bird. And I figured the cat must've gotten it off the fire escape, but we never open that window, and then I knew that someone else had been in our bed. So I asked Jeff, "Was someone else in this bed?", and he said "yes" and then he slept on the couch. And this morning he was gone.

REGINA: I am going to find Jeff and I am going to kill Jeff.

MARIE: Oh honey.

IZZY: I just want to have dinner with my sisters. I don't want to feel any worse than I already do, and having John Patrick Shanley at the end of the bar makes me feel worse.

REGINA: Alright listen. I'm going to go over there and I'm going to tell that John Patrick Shanley that my sister is having a rough day and that his presence in this establishment is making it worse so could he please go.

(Slight pause.)

IZZY: Okay.

REGINA: Okay? Really?

IZZY: Yeah. Go tell him.

MARIE: Go Gina!

REGINA: You bet your ass.

(REGINA starts to go.)

IZZY: Wait! No. I should do it.

MARIE: Honey you don't have to.

IZZY: I can do this.

MARIE: You sure?

IZZY: It's my problem. I should handle it.

MARIE: You have nothing to be afraid of. He's just a guy. Stomp. Stomp.

REGINA: Puts his pants on the same as the rest of us. Stomp. Stomp.

IZZY: Stomp. Stomp.

(IZZY goes to the bar.)

IZZY: Mr. Shanley you probably don't remember me but . . .

(Shanley holds his hand up and starts laughing. And

with that IZZY picks up Shanley's water and throws it in his face. MARIE and REGINA start grabbing their things and IZZY's as they head for the door. All three laughing.)

IZZY: And there's the scene when John Mahoney gets water in the face!

(They are to the door. Running out and laughing when REGINA turns back and yells.)

REGINA: Bully!

(And they are out. At that moment the waiter arrives with the breadbasket.)

The end.

ORIGINAL PRODUCTION

Originally produced as part of Artistic New Directions' Eclectic Evening of Shorts: Boxers and Briefs at Shetler Studios in New York, NY April 10-13, 2014.

Directed by Kathryn Long

CAST

LANA: Elanna White
MARJORIE: Jennifer Terrell
ASHLEY: Jennifer Terrell
ASHLEY: Marie Clair Roussel

Producer: Kristine Niven

CHARACTERS

LANA: Fourteen
ASHLEY: Fourteen
MARJORIE: Thirty-Nine, Lana's Mother.

A Tom Petty Concert at the Tweeter Center in Camden, NJ.

June 1998.

Lights up on a women's restroom. Tom Petty and the Heartbreakers are heard playing "Mary Jane's Last Dance," live. LANA crouches to find ASHLEY's feet, going stall to stall.

LANA: Ash?
  (Moves to next stall.)
  Ash?
  (Moves to next stall.)
  Ash?
  (Moves to next stall.)
  Ashley?
  (No luck. She goes to the mirror and digs in her purse. ASHLEY runs in.)
ASHLEY: I have to pee so bad.
  (She rushes past LANA and into a bathroom stall. The girls shout over the stall to each other.)
LANA: Oh my God where were you?
ASHLEY: With Brent.
LANA: The blonde guy? In the blue polo?
ASHLEY: Yeah.
LANA: He's cute.
ASHLEY: I think so.
LANA: I smell like Cool Water. Do you have any body spray?
ASHLEY: Did you guys make out?
LANA: Yeah.
ASHLEY: What was his name?
LANA: Tom.

ASHLEY: Tom! Right.

(She exits stall. Digs in her purse and hands LANA body spray.)

Sun-ripened raspberry.

(LANA spritzes it and applies lip gloss, which she then hands to ASHLEY, who then applies it also. ASHLEY flips over her head as LANA sprays a ton of aerosol hairspray onto her hair for her. ASHLEY then returns the favor for LANA and does the same. LANA flips her head back up.)

Oh my God.

LANA: What?

ASHLEY: You have a hickey.

LANA: What? Where?

(She rushes to the mirror.)

ASHLEY: It's like huge.

(LANA sees it.)

LANA: Oh my God! My mom is gonna kill me.

ASHLEY: It like could have its own zip code.

LANA: How did this happen?

ASHLEY: Didn't you notice he was like sucking your blood?

LANA: No.

ASHLEY: It looks like you got hit with a softball.

LANA: Shit. Do you have any concealer?

ASHLEY: Let me see.

(She rummages through her make-up bag.)

No.

LANA: Seriously? You have half the Clinique counter in there.

ASHLEY: I don't get pimples anymore, I'm on Accutane—but my lips bleed an awful lot.

LANA: Shit shit shit.

ASHLEY: You get pimples, don't you carry concealer?

LANA: No.

ASHLEY: I guess this is one of those moments where we learn we need to always carry concealer cuz you never know.

LANA: *(sarcastically)* Thanks for that good advice.

ASHLEY: Hey, maybe one of Tom's friends has some.

LANA: I don't know where he went.

ASHLEY: Really?

LANA: He might have like left. *(Pause)* We were making out, right? On someone's blanket. And I thought we were having a really good time. And then he said he was going to go get us some Zimas and I waited like twenty minutes, but he didn't come back. I went to find him or his friends. But they were gone. So then I tried to find you. And you were gone.

ASHLEY: I was with Brent by the Margarita machines.

LANA: And so then I came in here. After the concert we have to go meet my mom at the car. She's gonna kill me.

ASHLEY: Speaking of your mom . . .

LANA: What?

ASHLEY: I ran into Tara Sanders by the concessions and she told me she saw your mom and Mr. DeBenedetto like dancing together.

LANA: Mr. DeBenedetto the biology teacher?

ASHLEY: Yeah. Like grinding.

LANA: Grinding? Gross.

ASHLEY: I know.

LANA: Tara has such a big mouth. She's gonna tell everyone. *(beat)* This is the worst night of my life.

ASHLEY: Well I had a pretty good time.

LANA: What am I gonna do?

ASHLEY: Try putting your hair in front of it.

(LANA tries that.)

Let me spray it to hold it there.

(She sprays it all over. LANA coughs. Looks in mirror.)

LANA: It's not working.

ASHLEY: Hold your neck like this.

(She indicates tilting her head down.)

I saw a *Who's the Boss* where Alyssa Milano had to hide a hickey.

LANA: Did it work?

ASHLEY: Well, no . . .

LANA: I am gonna be so grounded for life. I'm not going to

be able to go to any pool parties this summer.

ASHLEY: Ok, calm down . . .

LANA: How am I supposed to calm down?

ASHLEY: There is no way your mom is going to see that you have a hickey. First of all, it's like totally dark outside in the parking lot. Like we could get mugged. *(Beat)*

LANA: It is pretty dark.

ASHLEY: It's totally dark.

> *(She grabs LANA's shoulders like they're in a sports huddle debating the next play in a game.)*

All you have to do is make it into the car and then out of the car and into the house and into your room before your mom turns on the lights and gets a good look at you. Don't stand directly under any street lamps or your porch light and you'll be good.

LANA: You positive?

ASHLEY: We gotta go out there. Are you ready?

LANA: Yes.

ASHLEY: Go get 'em!

> *(They exit. A beat, and then we hear a bloodcurdling scream off-stage.)*

MARJORIE (O.S.): What in the hell?!!!!!!!!!!!!!!!!!

> *(MARJORIE storms into the bathroom, dragging LANA by her ear. ASHLEY follows. MARJORIE gets LANA under the light and then pushes her hair away to look at her neck.)*

A hickey?! Are you kidding me?

LANA: I can explain . . .

MARJORIE: I left you alone for an hour for Christsake.

LANA: Mom, I/

MARJORIE: How in the hell did you get a hickey?

LANA: . . . making out.

MARJORIE: Jesus!

ASHLEY: Mrs. Lawrence, in Lana's defense/

MARJORIE: Ashley.

LANA: Yes.

MARJORIE: Quiet!

ASHLEY: Ok.

LANA: God, you act like I just shot someone. And you're not Ms. Innocent. I heard you were grinding with Mr. DeBenedetto.

MARJORIE: Who did you hear that from?

LANA: Ashley.

(MARJORIE glares at ASHLEY.)

ASHLEY: I heard it from Tara Sanders.

LANA: He's a teacher at the high school, Mom. He like just graduated college.

MARJORIE: . . . We're adults and we can do what we want.

LANA: Well I'll keep that in mind for when I'm old like you.

MARJORIE: Do you know how hard I work, huh? To put a roof over your head and buy you this Abercrombie?

LANA: You should have taken us to NSYNC instead . . .

MARJORIE: If your father was here I'm sure he'd smack you for having such a smart mouth.

LANA: Then lucky for me he's in Florida with that waitress from Chi-Chi's.

MARJORIE: Watch it.

LANA: I hope he gets eaten by an alligator.

MARJORIE: You're grounded.

LANA: Mom!

MARJORIE: Until August. And no more concerts. For life.

LANA: That is so unfair.

MARJORIE: And Ashley, I'm sure you weren't just sitting there while this was happening. Let this be a lesson to you too. Next time . . . I will call Deborah.

(Ashley gasps. Marjorie exits.)

ASHLEY: On the bright side, you are gonna have the best weekend story in homeroom Monday. I mean, aside from Tara.

LANA: You think so?

ASHLEY: Absolutely.

(The girls exit as we hear "Mary Jane's Last Dance.")

END OF PLAY

ORIGINAL PRODUCTION

POLLY was produced at Heartland Theatre Company (Julie Kistler, Artistic Director; Gail Dobbins, Director of Marketing and Operations) in Normal, Illinois on June 5, 2014. It was directed by Julie Kistler; the set design was by Katie McCasland; the costume design was by Nikki Wheeler; the lighting design was by Anita McDaniel; the sound design was by Isaac Mandel; and the production stage manager was Matthew Harter.

CAST

JOHN: Robert Goode
MAUREEN: Gabrielle Lott-Rogers
POLLY: Andrea Henderson

CHARACTERS:

JOHN: a man in his thirties. Any race.

MAUREEN: a woman in her thirties. Any race.

POLLY: a woman in her thirties, who is also a parrot. Any race.

LOCATION:

John's living room.

TIME:

Late afternoon.

A living room. JOHN, in his thirties, leads MAUREEN, in her thirties, into the room.

JOHN: . . . And I'm so excited for you to meet her, Maureen.

MAUREEN: You haven't said anything about her.

JOHN: We were keeping it sort of quiet.

MAUREEN: Why?

JOHN: You know, first real thing since my divorce.

MAUREEN: I think it's wonderful.

JOHN: How's Charlie and Charlie Jr.?

MAUREEN: They're great. I know we keep saying this but you have to come over and have dinner with us. So where is she?

JOHN: In the other room.
(calling)
Polly!
(POLLY, a woman in her 30s, "flies" into the room, using her arms. She wears a fake beak on her nose as if she's a parrot. She flies over to John and perches near him.)

JOHN: Maureen, this is Polly. Polly, this is Maureen.
(Polly speaks in a parrot-like manner unless otherwise indicated.)

POLLY: Hello!

MAUREEN: Hello.

POLLY: Hello!

MAUREEN: Uh, hi.

(John scratches POLLY.)

JOHN: Aren't you a pretty girl?

POLLY: Pretty girl, pretty girl.

JOHN: *(to Maureen)* I know you're shocked.

MAUREEN: I am a bit confused, John.

JOHN: Polly is a parrot. I got her and have fallen absolutely in love with her.

MAUREEN: She's a parrot.

JOHN: Isn't she's gorgeous?

POLLY: Pretty girl. Hello!

JOHN: Hello.

MAUREEN: John, something here is not right.

JOHN: I know. I'm not supposed to be so crazy about my pet but I love her.

MAUREEN: Really? Love?

JOHN: We all need it.

MAUREEN: I thought you were talking about a girlfriend.

JOHN: Well, she's my pet. But I'm the happiest I've ever been.

POLLY: Hello!

MAUREEN: But, John, she's not a parrot, she's—

POLLY: RICE!

MAUREEN: What?

POLLY: RICE!

MAUREEN: What is she saying?

JOHN: Oh, she wants her rice. It must be getting close to dinner.

POLLY: Rice.

JOHN: Okay, Polly, in a little bit.

POLLY: I love you!

JOHN: Aww, isn't she sweet.

MAUREEN: Uh, yeah. But, John, she's a not—

POLLY: RICE! RICE ! RICE!

JOHN: Polly, what's gotten into you?

POLLY: I love you.

(Polly starts to bob her head up and down to regurgitate food for John.)

MAUREEN: What is she doing?

JOHN: She's showing me that she loves me by regurgitating her food to share with me.

MAUREEN: Ew! Make her stop.

JOHN: Okay, that's enough, Polly.

MAUREEN: John, really—

POLLY: RICE!

JOHN: Okay, okay, I'm sorry, Maureen. Just give me a second while I get her dinner. Will you be okay with her?

MAUREEN: I guess.

POLLY: I love Maureen.

JOHN: She learned your name. Isn't that sweet? I'll be right back.

(John exits. Polly preens.)

MAUREEN: I know you're not a parrot.

POLLY: Asshole.

MAUREEN: What did you say to me?

POLLY: Bitch.

MAUREEN: I'm going to talk to John.

(As Maureen stands, Polly bites her.)

MAUREEN: AHH!

(John hurries in.)

JOHN: What's wrong?

MAUREEN: She bit me!

JOHN: You didn't antagonize her, did you?

MAUREEN: No!

JOHN: She's never bit me. Polly, no!

POLLY: I'm sorry.

JOHN: She didn't mean it, Maureen. Just don't get too close. I'll be right back.

(He exits.)

MAUREEN: I don't know what your game is but I don't like it.

POLLY: Slut.

MAUREEN: What did you just call me?

POLLY: Whore.

MAUREEN: You're not going to convince me that you're a parrot. I don't know how you convinced John, although he was always a pushover when it came to women he liked, but you're not going to get away with it.

(POLLY "flies" closer.)

POLLY: *(speaking normally)* Listen, Maureen, John and I have a nice thing going. Think of it as man's interaction with nature. And don't be a cunt.

MAUREEN: You have such a dirty mouth.

POLLY: My first boyfriend was a sailor.

MAUREEN: I don't care. I don't think John should be dating a "parrot."

POLLY: What're you, an animal hater?

MAUREEN: No.

POLLY: You got something against parrots? You're probably one of those cat people.

MAUREEN: I don't own a cat. I don't have any pets.

POLLY: Oh you're one of those. Even worse.

MAUREEN: I don't have anything against parrots. I have a problem with people who act like parrots and try to date my best friend.

POLLY: What does it matter what shape love comes in?

(John enters with a bowl of food. Polly goes back to speaking like a parrot.)

POLLY: Ready!

(He puts the dish in front of Polly. She eats with her hands.)

JOHN: Isn't it amazing that parrots eat with their feet?

MAUREEN: Yeah.

JOHN: And she can live 60, 70 years.

MAUREEN: Uh huh, that's amazing.

JOHN: Her breed, interestingly enough, is originally from—

MAUREEN: John, for Christ's sake, it's a fake beak!

(Maureen removes Polly's fake beak.)

MAUREEN: She can't fly! She's not eating with her feet, she's eating with her hands!

JOHN: What're you saying?

MAUREEN: She's not a parrot!

(John looks at Polly and then back to Maureen.)

JOHN: *(to Maureen)* How could you do that? Parrots are sensitive birds.

MAUREEN: John, I'm your friend and whatever weird thing is going on, I want you to know the truth. This isn't normal.

JOHN: Maybe I don't want normal.

MAUREEN: Well, you two clearly like each other. Why can't you like her as a normal girl? Hey, bird girl, what is your real name?

POLLY: Polly.

MAUREEN: Oh for the love of god.

JOHN: Maureen, after my divorce, it was a hard time for me. I shut down. I didn't have anyone. You were busy with your husband and little Charlie, your family.

MAUREEN: I tried to be there.

JOHN: I know. But you had your own life. It's no longer how it was. And then I found Polly. Like this. I didn't question it. She gave me comfort, a companion at a time when I need a companion. She was there and I am very grateful for that.

MAUREEN: She's not a fucking parrot!

JOHN: Maybe that doesn't matter to me.

MAUREEN: You're not seeing what is real. This is wrong.

JOHN: Not to me.

MAUREEN: Okay. Fine, whatever. Here, Polly.

(Maureen hands the beak back to Polly, who puts it back on.)

POLLY: *(parrot like)*Thank you!

MAUREEN: Unbelievable.

JOHN: Maureen.

MAUREEN: John, I can't be a part of this.

JOHN: You're my oldest friend.

MAUREEN: I'm sorry.

(Maureen exits. Beat as John and Polly sit there.)

JOHN: Maybe she's right. Maybe this is wrong.

POLLY: I love you.

(He reaches over and gently removes her beak.)

JOHN: I love you too, Polly.

(He scratches her head and she leans her head against him. As she makes happy whistling/bird sounds, the lights fade.)

END OF PLAY

RESEARCH SUBJECTS
OR THAT CREEPY GUY TAPING ME IN MY SLEEP
Erin Moughon

ORIGINAL PRODUCTION
Open Tent Theater Company
August 17, 2014, Fort Tryon Park
As part of Ourglass: A 24-hour play festival

Directed by Reuven Russell

CAST
DEBBIE: Arona Berow
ADINA: Kyra Young
JONATHAN: Danny Hoffman

CHARACTERS:

ADINA: Female, twenties, a free spirit, head in the clouds, and roommate of Debbie, allowed Jonathan into their home to observe them.

DEBBIE: Female, twenties, roommate and level head.

JONATHAN: Male, twenties, Debbie believes he's a creepy guy. Adina thinks he's an alien observing them. Take that as you will.

SETTING:

Debbie and Adina's home.

TIME:

Now.

Three chairs. A table.
Adina is doing a headstand (or if it is easier for all involved, she could be sitting upside down on a chair, feet in air, head facing audience). Debbie walks in, carrying a grocery bag. She puts the bag on the table.

DEBBIE: What are you doing?

ADINA: Helping my hair grow.

DEBBIE: What?

ADINA: I read somewhere that if you let all your blood rush to your head it helps your hair grow.

DEBBIE: That is absurd.

ADINA: You should try it.

DEBBIE: I don't need the headache.

(Adina sits up.)

ADINA: Whoa. Head rush. What happened?

DEBBIE: Nothing happened.

ADINA: Really? Not buying it. You've got that something big happened look on your face. Something . . . big. Happened. Spill.

(Jonathan walks in during Adina's line, wearing a robe. He clearly has just woken up. He stumbles over

to the table, reaches into the bag, pulls out a cereal box, walks back off stage. Adina is nonplussed. Debbie does a double take.)

DEBBIE: Umm . . . who the? What the? Who the heck was that?

ADINA: Jonathan. Don't try to change the subject. What happened?

DEBBIE: I think he changed the subject. Adina, what is he doing in our house?

ADINA: Research. So what happened?

DEBBIE: Research?

ADINA: Yeah. Something about the female experience or something for some sciencey thing. I think he made up most of the words he said. Something with outer space was involved.

DEBBIE: So you just let him in?!?

ADINA: Yeah. He's been in my room for a couple of days.

DEBBIE: A couple of days?!?

(Adina starts doing Krav Maga.)

ADINA: Yeah. It seemed really important. And I've always wanted to do something important.

DEBBIE: So you just let some random man who said he is doing something (air quotes) "sciencey" into our house for A COUPLE OF DAYS?

ADINA: He had papers. And a laser thing. And a space ship.

DEBBIE: A SPACE SHIP!

ADINA: Yeah. I mean how cool is that right? He said I could ride in it. Not drive it. But ride.

DEBBIE: This is unbelievable.

ADINA: I know, right? I'd totally be a great driver.

DEBBIE: Not that. The fact that you let a man, a strange man, into our house WITHOUT telling ME. STOP DOING KRAV MAGA!

(Adina stops. Jonathan walks in again, grabs a banana or other fruit from the bag, walks out.)

DEBBIE *(cont)*: And now he's eating my breakfast. You know how I feel about my breakfast. The banana! I was saving that for later.

ADINA: Yeah. Sorry. I'll talk to him about that.

DEBBIE: Not the point. Look. We have to get him out of here.

ADINA: But he's not done studying us!

DEBBIE: US!?!

ADINA: Yeah. He has some great footage of you sleeping.

DEBBIE: That's it. That's IT. I'm calling the police.

ADINA: Why?

DEBBIE: *(dialing on cell phone)* To see how their day is going. Why do you think?

ADINA: *(grabbing cell phone)* You're going to ruin everything!

DEBBIE: No, I'm going to get the creepy stalker out of my house. Give me back my phone!

(She tries to get the phone from Adina. Adina darts away.)

ADINA: But I love him!

DEBBIE: Oh for Pete's sake.

(Debbie starts to tickle Adina to get phone back.)

ADINA: No. No tickling! *(gets away)* He's important and dreamy and he told me I'm his most fascinating research subject EVER. Me! Fascinating!

DEBBIE: Adina. You don't love him. You just love the fact that he pays attention to you.

ADINA: You don't understand!

DEBBIE: He's using you.

ADINA: I know.

DEBBIE: And . . . wait. What? What do you mean you know?

ADINA: He's using me for his research.

DEBBIE: That's not what I meant. Adina. He's not really doing research.

ADINA: Yes. He is. I've seen all his files on us and the other women.

DEBBIE: That's what I mean. He's pulled this scam with . . . . how many other women?

ADINA: Umm . . . close to a thousand, I'd say.

DEBBIE: A thousand? And you let him stay? I cannot handle this today.

(Debbie puts her head down on the table and starts to

cry. Adina grabs a box of tissues and hands it to her.)
ADINA: It's going to be okay.
DEBBIE: No, it's not! I was late to work, again, and they fired me!
ADINA: Oh honey.
DEBBIE: *(crying more)* Then I went to David's apartment for sympathy, and he was in bed with another woman!
ADINA: I'm so sorry.
DEBBIE: And now . . . now there's some creepy potential serial killer eating my cereal!
(Debbie blows her nose loudly.)
ADINA: Look on the bright side. Your job sucked. David was a jerk. And Jonathan is only eating your cereal! He's not going to kill you.
DEBBIE: How do you know that?
ADINA: Because he's just observing behavior. We need to be alive for our behaviors to be observed. Besides, he said someone else was in charge of probes and dissections.
DEBBIE: Not a huge comfort.
ADINA: So. Details. What happened at work? With David? What did the skank look like?
DEBBIE: Why do you always have to push things?
ADINA: Why do you have to shut yourself off?
DEBBIE: I'm going to my room. And seeing if I have anything good to barricade the door with.
(Debbie exits.)
ADINA: Debbie. Debbie. Come back! Debbie!
(Just as she is about to leave, Jonathan re-enters, blocking her exit. He is carrying a notebook or other object/device to take notes on.)
ADINA *(cont)*: Oh! Hello!
JONATHAN: Hello.
ADINA: Sorry about Debbie. She's just had a rough day.
JONATHAN: *(writing notes)* No. No. Don't apologize. It's really good. It gives me a new perspective for my research. Female tragedies and how they affect their interactions with their environments. Fascinating stuff.
ADINA: I'm sure I have some tragedies that could . . . um . . .

---

affect my environment and stuff.

JONATHAN: What would you normally do? If I were not here.

ADINA: Umm . . . well . . . I'd . . . I'd go and see if I could get Debbie to come out of her room.

JONATHAN: *(writing notes)* Good. Good. You should do that.

ADINA: But . . . don't you want to interview me? Again?

JONATHAN: The closer you stick to your normal habits, the more authentic my research will be. I've already compromised my data by telling you about the project.

ADINA: Well . . . I don't know if I should give her her space or go talk to her . . .

JONATHAN: *(looking her directly in the eyes)* This would really help me out.

ADINA: Okay! I mean I want to help out.

JONATHAN: Thank you, Adina. I knew I could count on you.

ADINA: *(running out)* Debbie! Debbie! Come out!

(Jonathan looks around to make sure he's alone. He's very thorough. Then after a beat, he grabs the tissue box and digs through it. He pulls out a weird looking electronic device (NB actual prop could be made of cardboard or a cell phone with something on it to make it look like not a cell phone).

JONATHAN: This is J-Zero-Theta-Nnn reporting. Female subjects are displaying same behavior patterns as prior subjects. They have a strong bond, even though there is no blood relation, and they feel free to display erratic emotions, even in the near proximity of total strangers. These two have created a microcosm of the larger human community in their home. Further study is still required. The younger female seems willing to participate in offsite observations. Requesting permission to bring subject back to Vergon Eight for further study. *(pause)* Yes. Immediately. *(He hangs up. Adina walks back in. He shoves the device back into the tissue box. She doesn't see the device.)*

ADINA: Well, fine! Just stay in there.

JONATHAN: *(quickly taking note)* Fascinating. Fascinating.

ADINA: Some people. Am I right?

JONATHAN: I would not know.

ADINA: Trust me. I am. You should write that down.

JONATHAN: I actually have something more important to discuss with you.

ADINA: My mother told me this day would never come. But yes!

JONATHAN: You do not even know the question.

ADINA: Oh. Right. Sorry. Go ahead.

JONATHAN: I have received permission from my commander to bring you back to Vergon Eight for further study. I am requesting that you join me on my home planet so that I may see how a human female functions when forced into a new perspective.

ADINA: Oh.

JONATHAN: Oh? I do not understand this oh.

ADINA: Sorry. I just thought you were asking me a different question. Okay. I just . . . so you want me to go with you to your home?

JONATHAN: Yes. In my spaceship.

ADINA: Can I drive?

JONATHAN: The craft is linked to my biometrics. It would be near impossible to reconfigure it to your specifications here on Earth.

ADINA: Oh.

JONATHAN: Is that sadness?

ADINA: Disappointment. I just wanted to drive . . . no . . . pilot . . . pilot a spaceship. That's all.

JONATHAN: Well, once on Vergon Eight, it is a rather simple process that would allow you to, as you say, pilot a spaceship.

ADINA: Really?

JONATHAN: Yes. We even have much simpler crafts that we use to train our youths to pilot. I am certain I could find such a vehicle for you to try.

ADINA: Like a spaceship with training wheels?

JONATHAN: Our crafts do not have wheels.

ADINA: But I would really get to fly it? In space?

JONATHAN: Of course. If you come with me.

ADINA: I have to pack. And call my mom! And . . . there is so much to do!

JONATHAN: Please hurry. The best time for us to depart is fast approaching.

ADINA: Will do! This is so exciting! *(sing-song)* I'm going to fly a spaceship! I'm going to fly a spaceship!
(She bounces off the stage. Jonathan retrieves his communication device. Debbie walks in, un-noticed.)

JONATHAN: I have consent. The human female will be accompanying me on my next flight to Vergon Eight. We should arrive within two Earth years. *(pause)* Yes. I know I've gone native using Earth time, but since I'm here . . . *(He sees Debbie.)*

JONATHAN (cont): I have been spotted. I must end this communication.
(He puts down the device.)

DEBBIE: So Adina wasn't just talking her usual gibberish.

JONATHAN: *(taking note)* Fascinating how you demean someone you seem that you are about to defend.

DEBBIE: It's just my way. So you're going to leave now and never contact Adina again.

JONATHAN: You are not afraid of me?

DEBBIE: You have one minute to get out of my house.

JONATHAN: I believe the appropriate response here is "Or what?" Am I correct? Is that how this line of threatening works?

DEBBIE: Pretty much.

JONATHAN: Right then. Or what?

DEBBIE: You don't want to know.

JONATHAN: Amazing. Do humans do this often? Allowing the imagination of the other to create the worst scenario?

DEBBIE: Again, it's my way. Less than thirty seconds.

JONATHAN: You are going to have to follow through on that . . .

DEBBIE: There is a dimension known as the Shadow Space. It is a place between worlds that my people discovered while your planet was still rock particles floating through the universe. Once in this place, you are changed. In little ways at first. Maybe your nose becomes shorter. Your hair curls when it didn't before. Skin changes color. But slowly and surely, you begin to not recognize yourself. Then, it takes your name. You do not realize it at first. But then you cannot remember what you are called. It is there, on the tip of your tongue, but it never comes out. And that is when you realize that you are a shell, a shadow, a crude diluted sketch of your former self. And there is no way to get yourself back. And when you have reached that point of despair, I will pull you out of that dimension and place you back on your world. In a place where everything is familiar, but you know what nothing is. A place where you feel like you know everyone, but no one knows you. And I will sit and watch as this drives you slowly mad.

JONATHAN: How do you . . . ? No. The Shadow Space is just a story invented to scare small ones. You're lying. You couldn't . . .

DEBBIE: The inhabitants of Celestia never lie about the Shadow Space.

JONATHAN: Celestia?

DEBBIE: Go.

JONATHAN: But my data!

DEBBIE: Run!

(Jonathan runs out the door. Adina runs back in with a bag, wearing a wedding veil.)

ADINA: I'm ready! I'm ready! Jonathan?

DEBBIE: Adina, I'm so sorry.

ADINA: No.

DEBBIE: He just . . .

ADINA: What did you do?

DEBBIE: Nothing. I saw him in here, and he said he needed to find . . .

ADINA: What? What?

DEBBIE: More interesting subjects. Ones who wouldn't corrupt his data.

ADINA: *(near tears)* But . . . but . . . I worked so hard not to corrupt it. And . . . and . . . and . . .

DEBBIE: It's okay.

ADINA: He was going to let me drive a spaceship!

(She is sobbing loudly now. Debbie hands her some tissues. Adina blows her nose loudly.)

DEBBIE: There, there. Let it out.

ADINA: I LOVED HIM!

DEBBIE: Honey, I know.

ADINA: HOW COULD I BE SO STUPID?

(Blows nose again.)

DEBBIE: You're not stupid. Men are stupid. Jonathan. David. Stupid.

ADINA: You're . . . you're right.

DEBBIE: You know what we need? Ice cream. Cookie Dough. Thelma. Louise.

ADINA: Yeah. Yeah. Mint chocolate chip?

DEBBIE: Of course.

ADINA: Double chocolate chip cookie dough?

DEBBIE: Whatever you want. *(picking up keys)* I'll go get the food.

ADINA: I'll go find the DVD!

(Adina bounces offstage. Debbie pulls out her own communicator.)

DEBBIE: *(speaking in an alien voice)* Operative 226 reporting. Interfering party neutralized. Resuming data collection on subject immediately. *(pause)* No. Subject has no knowledge of the experiment. Data to be reported as found. Adina's new perspective on men should prove most fruitful in my observations.

ADINA: *(offstage)* Does Steel Magnolias work instead?

DEBBIE: *(yelling back to Adina, Alien voice)* Sure! *(normal voice)* I mean sure! Ben and Jerry's good for ice cream?

ADINA: *(offstage)* Perfect!

DEBBIE: *(Alien voice)* I must go engage subject. I will report back on the pre-arranged date. Over and out.

(Debbie puts communication device away, grabs her keys, and exits.)

End of play.

SARAH STEIN SENDS A SELFIE
Michael McKeever

ORIGINAL PRODUCTION

Island City Stage and City Theatre as part of Shorts Gone Wild, August 7 to September 7, 2014.

CAST

SARAH STEIN: Niki Fridh
ALLY: Gladys Ramirez
VERA: Renée Elizabeth Turner

CHARACTERS:

> SARAH STEIN: A bride-to-be, twenties
> ALLY: Her best friend, twenties
> VERA: A stylist, twenties

SETTING:

> Sarah Stein's apartment. Today.

Lights up on SARAH STEIN and her best friend ALLY. It is late morning in SARAH's apartment. SARAH has obviously, just woken up. She appears to be a little hung over. ALLY is showing her a photo on her cell phone. SARAH is mortified.

SARAH: *(looking at photo)* Oh my God.

ALLY: Uh huh.

SARAH: Oh. My. God.

ALLY: This is what I'm saying.

SARAH: I just . . . I mean . . . I just can't . . .

ALLY: Honey—

SARAH: I have no idea what to say.

ALLY: I'm not sure there really is anything to say.

SARAH: When did I send this?

ALLY: *(looking at the time on the text)* Uhhhh . . . 4:35. This morning.

SARAH: Oh my God.

ALLY: Yep.

SARAH: It's just . . . I mean . . . My clothes.

ALLY: What about them?

SARAH: Where are they?

ALLY: Why are you asking me?

SARAH: And what the hell am I doing?

ALLY: Well, from what I can tell, you are presenting your vagina as if it won First Place at the County Fair, while giving a sort of come-hither look, complete with raised eyebrow and a "don't-fuck-with-me-I'm-serious" grin. It's very 1970's Jane Fonda. In a porno sort of way. *(SARAH glares at her)*

ALLY: Hey, you asked.

SARAH: Well, obviously, I was a little loopy when I sent it.

ALLY: You think?

SARAH: I mean, I have no recollection. None.

(beat. She squints at the photo)

And where am I?

ALLY: Well, from what I can make out from the signage in the background, you're standing on one of the tables outside the Starbucks across the street from the gazebo in Downtown.

(beat. Once again, SARAH just stares at her, horrified)

ALLY: Seriously, if you look just under your left boob, you can clearly see the little green and white mermaid lady on the window.

SARAH: That's like four blocks from here.

ALLY: Six.

SARAH: I walked six blocks naked to take a selfie at Starbucks?

ALLY: Apparently.

SARAH: Was I that drunk last night?

ALLY: You didn't seem it. At the rehearsal dinner, you just had wine.

SARAH: How much wine?

ALLY: I don't know. A bottle?

SARAH: *(remembering)* It was a Malbec. It was very good.

ALLY: So you kept saying. And then, right before midnight you made a big deal about Seth seeing you before the wedding and so we all said our goodbyes, and Kendra and I took you home.

SARAH: See now that I remember. I also remember putting on Billie Holiday and opening the bottle of Kahlua that my aunt gave me.

(ALLY picks up an empty bottle of Kahlua)

ALLY: And suddenly, things become clearer.

SARAH: So let me see if I've got this straight. Last night - in the middle of the night - after drinking a entire bottle of wine—

Lawrence Harbison 379

ALLY: And Kahlua.

SARAH: And Kahlua. I got completely undressed and traipsed four—

ALLY: Six.

SARAH: Six blocks to stand on a table outside of Starbucks and send you a naked selfie.

ALLY: Oh, you didn't send me the naked selfie.

SARAH: I didn't?

ALLY: You sent it to someone else.

SARAH: Who?

ALLY: My mother.

SARAH: OH MY GOD!

(ALLY just nods)

SARAH: I texted a naked selfie of myself to your mother.

ALLY: At 4:35 in the morning.

SARAH: What did she say?

ALLY: She said that she still loves you and is going to recommend a really good twelve-step program when she sees your mother at the wedding today.

SARAH: Okay, I'm going to lay back down for a minute.

ALLY: But wait, there's more.

SARAH: Oh please honey, I don't think I can take anymore.

ALLY: There's a text that went along with it.

SARAH: Of course there is. Why wouldn't there be?

ALLY: Wanna read it?

SARAH: No.

ALLY: I think you should.

SARAH: And yet, I'm not.

ALLY: It's not that long.

SARAH: Wouldn't it be easier if you just shot me in the head?

ALLY: Here . . .

(ALLY holds out the phone)

SARAH: Seriously, the stylist is going to be here any minute. And the way I feel right now, it's going to take her hours to make me look like I wasn't hit by a Mac Truck.

ALLY: Read it.

SARAH: It's my wedding day Ally!!! *(beat, quietly)* I can't

(ALLY reads her the text)

ALLY: *(reading)* "My dearest sexy love . . ."

SARAH: Oh God.

ALLY: "I love you. I always have. I always will. I so want you to know that. Especially on this day. Seth might have my hand in marriage, but you will always have my heart."
(beat)

SARAH: Anything else? I mean, are there videos of me dry-humping a homeless person or setting the Starbucks on fire?

ALLY: No. That's pretty much it.

SARAH: Oh please, don't make it sound so trivial. I mean, texting a naked selfie and poorly written love note to my best friend's mother in the wee hours of my wedding day is some pretty major shit.

ALLY: Know what I think?

SARAH: That Kahlua is the devil's milk?

ALLY: I think that you sent that text to the wrong person.

SARAH: Oh?

ALLY: I think that you meant to send that text to someone else.

SARAH: Who?

ALLY: Me.
(The longest beat ever)
(Then SARAH laughs)

ALLY: I'm serious.
(SARAH stops laughing)
(beat)

SARAH: *(finally)* So. Like I said, the stylist is going to be here any minute and then the others will—

ALLY: Sarah—

SARAH: Ally. Honey. Let's not. I got trashed last night. That's all. Don't start creating melodrama where there isn't—

ALLY: Who's creating melodrama? I'm just making an observation.

SARAH: What observation?

ALLY: The gazebo.

SARAH: What about it?

ALLY: It's where—

SARAH: Oh, Ally. Stop.

ALLY: *(overlapping)* It's where we had our first kiss.

SARAH: Look—

ALLY: We had gone for coffee and ended up walking across—

SARAH: Stop! *(beat)* That was a lifetime ago. We were . . . I was a different person then. It was just—

ALLY: If you say it was just a phase, I will hit you over the head with this Kahlua bottle.

SARAH: Look. I'm not, in any way, discounting . . . *(beat)* . . . It's just . . . Those six months. It was a long time ago. We were both very young. I was never—

ALLY: It wasn't that long ago. We weren't that young.

SARAH: Really? Today? We have to do this today?

ALLY: It was the best six months of my life.

SARAH: Why are you saying this?

ALLY: Because it's true. And because I know you. Better than anyone else, I know you. And after reading that text—

SARAH: Honey—

ALLY: I just want you to know that if that's really how you feel—and I think it is—there's no reason to go through with the wedding.

SARAH: What the hell are you talking about?

ALLY: We could just leave.

SARAH: Leave?

ALLY: Yes leave. Right now.

SARAH: And go where?

ALLY: Anywhere. We could just jump in the car and drive. Anywhere you want. Just the two of us. Sarah and Ally. Thelma and Louis. Anywhere you want.

(beat)

SARAH: Don't you think you're being a little narcissistic here?

ALLY: Come again?

SARAH: I mean, making this all about you?

ALLY: I'm not the one who sent me a naked selfie.

SARAH: Well, you're wrong. I didn't send it to you.

ALLY: You didn't?

SARAH: No. *(beat)* As a matter of fact, I've always found your mother to be a very handsome woman and—

ALLY: Look—

SARAH: No, you look! I can't do this. Not this morning. Not today. I am getting married in less than five hours and I don't have the time or inclination to skip down lesbian memory lane. *(beat)* What we had was lovely. But it's done. For whatever reason, it's done. *(beat)* I'm sorry. I know you care about me. But you're wrong about this. You're projecting something onto me that simply isn't there.

ALLY: Am I?

SARAH: Yes. You are. *(beat)* In five hours, I am going to walk down that isle and say "I do."

ALLY: Why?

SARAH: Because that is what everyone is expecting me to do.

ALLY: Wrong answer.

VERA: Hello?

(They turn to find VERA standing there. She carries a large make-up case in one hand, and an oversized bag over her shoulder. She wears an apron around her waist, containing scissors, brushes and such.)

SARAH: Oh, Vera.

VERA: I'm sorry, but the door was open. I hope it's okay I just walked in.

SARAH: Of course.

VERA: I'm a little early.

SARAH: Actually, your timing is perfect. *(To ALLY)* This is Vera. She's doing our hair and make-up.

VERA: Nice to meet you.

SARAH: And this is Ally, my Maid of Honor.

ALLY: Hello.

SARAH: *(pointing offstage)* Why don't you get set up in the other room. The other two bridesmaids will be here in about a half-hour.

VERA: Perfect.

Lawrence Harbison　　　　383

SARAH: Do you need anything from me?

VERA: Nope. *(indicating her case)* Everything I need is right here.

SARAH: Alright then. Let me know.

(VERA goes to exit, stops)

VERA: Smile! It's your special day!

(She exits)

(An awkward beat)

ALLY: *(finally)* I guess I'll go out to the car and get that hideous dress you want me to wear.

SARAH: It's not hideous. It's apricot silk.

ALLY: Need I say more?

(ALLY turns to exit)

SARAH: Ally.

(ALLY stops)

SARAH: We're alright then?

ALLY: Why wouldn't we be?

SARAH: You're my best friend in the whole world. I never want to hurt you. *(beat)* I love you, Allison Swanson. I really do. I just . . . I can't. *(beat)* I hope—

(Suddenly ALLY kisses her. It is simple and honest and beautiful. It is a kiss between two people who love each other. After a moment, they separate)

(beat. The two women just look at each other. For a moment. For a lifetime)

ALLY: So. I will now go get that hideous dress. And that girl will do our hair and make us beautiful. And I'll stand next to you as you say your vows. And I'll raise my glass to the handsome new couple. And my toast will be lovely and funny and gracious. And at the end of the day, when the guests have gone home and you've left for your honeymoon, I will sit in the quiet of my room and delete both the photo and the text from this phone. Because that is what you want. *(beat)* Just don't think—for one moment—that any of that changes what you and I both know to be the truth.

(She exits)

(SARAH stares after her. After a moment, VERA re-

enters. She carries a glass of champagne)

VERA: Alright, I'm all set up in there. *(handing SARAH the champagne)* This is for you.

SARAH: *(repulsed by the sight of alcohol)* Dear God, why?

VERA: *(confused)* Because you're the bride.

SARAH: Oh. Right.

(She takes the glass but doesn't drink)

VERA: So, let's talk.

SARAH: *(not really listening)* What about?

VERA: About your look. About what we're going to do. I know we talked about leaving your hair down, but looking at it now, I'm thinking maybe up is better. What do you think?

SARAH: I, um . . . I really don't . . . whatever you want.

VERA: It's not what I want. It's what you want.

SARAH: I'm sorry?

VERA: Sweetie, this is your day. It's all about you. I can make you anything you want: Sophisticated and elegant, wholesome and sweet, classic and demure. All you need to do is tell me who you want to be.

(SARAH looks to where ALLY exited)

SARAH: It doesn't really matter. Any of those will do. Any of them. *(beat)* Anything but me.

CURTAIN

THE SCOTTISH PLAY
Theo Reyna

ORIGINAL PRODUCTION

The Scottish Play premiered on January 3, 2014, at the Sandbox at Miami Theater Center as part of Mad Cat Theatre Company's Mixtape 2: Ummagumma Forza Zuma!

Directed by Theo Reyna

THE CAST
SCOTLAND: Erin Joy Schmidt
U.K. (OR BRITAIN): Noah Levine
AMERICA: Joe Kimble
OIL: Jessica Farr

Produced by Paul Tei

SUBSEQUENT PRODUCTION

The Scottish Play was produced on June 12th, 2014, on the Susan Westfall Stage at the Adrienne Arsht Center for the Performing Arts as part of City Theatre's Summer Shorts 2014.

Directed by Paul Tei

THE CAST
SCOTLAND: Elizabeth Dimon
U.K. (OR BRITAIN): Tom Wahl
AMERICA: Mcley Lafrance
OIL: Mary Sansone

Produced by John Manzelli

CHARACTERS:

SCOTLAND: a woman on the verge of divorce
UK: her husband
AMERICA: Scotland's 'special' friend (a man)
OIL: Scotland and UK's teenage daughter

Lights up. Scotland is packing a couple of suitcases. UK paces around restlessly. Oil sits downstage listening to her Walkman/Disc-man/Ipod/whichever music-playing device is in use and is reading a magazine. Scotland's and UK's first few lines are spoken with American accents, it's only after Oil's monologue that they take on their accents and mannerisms. Oil has a neutral American accent throughout.

SCOTLAND: Well if that isn't the dumbest thing I ever heard—

UK: That? You think that was dumb? Well clearly you don't remember a damn thing you said yesterday because—

OIL: *(UK and Scotland freeze as Oil begins to speak)* Not too long ago there was a couple who were arguing. They had argued before and would likely argue again but on this particular day, not too long ago at all in fact, they argued in such a way that it seemed as though it was time for them to decide whether they were going to continue on together or alone. But separation is never easy. There are ties, physical and emotional, that have to be considered. In this particular case, there was land, lots and lots of land. And a child, me. But rather than examine this as it is, an unfortunate, yet commonplace event, let us look at it through the lens of the question of an independent Scotland. The father will be Britain, the UK, royal Britannia, the mother, Scotland, and their child, their lovely little adolescent, me, will be oil. Or more specifically, the drilling rights to all the oil in the North Sea.

UK: You're only in it for the money.

(Scotland ignores UK, keeps looking)

UK: I said you're only in it for the money!

SCOTLAND: An' yer not?

OIL: *(singing along to the song on her disc-man)* Help I'm a rock!

UK: No, of course not, it's just—

OIL: Help I'm a cop!

UK: Don't you think we'd be better together?

OIL: Help I'm a rock! Help I'm a cop!

UK: Oil!

OIL: Yes, father?

UK: Just go watch tele for a minute, would you?

OIL: Why?

UK: Your mother and I are having a conversation.

OIL: Sounds more like a referendum to me!

SCOTLAND: It's alright Oil, ma' dear. You'll be comin' with mum soon enough, don't you worry.

OIL: *(she exits singing to her parents)* TV dinners by the pool, I'm so glad I finished school.

SCOTLAND: Ooh, that girl—

UK: I know, I know.

SCOTLAND: You know what her teacher said to me the other day? He said, "Oil is one of the most resourceful students in this entire class but sometimes she can be so crude."

UK: It's not her fault though, it's just a phase. Deep down she just feels out of place. And she needs both of us.

SCOTLAND: No, no, don't you make this about Oil now, big man.

UK: But of course it's about Oil, you know how the courts are. They'll take your side. You'll get her 95% of the time—

SCOTLAND: She's my daughter.

UK: But we raised her together! What am I going to do with Oil 5% of the time? Without you, Scotland . . . without you and Oil, I don't think I'll manage.

SCOTLAND: Oh England . . .

UK: You know I don't like it when you call me that.

Scotland: Oh jeez—o, that's right. It's Britain isn't it? I'm sorry, Britain.

UK: I took that name when we got together.

SCOTLAND: Oh aye, I remember. As if you'd ever let me

forget.

UK: It was a symbol. It is a symbol. A symbol of everything we've shared.

SCOTLAND: I suppose.

UK: There was a time you called yourself that too. Remember? *(He draws her close)* Britain?

SCOTLAND: But we were young then.

UK: Well, younger.

SCOTLAND: Easy, you. Your not outta this yet.

UK: Sorry.   Scotland: Aye, we were young. So young.. And we were gonna conquer the world! And we did, darling, we did!

SCOTLAND: Those trains in India. Miles and miles of track, eh? Kashmir to Bombay. Bombay to Calcutta.

UK: And that wasn't all . . .

SCOTLAND: No, no it wasn't. We had the Caribbean. Jamaica. Those beaches, that sugar—

UK: That rum . . .

SCOTLAND: That rum . . . I remember that rum. Though I've always been a whiskey girl, I remember that rum. And Hong Kong. We had a good run there, cannae' you remember? All those ships . . .

UK: And you built them all. Finest shipyards in the world.

SCOTLAND: And some of the finest mines too . . . *(pulling away)* but you had me shut them, didn't you? And my shipyards, fine as they were.

UK: We needed the money.

SCOTLAND: You needed the money.

UK: It was a difficult time. It needed to be done.

SCOTLAND: You didn't bother to ask.

UK: That's not true. I asked. I might not have listened but I asked. Look, I'll admit I haven't been perfect, but neither have you.

SCOTLAND: Oh, now it all comes out.

UK: What about all those years you didn't work?

SCOTLAND: You mean all those years I couldnae work.

UK: You could have. You're bright. You've always had a good head for business.

SCOTLAND: Then why isn't my fookin' name on our chequebook?

UK: *(Doesn't reply)*

SCOTLAND: Nothing to say, big man?

UK: I always gave you what you needed.

SCOTLAND: It was my money.

UK: It was our money. We both paid. That was the deal. Remember? We both work, we both pay. I just took care of the bills because I didn't want to bother you with all of that. You were busy and—

SCOTLAND: I was busy?

UK: We both know it's not really your thing.

SCOTLAND: Not my thing?

UK: No I didn't mean—

SCOTLAND: And to think, I let you stick your little 'Trident' in me.

(They freeze and Oil re-enters)

OIL: Oh, hey. Yeah, so they're saying Trident, which is a nuclear weapons facility on the west coast of Scotland. Britain doesn't want to lose the base, but Scotland doesn't want nukes and has no interest in keeping it there if they become independent. So yeah, for our purposes, Trident, but really, you know, they mean his penis.

(Oil exits again)

UK: Now that's not fair.

SCOTLAND: Isn't it?

UK: Me and my, our Trident, that was for both of us.

SCOTLAND: Oh that's it, isn't it? Your worried you're not gonna have anywhere to stick that stupid little thing.

UK: You used to like it just fine. Never heard a peep out of you until—

(The doorbell rings)

SCOTLAND: That'll be for me.

UK: You didn't tell me anyone was coming over.

SCOTLAND: I donnae tell you everything.

(The doorbell rings again)

UK: Well, clearly.

SCOTLAND: Look, I thought things might get a bit complicated so I rang up me mate to help out for a wee bit.

UK: You were already planning on leaving?

SCOTLAND: Not forever. And I'm not leaving, leaving. I'll just be across the way. I need some time to figure out what I'd like to do. It's been a while since I've thought about that.

UK: What are you going to build ships again?

SCOTLAND: I very well fookin' might. If that's what I decide to do. But whatever it is, I'll be doing it across the street with my own fookin' chequebook.

(Doorbell rings again and UK crosses to open the door)

UK: Fine. If it's what you feel you need.

SCOTLAND: Oh aye, 'tis.

UK: Even though, and I'm sorry to remind you of this, but we are both in quite a bit of debt and I'm not sure how you think taking care of this by ourselves is going to make things any easier than—

(He opens the door and America enters)

AMERICA: Yo.

UK: America?!

AMERICA: Most people say the U.S. these days, but, you know, I'm cool.

UK: You need a bit of space and so you called America?!

SCOTLAND: He's just helping me move a couple of things.

America: Hey, hey. Is Oil here? Hey, Oil! Guess who?!

OIL: *(running in excited)* Heeeey!!!!! China!!! *(sees America)* Oh. Hey America.

AMERICA: China?

SCOTLAND: Oh no.

AMERICA: China's been here? *(Oil starts looking around suspiciously)* Because, I don't know what kind of set-up you got going here but, look, I said I'd help you move a few things, spend a little time with Oil, but if China's coming round, you know? Aww, I mean, China, you know? That changes things.

SCOTLAND: No, Oil, was just teasing. Weren't you Oil?

UK: Now wait a minute, this is my house and I am not going to stand for this sort of wild, yankee—

AMERICA: Look, I'm sorry, England—I mean, Britain. I'm sorry, Britain. I honestly just came over to lend a hand. Nothing funny, no special relationship, just—just—and you gotta level with me here, alright buddy? Has China been here?

UK: Well, just for a visit last week, but that was to see both of us—

AMERICA: Goddamnit!

UK: No, it wasn't like that. We just had a chat about the opera.

AMERICA: Yeah, yeah, ok, but did they talk alone?

SCOTLAND: I'm right here, you know? And I'd prefer it if you talked to me.

AMERICA: I'm sure you would, and I want to. Believe me, I want to, but CHINA, you know? China.

UK: Come to think of it, I did go out back and have a chat with Oil in the garden.

AMERICA: No. No. No, No, No!

SCOTLAND: If ye could just lend us a hand with these boxes here. I'll go fetch Oil.

UK: You're not taking Oil.

SCOTLAND: She's mine. We already talked about this. We might have raised her together, but Oil is mine.

AMERICA: Doesn't matter now.

SCOTLAND: Excuse me?

AMERICA: Doesn't matter. You called China.

SCOTLAND: So?

AMERICA: China's cool.

UK: China's cool?

AMERICA: To Oil. I mean Oil's at that age when she wants to start going out.

UK: And?   America: And? Jesus, no wonder you lost the empire. China goes out all the time. Everywhere. China will take Oil wherever she wants to go. China can even get in to places that I can't.

UK: I don't—

AMERICA: Look—I'm sorry about the empire thing -

but remember when you had yours? Remember that feeling? You were going out all the time. Everyone wanted to see you. Not that they don't now, it's just different now, right? Anyway, you had it and then you sorta, let it go, or found out you were wrong, or lost it or whatever. Not important. And you know how since then I was kinda the cool one. I mean rock n roll, right? You're welcome. But yeah, I've doing alright for a while now but I will admit that things are getting a bit trickier. I mean, I still go out a lot, just not every night. And well, China does. So to Oil, China's looking pretty good. And on that note, thank you and good night.

SCOTLAND: But you said you'd help.

AMERICA: Yeah and I might. Just, not gonna fuck with China today. Sorry. Oh, and good luck to the two of you, really. Hope you guys work it out. Peace.

(America exits)

SCOTLAND: Well, shite.

UK: You still leaving?

SCOTLAND: I have to.

UK: I'd rather you'd stay.

SCOTLAND: I know. Maybe just a wee break. I'll still come round every now and then, though I will be getting that chequebook.

UK: What about Oil?

SCOTLAND: I think America was right, she's getting to that age. Maybe we ought to let her decide for herself.

UK: Sounds fair to me. Oil!

(Oil enters)

SCOTLAND: Mummy's gonna leave for a while, Oil. Just going across the street though, bit of a trial run. And your father and I were wonderin' which one of us you'd like to live with? It's alright, you can be honest.

OIL: Really?

UK: Really. It's your decision. We'll still love you either way.

OIL: Ok, cool. I choose . . . China.

SCOTLAND: What?

OIL: Yeah, he's out front. I'm just gonna go grab my helmet. Safety first, right? *(Oil kisses UK and Scotland, begins to exit)*
Love you.
UK: But why?
OIL: Like you said, dad. I'm only in it for the money!
(Lights down. End of play.)

SUPERATURAL SEMINAR
Jenny Lyn Bader

ORIGINAL PRODUCTION
The play was commissioned by Half Moon Theatre in Poughkeepsie, NY and was first presented in their Annual Ten-Minute Play Festival in June 2014. Curated by Darrah Cloud and David Simpatico. Produced by Jen Dobies. Directed by Amy Lemon Olson.

CAST
CLAUDIA: Deborah Coconis
VIV: Audrey Rapoport
ZEKE: Phillip Douglas
MIRIAM: Amy Lemon Olson
ANNIKA: Kathleen Saumure.

The playwright would like to thank John Markus for sharing his expert insight into barbecue sauce.

CHARACTERS:

CLAUDIA: a woman dedicated to her family and friends, in need of a retreat, forties to fifties.

VIV: a wry woman on her forties to fifties, maybe a little older, who's counting?

ZEKE: late twenties, a local guy.

MIRIAM: a spirit medium. Of indeterminate age, but has been at this a while.

ANNIKA: Miriam's assistant, late twenties to early thirties.

SETTING:

The Omega Institute for Holistic Studies in Rhinebeck, NY.

TIME:

The present.

An empty classroom at the Omega Institute for Holistic Studies. Two women, CLAUDIA and VIV, enter.

CLAUDIA: We're the first ones here!

VIV: We're the only ones here.

CLAUDIA: I am so excited to meet Miriam! I can't contain myself.

VIV: Yeah, neither can she.

CLAUDIA: What's that supposed to mean?

VIV: That's her schtick. Not containing herself. Containing . . . others.

CLAUDIA: It's not a schtick.

VIV: Okay, I'm just kidding around. I'm happy to be here. I want to be here.

CLAUDIA: Good.

VIV: *(glancing out the window)* Oh no! We're missing outdoor yoga!

CLAUDIA: Aw, I know you really wanted to go to that, but you know I need you here. Can you do it another time?

VIV: *(checking her schedule)* No. This is only remaining

outdoor yoga session during our whole stay at the Omega Institute for Holistic Studies . . . . Oh no, you want me to skip it don't you?

CLAUDIA: You said you were happy to be here.

VIV: Sure I am but . . . it's outdoor yoga at sunset, by the lake . . . it's a little bit of perfection. Not the big, opera house kind of perfection. Just—just what it is. That's what I came here for. A perfect moment. Not this semi-nar where—Oh no. You're really taking this seriously.

CLAUDIA: Of course I'm taking it seriously! I thought you were too! Alan took it seriously.

VIV: Of course he did, he prided himself on being eccentric.

CLAUDIA: So do you.

VIV: Not like him. You're talking about someone given to wearing hats indoors and playing "You're a Grand Old Flag" on the kazoo.

CLAUDIA: Point taken. But my parents took this seriously. They both did.

VIV: We're not your parents. Your parents gave up their doctor to see a medicine man. What if this Miriam person never even appears? I hear she's always late, and sometimes doesn't even show up.

CLAUDIA: That's because she's otherworldly.

VIV: I wasn't going to tell you this but now that she's not here . . .

(a confession:)

I only agreed to come because I misunderstood your invitation.

CLAUDIA: What?

VIV: In your email, you said the most important thing to you this weekend was attending the Supernatural Seminar and I assumed it was a typo and you didn't mean Supernatural but Super.—Natural. With a hyphen.

CLAUDIA: A hyphen?

VIV: As in, a seminar about things that are super-natural. Very, very natural. No processing, no additives . . . .

CLAUDIA: Why would I make a typo?

VIV: You're not very precise. And you know how much I love gardening. And, frankly, I didn't think a—seminar on the supernatural was even possible.

CLAUDIA: Your mind is very closed. Deeply closed. It's maddening.

VIV: No, what's maddening is when you . . .

(ZEKE enters.)

ZEKE: This the supernatural seminar?

CLAUDIA and VIV (at the same time): Yes!

(ZEKE sits down. He looks around.)

ZEKE: Hey. I'm Zeke.

CLAUDIA. I'm Claudia. That's Viv.

ZEKE: You sisters?

CLAUDIA: No. Friends. I don't have a sister. I mean. I used to. That's partly why.

ZEKE: I'm sorry.

CLAUDIA: Thanks.

ZEKE: I love Miriam.

CLAUDIA: Me too.

ZEKE: She's so great. I can't believe she's here.

VIV: She's actually not.

CLAUDIA: *(indicating VIV)* She thinks this is just—bullshit.

ZEKE: Oh yeah? That's too bad. Why'd she come?

CLAUDIA: Just to support me.

ZEKE: So nice. I always support the bullshit of my good friends. Always.

CLAUDIA: Yeah. She wants to leave to go to outdoor yoga.

ZEKE: Oh, no she doesn't. The lake's a little buggy right now since it rained yesterday? I saw two ladies trying to hold shoulder stands but nearly falling over 'cause they started slapping mosquitoes off their thighs. Seriously.

CLAUDIA: She think it's gonna be some perfect sunset moment.

ZEKE: Yeah, no it's not that.

(MIRIAM enters, her assistant ANNIKA trailing behind.)

MIRIAM: Hello, so sorry to keep you waiting . . . The energy here is divine, isn't it? All of the auras I see here are rippling, just rippling, and vibrating . . . And the spirits are so vivid too . . . I am Miriam. I know that you are here not to talk to me. You are here to talk to those who have been taken away from the visible dimension but exist in the dimension just next door. Welcome. Welcome to my seminar of the supernatural where anything can happen if we listen, by which I mean, when I listen. My assistant Annika has ginseng tea with lemon for all of us, just let her know if you want yours iced or hot. Both have a cooling, decompressing effect on the system.

ANNIKA: Or there's water.

MIRIAM: Lovely, Annika.

ANNIKA: And if anybody needs anything, I'm—

MIRIAM: *(sharply)* That's enough Annika.

ANNIKA: Right. Sorry.

(ANNIKA brings a tray around, offering drinks.)

VIV: Does she always talk to you like that?

(ANNIKA shrugs.)

MIRIAM: Let's begin.

(A beat as she takes in the room, eyelids closed, inhaling.)

There is a spirit here. Speaking softly.

(Her voice gets more high-pitched as she "does" the spirit; as the spirit:)

"I'm here. I'm here."

VIV: That's what it sounds like?

ZEKE: Jesus.

CLAUDIA: This is not the time for one of your comments. She's trying to hear a spirit who is whispering to her through molecular energy!

MIRIAM: *(smiles at CLAUDIA)* Someone here has read my book. But others have not so let me explain. Most mediums tell you what the spirit is expressing. I go further by "doing" the spirit. Your comment on how that sounds to you is not helpful as I establish my rapport. They may just be energy but they understand negativity as well as the next person. Please be more respectful.

VIV: *(amazed)* So basically, you're doing impressions of them?

MIRIAM: It's not a comedy act! I'm doing them. Not an "impression." I do an approximation of what they sound like to me. Of how I am hearing them, adjusting my voice just a little in whichever direction it . . . *(realizing)* I guess it is an impression! Actually I like that. Because an impression is not exact. Now everyone sssh . . .

ANNIKA: She needs quiet to channel.

MIRIAM: They know that, Annika! I told them "sssh"! So you "sshh"! *(to the spirit)* Where'd you go? *(as the spirit:)* "I'm here" *(as Miriam)* There. There. *(as spirit:)* "I'm here for you." *(as self)* Yes I got that. (as spirit:) "I miss you. It's so good to see you here." *(as herself:)* This is a loving spirit, people. Who is this spirit here for?

CLAUDIA: Oh God. I was expecting my parents because they loved the Omega Institute, but it sounds a little bit like my sister!

VIV: Was she really that sentimental?

MIRIAM: *(as spirit)* "I can't stand the pain I've caused you. I know you weren't expecting me to leave quite so soon . . . and to leave you with so many loose ends to tie up."

CLAUDIA: Leave so soon. That is my sister! Oh Viv this is so raw, I think I must have been hoping it would be her, but I'm just not ready.

ZEKE: I'm sorry, but actually, I think it may not be your sister.

MIRIAM: "I wish I could hold you and sing to you."

CLAUDIA: My sister loved to sing. Didn't she love to sing? Oh my god it's her.

ZEKE: Are you sure? Because . . . my mom sang in her church choir.

MIRIAM: "It was so cold the day I left but it's so warm now. I want you to be warm. To know I'm nearby."

CLAUDIA: Patty! *(to Zeke)* I'm feeling more certain. Patty always hated cold weather.

ZEKE: *(to CLAUDIA, with hostility)* My mom passed away on the coldest day of the year.

MIRIAM: This spirit has some possiiblities. *(to the spirit)*

Tell us more, please. *(as the spirit)* "If I were there I would make you your favorite food." *(as Miriam)* That's so sweet.

(MIRIAM concentrates hard, trying to hear the spirit, during the following)

CLAUDIA: *(disappointed)* Not my sister. She hated cooking.

ZEKE: *(overjoyed, to MIRIAM)* Mom!

VIV: *(not convinced, to ZEKE)* Don't you need a few more details?

ZEKE: *(to VIV)* My mom died last year, and was taken before her time, botched routine surgery, so . . .

VIV: I'm sorry!

ZEKE: So yeah, all of a sudden, unexpected, tons of loose ends—just like Miriam said. Loose ends. The paperwork, taxes, the nineteen things she was selling on eBay to pay for the surgery . . . This is all so her, especially the food thing! Cooking for me was her whole purpose. That sounds bad. I mean, she truly enjoyed making a meal. Especially for me.

VIV: But so many family members do. Why do you assume it's your mom?

ZEKE: The spirit's in this room, looking for one of us. I feel it's me.

MIRIAM: *(to the spirit)* Can you give us more? *(as spirit)* "This time of year, I would barbecue chicken for you."

ZEKE: *(crushed)* It's not my mom.

CLAUDIA: Why not?

ZEKE: Because the spirit barbecues chicken every summer, and I'm a vegetarian.

CLAUDIA: *(to VIV, suddenly hopeful again)* Do you think Patty could have learned to grill chicken in the other dimension?

VIV: I don't know how to answer that.

MIRIAM: *(as spirit)* "You aren't close to a lot of people. I'm so grateful that you let me in. You let me get so close to you." (as self:) Someone here was very close to this spirit.

VIV: "You aren't close to a lot of people but you let me in?" Couldn't that be said by most of returning spirits to most

people they might want to haunt? I've seen enough.
(to Claudia)
I'm gonna go catch the rest of yoga . . .
(VIV collects her jacket and bag, gets ready to go,)

MIRIAM: Oh dear, the spirit is getting restless. *(voice now high-pitched and urgent)* "I'm trying to speeeeeek." *(as MIRIAM, anxious:)* This spirit is agitated!

VIV: Nice meeting you all.
(from the doorway, waves to Claudia, trying to get her attention)
And Claudia I'll see you back at the . . .

MIRIAM: *(urgently)* Now it's making a sound!
(VIV turns her attention to MIRIAM. And in a clear, pure tone, Miriam starts whistling "You're a Grand Old Flag." VIV, at the door, stops in her tracks, stunned. She and CLAUDIA stare at each other)

VIV: She just . . .

MIRIAM: *(as the spirit:)* "The security code at the house is 2-9-4-5"
(A beat.)

VIV: *(shocked)* Alan?

MIRIAM: *(as spirit)* "The barbecued chicken wasn't enough proof? What is wrong with you? You need the kazoo? And a security code? Now everyone knows how to get into our house!"

VIV: It is you!

CLAUDIA: Oh my god. Alan, how are you?

VIV: Alan, I'm so sorry I didn't recognize you. You know I don't believe in this stuff.

MIRIAM: *(as spirit)* "But the chicken."

VIV: I always loved your barbecued chicken. I just thought . . . it's such a cliché . . .

MIRIAM: "My chicken is not a cliché because I grate an entire Granny Smith apple into the barbecue sauce, add five tablespoons of Crown maple syrup, and then press a cup of blackberry preserves through a sieve into the sauce."

VIV: You're giving your secret recipe now? That was your mother's recipe.

MIRIAM: *(as spirit)* "It's worth it to talk to you."

(VIV looks up, stunned)

(as spirit)

"Vivi. You don't have to go outside to get the perfect moment."

VIV: Oh Alan. You always hated nature.

MIRIAM: *(as spirit)* "I mean, you can stay where you are . . . and . . ."

VIV: Yes, yes. I see.

MIRIAM: *(as spirit)* "Just relax so I don't have to worry about you worrying about me the whole afterlife. Okay?"

VIV: Okay.

MIRIAM: *(as spirit)* "That's all. I am fine." "I am fine." *(as Miriam)* He keeps saying he's fine. *(to VIV)* That was your husband?

VIV: Yes.

MIRIAM: He really wanted to get that message through that he's fine. And he is. One of the more articulate spirits I've met in a while. In very good shape.

VIV: So I won't talk to him again?

MIRIAM: You never know. I give an advanced seminar where it may be possible. This one's for beginners. Here's my card. Go to my web site for updates.

VIV: I'm sorry I was so disruptive earlier.

CLAUDIA: I can't believe Alan showed up. It's just like him. Always so reliable.

VIV: I know.

CLAUDIA: *(to Miriam)* But can't you let them talk for longer? Alan likes a good conversation. We came all the way here for a little quality time.

MIRIAM: *(annoyed)* That was quality time. You're asking for more quantity time.

VIV: Claudia it's good, I'm . . .

CLAUDIA: I just want you to have what you deserve.

(VIV nods.)

MIRIAM: And a new spirit has joined us. *(as spirit)* "I'm

sorry, I'm sorry."

CLAUDIA: Ha! This has got to be Patty. She was always late to any class. Honey, you don't have to be so sorry! You were terrible to me a lot of times but it's all right. I forgive you.

ZEKE: This one's not my mom. She never apologized for shit. *(to Annika:)* Could I get a little more tea?

(ANNIKA goes to get tea.)

MIRIAM: Annika as usual you are moving around the room wrong. If you go in straight lines instead of circles I can't hear the spirit.

ANNIKA: . . . That's it, Miriam . . . I can't take it anymore . . . I quit!

MIRIAM: What?

ANNIKA: You communicate through the ether with the other dimension and yet you are a complete control freak about every little thing in our dimension! The color of your tea, the size of each lemon wedge, whether I walk straight or in circles. And your spiritual work . . . what are you doing with it? (to VIV) She's never gotten a security code before or anything like that. Usually her readings could apply to nineteen people. That was the best one she's ever done, and you know what? She's as shocked as you are. Sure she has some weird intuitive gift, she can guess the number of jellybeans in a jar, but she has no clue how it works or what it means. Maybe she'll figure it out one day and maybe she won't, but I don't have the patience to find out while dealing with her relentless demands. I'm done.

ZEKE: Wow.

CLAUDIA: Good for you!

MIRIAM: And you felt the need to say all that now, during the supernatural seminar at the Omega Institute, where holistic practitioners journey from all over the world?

ANNIKA: I'm sorry. Wow, that was really inappropriate.

VIV: Beyond inappropriate.

CLAUDIA: I don't know. Sometimes people just snap . . . she's in touch with her anger. And she's right! Some of this is feeling not good to me. I'm starting to have questions.

VIV: *(startled)* You are? After that?

CLAUDIA: It's not enough to have a gift, it's how you use it. And how you treat others.

ZEKE: Totally. This is starting to feel like class-A bullshit.

VIV: But the security code . . .

CLAUDIA: Lucky guess. Like jellybeans in a jar.

VIV: But I just had the . . .

MIRIAM: *(still absorbed in her reading)* Typically an outburst like that would drive a spirit away but this one here is getting louder.

ANNIKA: Because you continue to abound with insane paradoxes.

CLAUDIA: Patty was always loud.

(As ANNIKA is putting down the tea tray on her way out:)

MIRIAM: *(as spirit:)* "Listen . . . I think about you and I'm so pleased by how you turned out. I'm sorry I used to call you Squidgyface when you were in grade school. It was your brother's idea and I shouldn't have followed. You deserved a better nickname."

ANNIKA: *(stunned)* Mom?

VIV: Your mother called you Squidgyface?

ANNIKA: *(chastened, comes back and sits down)* Yep. *(to MIRIAM:)* Hi mom.

CLAUDIA: I'm so surprised she can't conjure up Patty, who seems like she'd be so easy to get here, y'know? It's a disappointment. Do you have your yoga mat? *(VIV nods)*

VIV: You have yours?

CLAUDIA: *(nods)* And I have bug repellent. Ready to go?

VIV: Yeah. I'm ready.

CURTAIN

TEEMING SHORE

Nick Gandiello

ORIGINAL PRODUCTION

August 26, 2014
Summer Shorts presented by Crashbox Theater
Company
Meredith Jones, Artistic Director
Brittany Crowell, Managing Director
The Clarion Theatre, NYC

Directed by Sharone Halevy

CAST
JOSEPH: David Gazzo
MICHAEL: Greg Carere
MARY: Sarah Cook

CHARACTERS:

JOSEPH: Twenty-one. Sensitive, thoughtful—sometimes to the point of indulgence.

MICHAEL: Twenty-seven. Joseph's brother. Aggressive, tough, thoughtful though guarded, and loving of his family.

MARY: Their aunt. Of age to have a teenaged daughter. When we meet her, she is in a fragile state, but is smiling and exclaiming and loving her way through it.

TIME:

Summer, 2014.

PLACE:

On the border.

Notes: Slashes indicate overlap. Absent punctuation is intentional.

Oh, I dream a highway back to you, love
A winding ribbon with a band of gold
A silver vision: come and rest my soul
I dream a highway back to you
—Gillian Welch, *I Dream a Highway*

Harsh white sunlight on rust and cream sand and dirt. A crude fence of strings running from thin metal pole to another. Small American flags are arranged on the fence. The light falls on JOSEPH and MICHAEL; both young men are armed; guns holstered and easily accessible. Tucked in shirts; work jeans, work gloves.

Michael is staring at Joseph, his mouth hanging open. Joseph gestures as if to find and explanation, but:

MICHAEL: I'm trying to understand what put that in your mind just now.

JOSEPH: If you don't wanna talk about it, Mike.

MICHAEL: I don't know if I wanna talk about it, I wanna know what put it in your mind to ask about Uncle Andrew.

JOSEPH: I don't keep track of my mind like that. Do you keep track of your mind like that?

Aunt Mary's bringing our lunch in five minutes, maybe I thought of Uncle Andrew.

MICHAEL: Well I find it disturbing, the question you asked. I got an important job to do here and you go on with a disturbing question like that.

I'mma keep watching that hill. Looks to me there's an American flag still need to go up.

(Joseph hops to and begins unfolding a flag, delicately. Michael begins a lion's prowl, eyes surveying a stretch of land in front of him.)

MICHAEL: They can't see these little flags down that hill.

JOSEPH: Okay, Mike.

MICHAEL: You go on and put that big flag up, let'em see it.

JOSEPH: Alright, Mike.

(Michael stops, observes his brother and the flag.)

MICHAEL: You mad at me now?

JOSEPH: You trying to make me mad at you now?

MICHAEL: Don't give me sass, okay, I get enough sass every night I come home, okay?

Joe, it's not that I don't care about your feelings.

It's that we're here doing something for the Movement and my mind wasn't, engaged with, ya know, Uncle Andrew, all that.

JOSEPH: If your mind is engaged with it now? If I engaged your mind with it now? Then:

I just wanna know: Who found him?

Was it Christina or Aunt Mary found him? / No one told me.

MICHAEL: Fuck's sake, man! Why you wanna know an ugly thing like that?

JOSEPH: Could I just know if you know? If you know who found him, / because no one told me.

MICHAEL: Why would I wanna know an ugly thing like that?

You letting the flag touch the ground, man!
Fuck's sake, let me do my job and watch this hill!
(Joseph struggles to arrange the flag.
There is a rattling somewhere nearby.
Only Michael seems to notice it.)

JOSEPH: It's a big flag, Mike.

MICHAEL: Huh, what?

JOSEPH: I can't do it myself.

MICHAEL: I swear man, you'd still make me tie your shoes
    with bunny ears if I let you.
    Make me pick you up outside your college classes for a
    piggy-back home, I let you.
    If any'a them Illegals come sneaking by while you dis-
    tracting me, it's on you.
    If Dad gets word we let an Illegal sneak by, I'm telling
    him it's on you.
    (They work on the flag together for a moment. As it's
    just about secure:)

MICHAEL: (*Sincerely*)
    Why you wanna know an ugly thing like that, Joe?
    (They finish the flag. Michael goes back to his prowl
    and Joseph takes up a posted watch of the hill under:)

JOSEPH: I guess I see it like this:
    There's a world where Christina . . . found her dad, like
    that.
    Or there's a world where Aunt Mary found him like that.
    And we talk, Mike, we talk like we don't live in either
    world. We talk like neither world exists.

MICHAEL: What kind of talk is there to have?

JOSEPH: I don't know—for comfort? Healing.

MICHAEL: The man was cleaning his weapon. He wasn't
    careful, cleaning his weapon, and. And we couldn't have
    an open casket. How you gonna heal that by talking?

JOSEPH: They should know they can come to me. To us,
    they should know they can come to us.

MICHAEL: They do know that, and they would if they
    wanted, so maybe they don't want to.
    Christina's gotta focus on Senior Year. Come September,

she's in charge of Sports Nite for the girls. Aunt Mary wants to help her with college applications. And she's got the fundraising for the choir. Not your job to bring up the worst thing ever happened to them and shove it in they face every time you feel like it.

JOSEPH: I just thought. We're out here. It's quiet, peaceful. Away from everybody.

She's coming with our lunch, and

MICHAEL: Do not go bringing that up with her! Especially here. Especially with the job we doing here.

You watching that hill?

JOSEPH: Yeah, man.

MICHAEL: You really watching or is your mind somewhere else?

JOSEPH: I'm really watching, man.

MICHAEL: You looking for movement or just a human shape?

JOSEPH: I said I'm really watching.

MICHAEL: Because you know they could be disguised, right?

Like we out here for reflection time when we got a job to do.

(The rattle again, closer.)

MICHAEL: Fuck, man, you hear that?

JOSEPH: (*Mocking*) Hear what, an Illegal?

MICHAEL: Nah, man, a rattlesnake. You ain't hear that rattle?

JOSEPH: Too busy watching.

MICHAEL: Second time I heard that thing. I'mma kill it if I see it.

(A few breaths, watching the hill.)

JOSEPH: He wasn't cleaning his weapon.

MICHAEL: What?

JOSEPH: Mike. Mikey. He wasn't cleaning his weapon.

You know how Uncle Andrew . . . was. And I want Aunt Mary, I want Christina to be able to—say that. That they know that. And that's it okay and that there wasn't a thing they could do. I want them to be able to / acknowledge that.

(Michael abruptly slices through the air toward his brother; he is close into his face.)

MICHAEL: Listen to me now.

Not everyone is sensitive like you. Not everyone finds words for it like you.

You don't obligate someone you love to grab at they feelings and rip 'em out and hand them to you. You wanna comfort them? You wanna help them heal?

Then you let them deal with it in they own way.

Do not bring it up when she gets here.

JOSEPH: When am I allowed to bring it up?!

MICHAEL: Keep your voice down.

JOSEPH: When's it gonna matter that I feel something and / I need to say something?

MICHAEL: Keep your voice down—and stop thinking of yourself! Your feelings aren't at the center of the world! Now don't stand there like a puppy just got kicked. Don't—don't be sad, Joe, fuck—

You remember what dad told us to say on this line here? *(Joseph nods.)*

MICHAEL: So say it. Say it so you remember what we're doing here.

JOSEPH: 'Turn back or you will be shot.'

MICHAEL: That's right. Turn back or you will be shot! And we have to be ready to do the job. We are in a crisis here. There's free-loaders and drug dealers coming across this line, with they own weapons, onto your neighbor's property. They trying to cross this line into your family's home. Keep your mind on the job. Stand up straight. Compose your face, Joey. Straighten your spine. Keep your eyes focused.

Compose your face, Joe.

JOSEPH: It's eating at me.

MICHAEL: Eating what?

JOSEPH: I lay in my bed at night, sweating, thinking of him. I catch myself drifting at the wheel, wondering: How many days do I remember wrong? How many times was he trying to tell me something and I wasn't listening?

(Sincerely)

How long until I can say something?

MICHAEL: You've always been the one with his heart right
below the surface.

But Aunt Mary gets through her days keeping her heart
further down than that.

You'll break her heart if you try to bring it up to where
you keep it.

You hear me? You'll kill her, you talk to her like that.

You woulda heard him if he was trying to tell you something, Joey.

(A voice, abruptly from nearby.)

MARY: Boys? Boys?

JOSEPH: Over here, Aunt Mary, follow the fence!

MICHAEL: Keep quiet on it, please.

The boys try to compose themselves.

*(Aunt Mary comes along—work jeans, work boots,
gun holstered—carrying some bags for lunch.)*

MARY: There could not have been a hotter week for this,
huh? I am sweating in—in places I cannot say. Hi
sweetheart.

MICHAEL: Hey Aunt Mary.

(She kisses his forehead.)

MARY: Oo, you sweating too, and you just got beer coming
out of your pores, Michael, I swear.

(She kisses Joseph.)

Hi baby.

Oh you boys. I am so proud of you, doing such a good
job—your father is so proud of you.

Now I brought chicken salad with the apples and potato
salad with some bacon mixed in. You can fight over who
gets what.

But I got some troubling news.

MICHAEL: What, what's the matter?

MARY: Mr. Davis is gone into hiding.

MICHAEL: Hiding?

MARY: He took the YouTube video down, he took the
Facebook page down, he canceled his interviews with

Fox News—

MICHAEL: What?

MARY: I know but that's the world we live in. A man starts a movement for his country and then fears for his own security.

Sent word to the members that he's 'going black.'

So we don't have the press we thought we would but you just keep on doing what's right.

Don't need to be famous to do what's right.

That's what I tell your cousin.

I tell her Michael and Joe are standing guard. Michael and Joe are out there protecting us.

When she'll listen. She's busy getting the uniforms together for the Sports Nite.

And maybe that's better.

Oh well, listen to me! You get me out that house for five minutes and I jabber away!

I gotta get back up to the station but—

JOSEPH: (*Urgently*) Aunt Mary—

MARY: / Yes baby?

MICHAEL: Shut your mouth!

JOSEPH: I just / want to say

MARY: What on earth?

MICHAEL: Don't listen to him—Shut your mouth I said!

JOSEPH: I just want to say that I believe in Heaven,

MARY: You

JOSEPH: That I truly believe in Heaven.

And I don't think it's a place, really, or

MARY: Why are you

JOSEPH: or that's it, like, infinite joy?

I think it's absence of pain.

Absence of any pain or confusion.

And you don't have to do a thing to get there, you just go.

That's what I truly believe and I wanted to say it to you, so.

MARY: (*Moved*) What has gotten into you?

(*She goes over to him, touches his face flightily,*

brushes a strand of hair, straightens his collar.)
My Lord, Joe, what has gotten into you?
*(She pats his chest. She looks from her one nephew
to the other. She looks out toward the hill.)*
Hard to be sad when there's a sky like that, huh?
You boys. We're all so proud of you.
I'll be at the station til sundown, you enjoy that lunch.
*(She goes off quickly. Joseph and Michael stand,
still, silent for a few moments.)*

MICHAEL: Joe, go on home.

JOSEPH: Home?

MICHAEL: Go on, man. I'm not rejecting you or whatever,
I'm saying you shouldn't be out here.

JOSEPH: I'm not gonna leave you alone.

MICHAEL: Then tell dad to come down. Tell him get his
rifle and come down here.
He's the one signed us up for this.
*(Joseph moves toward his brother. He hesitates then
puts a hand on his shoulder.)*

MICHAEL: I'll be alright. She's gonna be alright. Christina's
gonna be alright.

JOSEPH: Mike, I don't wanna leave you here.

MICHAEL: Gotta watch for movement, not just human
shape.
*(Joseph nods. He takes one of the lunch bags and
starts heading out.)*

MICHAEL: Hey Joe don't come back tomorrow morning.
Don't need you here tomorrow either so don't come back.
(Joseph leaves.)

JOSEPH: Aunt Mary! Wait up!
*(Michael watches the horizon. he rattling starts up
again, closer.)*

MICHAEL: Ah, hell—WHERE YOU AT? HUH?
I find you, I'mma kill you, just you wait.
(The rattling goes on.)

MICHAEL: Just you wait.
*(Michael begins his prowl again. The rattling con-
tinues. He breathes heavier and heavier as he scans*

the landscape ahead of him—then abruptly stops,
and looks up to the Heavens desperately.)

End of play

TOO TOO SOLID FLESH
Peter M. Floyd

ORIGINAL PRODUCTION
The Boston Theater Marathon XVI, May 11, 2014,
by Hovey Players

Directed by J. Mark Baumhardt

CAST
CHLOE: Alexandra Corwin
ISABEL: Brooke Casanova
MAX: Michael Carr

CHARACTERS:
>CHLOE: female, twenty to thirty-five.
>ISABEL: female, twenty to thirty-five.
>MAX: male, twenty to thirty-five.

SETTING:
>A table or booth in a bar, after midnight.

A bar. CHLOE, ISABEL and MAX sit at a counter, or around the table. Each has a pilsner in front of them. ISABEL's is about half-filled with beer, CHLOE's is nearly empty, and MAX's appears to be untouched. They are all drunk, especially CHLOE. ISABEL has her hand stretched out on the table/bar, and MAX casually holds it with his own, as boyfriends do. CHLOE is expostulating, and is the center of attention. We begin in the midst of a conversation.

CHLOE: No, listen. I'm serious.

ISABEL: Sure.

MAX: 'Course you are.

CHLOE: Fuck you, I am! This is a real, honest-to-shit scholarly theory. Creation is creation, right?

MAX: Can't argue with that, Chloe. That's some profound thinking there.

CHLOE: Creation is creation. Whether you're God or a poet. So, here's the thing: whenever a writer, an artist makes something, it becomes real. The word is made flesh. Right?

ISABEL: I honestly have no idea what you're trying to say.

CHLOE: So, let's say a writer creates a character. That character then comes into existence. See?

ISABEL: No.

CHLOE: Jesus. Okay, do this. Pick a character.

MAX: What?

CHLOE: A character. A fucking literary character. Anyone.

ISABEL: Fine. Um, I don't know . . . *Hamlet?*

CHLOE: *Hamlet.* Of course it's *Hamlet.* It's always *Hamlet.*

A thousand years of fucking English literature, and some-how it always comes back to fucking *Hamlet*.

ISABEL: Fine, I'll pick someone else.

CHLOE: No, too late. Actually, Hamlet's a good example.

(She takes a drink.)

MAX: . . . Of what?

(Pause.)

MAX: Chloe?

CHLOE: Is this Sam Adams? It doesn't taste like Sam Adams.

ISABEL: What is Hamlet an example of?

CHLOE: What? Oh, right. So, William Shakespeare wrote *Hamlet*. Okay? He creates this character. *(as Shake-speare)* "Here's me writing about this tight-assed Dane whose life is going down the crapper." And so, poof! Somewhere out there, Hamlet comes into existence. Like, a real person.

MAX: Hamlet is real?

CHLOE: As real as the nose on your chin.

ISABEL: Right. I mean, there was a historical Hamlet, wasn't there? Shakespeare took this story from like Danish history . . .

CHLOE: I'm not talking about fucking historical fucking Hamlet. I'm talking about fucking William fucking Shakespeare's fucking *Hamlet*.

ISABEL: Shakespeare's *Hamlet*?

CHLOE: Yeah.

MAX: From the play? With the iambic pentameter and everything?

CHLOE: Yes! When you create a work of fiction, you liter-ally create that world. It's out there. Somewhere. You are that world's god. And you don't even know it! Some-where there's a world where *Hamlet* really happened, and Shakespeare is god of that world. There's another world where Pride and Prejudice is true, and Jane Aus-ten is goddess there. And somewhere, in some pathetic shithole, there's a world where *Twilight* is real, and the god of that world is whoever the fuck that person is who wrote Twilight.

ISABEL: You really believe that?

CHLOE: It's a working theory. Just bear with me. So, get this. Imagine you're Hamlet.

MAX: Why?

CHLOE: Just do it. You're Hamlet, and your life is suckville. You're like, what is this? *(as Hamlet)* "My uncle kills my dad, my mom's a total whore, my girlfriend's this suicidal hippy-dippy bitch, and pretty much everyone I know is getting stabbed or poisoned. What's up with that?" You got a life like that, you'd pray to God, and say, "Hey, God, why does my life have to be this frickin' vale of tears? What's up with that shit?"

ISABEL: Not me, I'm an agnostic.

CHLOE: No. No agosti- agnozzig- *(She can't make it through the word.)* None of this not believing. This world has a god. I told you that. Remember? Remember who it is?

ISABEL and MAX: Shakespeare.

CHLOE: Right. Glad to see you're paying attention. So, imagine this scenario. Hamlet meets God, who's Shakespeare, and he's like, what the fuck, dude? Why'd you make my life such a mess? And what would Shakespeare say?

MAX: I don't know.

CHLOE: What could he say? "Sorry, guy, I had to make a your life be a shitstorm so that people could enjoy a good tragedy. No hard feelings." I mean, can you imagine that? Your life is a fucking carbonated cesspool just so a bunch of other people can be entertained.

ISABEL: Chloe . . .

CHLOE: And it's not just *Hamlet*, not just Shakespeare. Look at, what, Peter Rabbit. Peter Fucking Rabbit! His creator-goddess is Beatrix Potter and she sends that psychopathic bastard Mr. MacGregor after him. Why? Just to give the kids a laugh. Is that crazy, or what?

MAX: Yes. I think I can definitely say that that is crazy.

CHLOE: You think I'm wrong? You can't prove I'm wrong.

ISABEL: You know, there's something in what you're saying . . .

MAX: What?

ISABEL: I'm not saying you're right, but maybe you're not wrong, either.

MAX: Uh, Isabel, how much have you been drinking? 'Cause I think I can say with confidence that Chloe is pretty damn wrong here. I mean, she hit "wrong" ten minutes ago and just kept going. She's so wrong that even if everything she says is right, it'd still be dead wrong.

ISABEL *(still to CHLOE)*: Wait, wait, listen, listen. If what you're saying is true. And I'm saying "If."

MAX: Yay for "If"!

ISABEL: If what you're saying is true, then every writer is potentially a mass-murderer. I mean, if you're like, Stephen King, you'd be the most horrible god ever.

CHLOE: That's true.

MAX: It is not! None of this is. What is true is that you are very drunk . . .

ISABEL: I mean, the best god of all would be a crappy romance writer, because she'd always make everything come out happy at the end. Do you realize what this would mean? Good literature would be evil!

CHLOE: Well, some good literature has happy endings. Like, um . . . *(Thinks)* Nope, drawing a blank.

MAX: *Oliver Twist.*

CHLOE: Right, *Oliver Twist.* Oh, and *The Cat in the Hat.*

ISABEL: Jeez, I'm glad I'm not a writer, then. I couldn't bear that kind of responsibility.

CHLOE: Well, maybe it's not just literary works that create these realities.

ISABEL: What do you mean?

CHLOE: Here's where the theory gets really cool and twisted. Maybe it's any kind of tale you tell. If you make something up, pretend something's real, then Abraca-fucking-dabra! That thing becomes true.

MAX: You're really taking this as far as you can go, aren't you?

CHLOE *(to ISABEL)*: Well, take Max.

MAX: Me?

ISABEL: Max?

CHLOE: Twenty minutes ago, this douchebag tries to hit on you, right?

ISABEL: Right.

MAX: What? Are you calling me a douchebag?

CHLOE: And you have no interest in being hit on by any guy, let alone one who's operating under the influence of douchebaggery.

ISABEL: Of course not.

MAX: You're not talking about me, are you? Did someone hit on you when I was in the can?

CHLOE: So you say . . .

ISABEL: *(to the imaginary douchebag)* "Jeez, I'd love to have a drink with you, but I'm waiting for my boyfriend Max. He'll be along shortly."

MAX: Okay, so I was in the can.

ISABEL: *(still to the douchebag)* "Sorry. You seem real nice. Bye."

MAX: You didn't have to tell him he seemed nice.

CHLOE: Well, you lied. People do that.

ISABEL: Right . . .

CHLOE: You don't have a boyfriend named Max.

MAX: Wait, what? Yes, she does. Hello, Max the boyfriend is right here.

ISABEL: Well, obviously. It just seemed the best way to get rid of him.

MAX: Wait, what do you mean, "obviously"?

ISABEL: I mean, if I'd said I'd had a girlfriend, he'd probably try to pick both of us up.

CHLOE: So, you created this fictional boyfriend Max. You even bought him a Sam Adams.

ISABEL: Yeah, just to make sure Señor Douchebag really believed Max existed.

MAX: Hey, stop it! Very funny, ha ha. I don't exist. Now—

ISABEL: I figure I'll have it myself when I finish this one.

CHLOE: Now I'm saying that by telling that lie, you conjured an actual Max into existence.

MAX: What?

ISABEL: What?

CHLOE: You made a little tale about boyfriend Max, so somewhere you've created an actual Max, who is your boyfriend.

MAX: That's fucked up.

ISABEL: Whoa, that's fucked up.

MAX: Okay, this is getting a little too meta for me. I think—
(Max reaches for his beer, but seems unable to pick it up. His hand slides off it.)

ISABEL: So, where is this Max? If he's my alleged boy-friend, he can't be in some other universe, 'cause I'm not there.

MAX: What the hell is up with this glass?

CHLOE: Good point. Maybe when you conjured him up, you put him in a place where there's another version of yourself.
(MAX is now trying to lift the glass with both his hands, with no success.)

ISABEL: Well, wherever he is, I hope he's happy.
(She reaches for MAX's beer, picking it up without effort. She takes a drink.)

CHLOE: Well, just say he's happy then. You invented him, right? Say, Max is fuckin' happy.

ISABEL: Max is fuckin' happy!

MAX: *(suddenly relaxed)* Hey, you know, this is kinda cool.

ISABEL: Max is blissed to the max!
(MAX is now speechless with delight, nearly having an orgasm.)

CHLOE: You're nice to Max. You're a good girlfriend.

ISABEL: Yeah, I don't know. This feels weird. If there was a Max, and he knew I was manipulating him like this, he'd be pretty pissed.

MAX *(suddenly furious)*: You're god-damned right I'm pissed! What gives you the right to—

CHLOE: Hey, he should be happy you didn't have his uncle kill his dad, unlike some gods I could mention.

ISABEL: Yeah, but I could have him totally be head over heels for his true love, right?
(MAX gazes at ISABEL, his heart melting.)

CHLOE: Dummy, you're his true love. He's your boyfriend, right?

ISABEL: Oh, shit, that's right. But I can't be his girlfriend, I'm your girlfriend.

MAX: It's all right, honey, I'd be willing to share. I just want you to be happy.

CHLOE: Kind of a conundrum there, huh?

ISABEL: Yeah. *(She checks her watch.)* Holy crap, it's half past midnight. We gotta get home. We have to be at Beatrice's thing tomorrow morning.

CHLOE: Yeah, let's go. *(She and CHLOE stand up.)* God, my head is spinning circles. I'm gonna have a king-sized hangover tomorrow.

ISABEL: Drink like three glasses of water before you go to bed. That'll rehydrate you. So what happens to Max?

CHLOE: What?

ISABEL: What happens to Max when I've forgotten him?

CHLOE: A very good question. One of two things, I think. Either he disappears like that *(she snaps her fingers)* or he spends the rest of eternity alone, pining for you. Kinda sucks either way.

ISABEL: Yeah. Too bad for Max.

(They exit. As they do, the lights go down, except for one shining only on MAX, now the sole occupant of his own Universe.)

MAX: Fuck.

The light on MAX goes out.

TRANSFERRING KYLE
Jonathan Cook

ORIGINAL PRODUCTION

The first production of 'Transferring Kyle' was produced by the Playwrights' Round Table and took place at the John & Rita Lowndes Shakespeare Center in Orlando, FL on July 25, 2014. It was directed by Carol Jacqueline Palumbo and starred Stephanie Leibowitz, BeeJay Aubertin Clinton, and Craig Raymond.

> KYLE: Male of any adult age. Unkempt and reckless kind of guy. Not on the right path in life.
> NEW KYLE: Male of similar age to KYLE. KYLE'S replacement. Only recently came into existence, so he's a little slow but quickly learning about this thing called life. Does not need to look anything like KYLE.
> TINA: Female of any adult age. NEW KYLE'S caseworker. Professional-looking woman with a business attitude, but not very patient.

TIME:

> December 18, 2013.

PLACE:

> Mayor's Income, Tennessee—The residence of KYLE HENLEY.

SCENE: The stage is the living room of KYLE HENLEY. There is a chair with a small end table next to it. On top of the table rests a framed picture of KYLE and his wife. AT RISE: KYLE is hanging out in his house, sitting in the chair. Maybe he's having a drink, playing a video game, or browsing a TV Guide. TINA, a professional-looking female dressed in a suit, enters with a respectable-looking man, NEW KYLE.

TINA: This is the place.
NEW KYLE: Nice! Much bigger than I expected considering I don't have any kids.
TINA: Three bedrooms. Two and a half bathrooms.
NEW KYLE: Half bathroom?
TINA: You'll understand as soon as the transfer is complete. Just have a seat and—
KYLE: Who are you people?
TINA: *(Finally noticing KYLE sitting in the room.)*
 . . . and . . . and that's not good.

KYLE: *(Rises.)*What're you doing in my house?

NEW KYLE: Is that the . . . ?

TINA: Yes.

NEW KYLE: I thought you said that part was already taken care of.

TINA: It was supposed to be.

KYLE: Hey! I'm standing right here! Somebody tell me what's going on.

TINA: Did you speak with a man earlier?

KYLE: What man?

TINA: Harold. Dark hair. Very slender. Probably wearing a plaid suit. I'm not sure why he has this thing for plaid. Whatever. Never mind. I need to make a phone call. *(She gets a phone from her suit pocket.)*

KYLE: Did my wife do this? Did she sell our house without telling me or something?

TINA: Phone call. Just need to make a phone call. I'll be with you in a sec. *(TINA exits. KYLE and NEW KYLE stare at each other in an awkward silence.)*

NEW KYLE: Chairs, huh?

KYLE: Excuse me?

NEW KYLE: Chairs. They're all different. Nice places to sit. Well, you can sit anywhere really. But chairs are actually meant for sitting.

KYLE: Tell me what's going on here, okay.

NEW KYLE: I can't. It's not my place to say.

KYLE: Right. This is MY place. And I want you to say.

NEW KYLE: It's just that . . . it wasn't supposed to be like this.

KYLE: Oh? Then how was it supposed to be?

NEW KYLE: You're not supposed to be here. You were scheduled to be gone hours ago. Transferred as they say.

KYLE: As who says?

NEW KYLE: You're done. Alright? Your time is over. I hate to put it so bluntly, but I think you deserve an honest answer. You're being replaced.

KYLE: What does that even mean?

NEW KYLE: I'm your replacement.

KYLE: Replacement to what!?

NEW KYLE: To life.

KYLE: Huh?

NEW KYLE: Tina is going to have to explain everything.

KYLE: Who the Hell is Tina?

NEW KYLE: She's the one on the phone. My caseworker. I don't know anything else. I mean, I literally just came into existence about thirty minutes ago.

(NEW KYLE makes a "coming into existence" sound with his mouth. *Intepret that however you like*)

KYLE: I'm not in the mood for this.

TINA: *(Enters.)* Alright. I just spoke with Harold and, according to him, there was a bit of a mix up. He apparently had the wrong time marked on his calendar for your exit interview, which makes this very awkward.

KYLE: Listen up, you two lunatics. It's time for both of you to get the Hell outta here, okay.

TINA: Can I speak with you a moment?

KYLE: No. You can tell that crazy-ass "replacement" story to the police after I call them. How about that?

TINA: *(Frustratingly turns to NEW KYLE.)* You told him?

NEW KYLE: Sorry.

TINA: You went over the orientation manual didn't you?

NEW KYLE: I did.

TINA: Then you should have read that you're not supposed to—

NEW KYLE: I know. I know. I'm sorry.

TINA: Whatever. Never mind.

(To KYLE.)

Kyle?

KYLE and NEW KYLE: Yes?

TINA: *(To NEW KYLE.)*

Not you. TINA (cont.)

(To KYLE.)

You. Here's the deal. And I'm going to break this down as simply as I can. This is the new Kyle. He's here to take your place. And you're coming with me. You don't even need to pack or anything.

KYLE: I'm not going anywhere with you, lady.

TINA: Listen to me. This isn't a new concept. My department has been handling transfers for centuries. Here's what it comes down to. You suck at life. You have no motivation. You make no contribution to society. And you haven't inspired anyone for over a decade. Shall I continue?

KYLE: I contribute.

TINA: Let's not kid ourselves here.

KYLE: I do.

TINA: See. This is why they shouldn't let me do exit interviews. It's already been decided. Your transfer isn't up for debate.

NEW KYLE: Dude, don't make this weird. Just go.

KYLE: You shut your face! Okay!?

TINA: Just settle down.

KYLE: No. This is stupid. You think just because you walk up in here wearing your little fancy suit that I'm going to buy into this? I'm not an idiot. People don't get replaced in life. That doesn't happen.

TINA: It does happen. Even to people you know.

KYLE: Who?

TINA: What?

KYLE: Go on. Tell me who. If this is so common, then go ahead and—

TINA: Valerie Campbell.

KYLE: You replaced Valerie?

TINA: Not me. A coworker did. She wasn't my client.

KYLE: But Valerie is very successful. She even heads the Film-makers For a Cause group. They're non-profit. They visit the local high schools and get students involved. She won an award only a few months ago.

TINA: She IS very successful. Now.

KYLE: What is that supposed to mean?

TINA: It means four years ago, she was in the same place you are now. Being transferred.

KYLE: That's complete BS.

TINA: Robert Downey Jr.

KYLE: Iron Man?

TINA: Client of mine. Replaced him in 2005. He was a complete waste of space throughout the nineties. Now look at him.

KYLE: *(Regarding NEW KYLE.)*

But this guy? This guy doesn't even look like me.

TINA: Yeah. I know. There was a time long ago that we tried to match physical characteristics, but it got to be too much of a hassle. DNA is just so damn precise. Now we use the aura instead.

NEW KYLE: Ooh, that was mentioned in the manual. It's what changes the perception of you to others.

KYLE: Why are you talking!?

TINA: The aura is what allows new Kyle to blend in with your current life. Until the transfer is complete, he'll be emitting the aura and, like he said, it permanently alters how people perceive you.

KYLE: He's doing this right now?

TINA: Yes.

(NEW KYLE gives KYLE a proud look. He's proud of his aura.)

TINA: It's completely harmless though. It just changes photographs and memories. That sort of thing. Look for yourself.

(TINA points to a framed picture of KYLE with his wife. The picture has been altered and now shows NEW KYLE with his wife.)

KYLE: *(Looking at the picture.)* Woh, woh, woh . . . what's happening!? We took this photo three years ago. How did you . . . ? What's he doing in this picture?!

TINA: I told you.

NEW KYLE: The aura.

TINA: It's spreading over everything and very soon it's going to load him with all of your memories. And every memory that people have of you . . . they'll now remember those moments with new Kyle instead.

KYLE: Even my own mother?

TINA: Family. Friends. Coworkers. Basically, anyone you've

been in contact with in your entire life.

(Off of KYLE'S look.)

It's a lot to take in. And I don't do exits, so I'm sorry that I can't paint a pretty picture for you like Harold would be doing right now.

(Her phone rings.)

Speaking of Harold. Excuse me.

(She answers her phone.)

Do you know how inconvenient this is? Sorry isn't going to cut it. I'm reporting you to Frank. No, not mailroom Frank. Frank with the cane—

(She exits.)

KYLE: This is unreal.

NEW KYLE: Yeah. I know.

KYLE: I have to be dreaming.

NEW KYLE: Nope.

KYLE: Am I really THAT worthless?

NEW KYLE: From what I understand . . . yeah.

KYLE: Holy shit. Maybe I am.

NEW KYLE: So, is your wife hot?

KYLE: I'm sorry?

NEW KYLE: Wait, not YOUR wife. I meant to say MY wife. Is my wife hot?

KYLE: I don't want you talking about my wife.

NEW KYLE: *(Picks up the framed picture.)* Oh, wow! Look at her. That's gonna be fun.

KYLE: Give me that! It's mine.

NEW KYLE: I'm in that picture with MY wife. It's mine!

(They struggle over the picture as TINA enters.)

TINA: *(Still speaking in phone, raising her voice over their argument.)*

Damn it, Harold! Whatever. Never mind. Just let me call you back.

(Breaking up the two KYLES.)

Cool it. Both of you!

NEW KYLE: Old Kyle started it!

KYLE: No! Do NOT start calling me "old Kyle".

TINA: We need to get moving. Come on.

Lawrence Harbison

KYLE: This is bullshit. There are plenty of people that need to be replaced in life other than me! I can make you a list three miles long of people who are a lot worse, okay.

TINA: You're missing the point.

KYLE: Mikey Winchester. Now there's a worthless sonofabitch. Totally unmotivated and always reeks of piss and wine. He lives off of 8th and Main. And . . . uhh . . . Billy. Yeah, Billy. I forgot his last name, but he's a complete insignificant little douche bag.

TINA: The point is that Kyle Henley has a purpose.

KYLE: I'm Kyle Henley.

TINA: Not anymore.
(Points to NEW KYLE.)
This is Kyle Henley. And, if things go as planned, this Kyle Henley will accomplish the things in life that he's meant for.

KYLE: Just tell me what I need to do.

TINA: The decision has already been made.

KYLE: Who makes that call?

TINA: Management.

KYLE: But I can change.

TINA: Let me fill you in on a little secret. You're not the original Kyle either.
(Off of KYLE'S look.)
That's right. There was a time when YOU were the new Kyle. The fresh start we hoped would steer this soul into the appropriate direction.

KYLE: That's not true.

TINA: Yes. You're also a replacement. Like I said, this happens to people all the time. Sometimes it can take multiple transfers to get people on the right track.

KYLE: When? I don't remember anything like that.

TINA: Of course not. It would be impossible for you to live a normal life with memories like that. Just like new Kyle here won't remember any of this either. As soon as we're gone, the transfer will be complete. Things will be set in motion on the destined path.

NEW KYLE: I'm gonna miss you, Tina.

TINA: No. You won't. Just go sit down and wait over there or something.

NEW KYLE: I will though.

TINA: Whatever. Never mind. Old Kyle, we need to go.

(Off of KYLE'S depressed look.)

Okay. Sorry. Human being formerly known as Kyle, we need to go.

KYLE: That's it then?

TINA: Come on.

KYLE: Is it gonna hurt?

TINA: Excuse me?

KYLE: Where ever you're taking me. This whole transfer thing.

TINA: Basically, you'll just become non-existent. I don't really know if there is pain involved in that.

(To NEW KYLE.)

New Kyle? Did it hurt coming into existence?

NEW KYLE: I don't think so. I don't really remember.

TINA: Then I think you'll be fine. Let's go.

(KYLE walks with TINA to the door and he turns to NEW KYLE.)

KYLE: Take care of Elaine.

NEW KYLE: Elaine?

KYLE: My wife.

NEW KYLE: Oh, of course. Will do.

KYLE: There's beer in the fridge.

NEW KYLE: Thanks, but I don't drink.

(TINA and KYLE exit. NEW KYLE is sitting in the chair that KYLE was sitting in. His posture and expression makes a subtle change after the others leave. He's forgotten everything that just happened and has become Kyle Henley.)

End of play.

ORIGINAL PRODUCTION

2 + 1 = MURDER premiered in Bellarmine University Theatre's International MADthematics Festival (Louisville, KY) in March 2012.

Directed by Nelson Lopez

CAST

LIEUTENANT GRAFTON: Patrick Jerger
PONZI: Anne Marie Doran
BLAKE PASCAL: Lance Grimes
POLLY NOMIAL: Jessica Brannock

SUBSEQUENT PRODUCTION

2 + 1 = MURDER was produced in October 2014, as part of the Dewey Decimal Festival (Chappaqua, NY).

Directed by C.J. Ehrlich

CAST

LIEUTENANT GRAFTON: Matthew Silver/Ben Ehrlich
PONZI: Micaela Silver
BLAZE PASCAL: Adam Bayer
POLLY NOMIAL: Rebecca Ozer
Producer: Shobha Vanchiswar, Friends of the Chappaqua Library. Email chafriends@wlsmail.org.

LIEUTENANT FRANK GRAFTON (forties to fifties), the detective. Seen it all, while trying to look the other way. The only scenery he wants to see now is the sun setting over his retirement.

BLAZE PASCAL (30s-40s), the shamus, PI, private dick—pick your poison. Just don't double cross him. He needs a case, so he can go back to answering the landlord's phone calls.

PONZI (F/M, twenties), the eager rookie, gopher, dogsbody, definitely smarter than the boss. Female or male: adjust pronouns accordingly.

POLLY NOMIAL (twenties to thirties), the femme fatale. Daddy's little girl. Dressed in a tight outfit that shows off a few more curves than Bezier would have approved of.

(+) SHIFTY La POINTE (pronounced "Point"), the corpse, played by a dummy, or a very patient actor.

SETTING:

A dark alley, somewhere in Chicago. A 1940s noir atmosphere.

Playwright's Notes:

Keep it snappy.

(+) The actor playing Ponzi artfully creates the illusion of the voice and animation of the corpse, unless a very patient actor is willing to do the moaning.

SCENE: 2 A.M. IN DIMLY LIT ALLEY, A BODY LIES IN SHADOW.

DETECTIVE FRANK GRAFTON circles a CORPSE. His assistant PONZI is drawing a chalk line around the body. Maybe s/he takes some flash pictures with a 1940s style camera.
Grafton stashes his notepad, sticks his pencil in his hat.

GRAFTON: Deader than a greyhound after the ninth race.

PONZI: Yes sir. Uh, sorry, sir—

GRAFTON: Get used to it, Ponzi! Nobody ever solves these acts of senseless, animal violence—

PONZI: Thing is, sir.

GRAFTON: Yeah?

PONZI: You can't be deader than dead, sir. You can be less than or equal to dead. But not deader than—

(Grafton grabs him by the collar.)

GRAFTON: Don't mince apples and oranges with me, Ponzi. I got three weeks to retirement. Any more of your lip, and you'll be deader than dead, patrolling the South Side.

(They stand over the corpse and remove their hats.)

GRAFTON (cont'd): It's always some nameless sucker with five o'clock shadow. Four holes in the back from the three dollar petunia he was two-timing. Not one relative. Zero clues—

PONZI: And tomorrow, he'll be six feet under.

GRAFTON: Poor sap. End of the number line.

(They replace their hats.)

PONZI: It don't add up, sir.

GRAFTON: No, Ponzi. It subtracts. Why—? What's it look like?

(Ponzi bends his elbows at crazy angles.)

PONZI: Geometry. Can I frisk him, boss?

GRAFTON: No! Uh, I already did. He's nobody. Call him Mr. X. We're done here Ponzi. Let's drop Mr. X at the morgue, and go home to our frozen dinners, crippling loneliness, and three weeks to retirement. Nobody ever solves these brutal, random—

PONZI: Not even . . . For Mr. X?

GRAFTON: No, Ponzi. We are not solving for X. Stay back—Eww!

(Ponzi pries a pink cigarette out of X's hand as BLAZE PASCAL enters.)

PONZI: A clue, boss! To solve, for X?

PASCAL: Solving for X. That's algebra. Kid's stuff. What you need is calculus.

GRAFTON: Blaze Pascal! You're as welcome as a pop quiz in July.

PASCAL: Grafton. We're like two trains, passing in the night.

GRAFTON: Sure. But my train's going 60 mph eastbound from Cleveland, and yours is a rusty freighter outta Beantown making all the local stops. Where do we meet?

PONZI: Niagara Falls?

GRAFTON: In Hell! By which I mean Reno, where I left my ex-wife.

PASCAL: Guess I made a rounding error on the last curve.

GRAFTON: Beat it, Pascal. This is PD turf. Go pedal your papers.

PASCAL: Sure! I'll be at the all-night library. Writing them. They sell like hotcakes, with finals coming . . . ID the body yet?

GRAFTON: Just another John Doe. Uhh . . . right?

PASCAL: Sure, Grafton. Plant this zero in Potter's field. If he turns out to be worth a sideways 8-ball, you're the one laying a goose egg.

GRAFTON: Huh? Sure, why not? Pay your respects to the dear departed.

PASCAL: All those chalk lines. Makes him look like . . . a math teacher.

(Pascal frisks the body, extracts a wallet. He checks the IDs.)

PASCAL (cont'd): Drivers license, social, Shoeshine of the Month club. Poor guy, one shy of a free shine . . . Yep. He's nobody. See you in the funny papers, Grafton.

GRAFTON: Hold it, Pascal! You got a name for this loose variable?

PASCAL: How's about a retainer?

GRAFTON: How's about twenty bucks a day, if you solve the case.

PASCAL: How's about Shifty La Pointe?

GRAFTON: Who's Shifty La Pointe?

PASCAL: You never heard of Scientific Notation?

GRAFTON: No. Maybe. Don't they make notebooks?

PASCAL: Shifty was the black spot of the family. Moving target. Numbers runner. Guess he had one too many balls in the air—

PONZI: You mean, he had more than three balls? *(they look at him)* I mean, he had two hands. So two balls wouldn't be too many—but four balls would be—

GRAFTON: Go back to the squad car, bring me my coffee!

PONZI: You weren't drinking coffee.

GRAFTON: Improvise.

(Ponzi reluctantly exits.)

GRAFTON (cont'd): Why'd you say calculus, before?

PASCAL: Sum up his operations over the night, see what trends arise.

GRAFTON: Whoa, Pascal. Back up a semester.

PASCAL: That'd be trigonometry. You calculate the time a fink's gonna do in Cicero by measuring the shadow of the judge's gavel.

GRAFTON: Yeah . . . Go back to that "trends arise" thing. Stoolie, maybe? You think he ratted out the wrong guy? Or . . . dame?

PASCAL: Who said anything about a dame.

GRAFTON: She didn't say anything. You just have to look at her. C'mon out, sister. What's your name?

(POLLY, hiding in the shadows, slinks forward, very sexy, very noir.)

POLLY: What if I forget my name.

GRAFTON: Take a guess. It's better than leaving it blank.

PASCAL: Sure Polly. Eliminate the improbables. Your odds'll improve.

GRAFTON: You know this tomato?

PASCAL: Knew. Until she erased me from her life like a bad check, in the wrong bubble.

GRAFTON: So Paula, what's a nice girl like you doing on the wrong side of a bachelors degree?

POLLY: It's Polly. Polly Nomial. The rest is none of your beeswax.

PASCAL: And very confusing.

GRAFTON: Hang on. Nomial? Didn't your father make a small fortune? Out of a large one?

POLLY: Daddy made a killing . . . in the tutoring biz.

PASCAL: Suddenly, she was too rich to let me into study hall. I couldn't even sign up for detention.

(Polly taps out a pink cigarette from a pink pack. She lets Grafton light it.)

GRAFTON: What a coincidence, Pascal. You and your old cosine reunite at the crime scene.

PASCAL: Cosine! More like no sign. Of a heart!

POLLY: Quite the opposite! Daddy wouldn't let me see you.

(Ponzi returns with coffee.)

PONZI: Here's your coffee, boss!

Polly drops her butt into the cup.

GRAFTON: *(glaring at Ponzi)* Now get me MY coffee!

(Ponzi reluctantly exits.)

GRAFTON: *(cont'd) (back to Polly)* Any more diamonds in the rough like you back home, dollface?

POLLY: My sister. Mona. We call her "Legs." Leave her out of this!

GRAFTON: She a knockout, too? I'd join her, in a Venn diagram.

POLLY: You'd have nothing in common. She and I, we're similar, but "Legs" is prone to such, wild outbursts—

PASCAL: Especially after you steal her gentleman friends.

POLLY: You deserved me, Blaze! Not her!

PASCAL: I had it right the first time. But you wrecked it.

POLLY: You were a wreck, and a tangle, until I—

GRAFTON: I take it you and Miss Nomial have shared a phosphate or two.

PASCAL: Let's just say I know she has a fondness for pink cigarettes—

POLLY: The pleasure was all yours, Blaze—

PASCAL:—and breaking a guy's heart. She left a big icy hole where it used to be.

POLLY: How big and how icy?

PASCAL: You want Fahrenheit or Celsius?

POLLY: I don't care, but show your work for once.

GRAFTON: Knock it off you two! Explain this, Miss Nomial. Your pretty pink cancer stick, in the corpse's hand.

POLLY: Mine? Why, I borrowed this pack from my sister. Lot of people smoke custom-mades, in my circle.

GRAFTON: Well I don't run in those circles. I can't even find the perimeter. So, pi face, where were you this evening?

PASCAL: If you're sober enough to remember the general area.

(Ponzi returns with coffee.)

PONZI: Here's your coffee, boss!

GRAFTON: Quiet, Ponzi! I'm giving this case a hundred and ten percent!

PONZI: But, boss. You can't give— more than—

(Ponzi raises his finger, thinks better of it, and drinks the coffee.)

POLLY: I was at a gallery tonight on the South Side. With my sister. The work was . . . derivative.

GRAFTON: Which gallery? There are three on the South Side. One exhibits modern art, one, sculpture, and the third, etchings. Each of the owners keeps a different pet. One has a zebra—

POLLY: This owner keeps gorillas. They guard the door with 38s! Suddenly, Legs rushed out, why, she could have gone anywhere. I went to the Copa to drown my sorrows.

PASCAL: If a broad and a half needs a bar stool and a half to tell sob stories to half of Chicago, why'd you have to walk into mine.

POLLY: Your— what?

PASCAL: Exactly!

GRAFTON: Time's up! Who did it. You, him, her? The suspects keep multiplying. I oughta take you all down to division!

POLLY: You can't think I—Oh, Blaze, protect me!

(Polly falls into Blaze. Surprised, he holds her. She frisks him and pulls out a pack of cigarettes—pink.)

GRAFTON: When did you go pink, Pascal?

PASCAL: Just souvenirs, of a bad road trip, down the wrong hypotenuse. Should have stuck with the Legs.

(Pascal tosses the pack onto the corpse. Ponzi kneels to retrieve it and pulls a large number "3" from under the body.)

PONZI: Boss, look! He was a numbers runner! And, I think he's alive!

GRAFTON: Paperwork on this'll be unbelievable. Shifty! What happened?

(Ponzi puts an ear to Shifty's head. Ponzi (the actor) groans; it should seem to come from Shifty. Polly gasps.)

PONZI: He says, "Uggghhhh . . . I was . . . shot."

GRAFTON: I know! I know! Who shot you?

PONZI: Is that an extra credit question?

(he listens to the corpse)

He says, "The angle of incidence . . . doesn't equal the . . . angle of refraction . . . " Of course!

GRAFTON: Speak American!

PASCAL: The bullets. The gozinta doesn't match the gozouta!

GRAFTON: Wow. If Miss Dixon explained it like that, I mighta graduated 8th grade.

PASCAL: In the back, out the labonza—

PONZI: Look! He was shot and stabbed.

GRAFTON: So—what? An amateur did this? Two amateurs? Who, Shifty, who? Those two, with their pink butts?

PONZI: He says . . . "Euuuhh."

GRAFTON: Three weeks to retirement, and I get "Euuuhh"!

(Shifty re-expires. Pascal frisks the body, finds a photo. He shows Grafton.)

PASCAL: Lieutenant. Meet Mona Nomial. "Legs".

POLLY: She has no shame! Oh, don't look! It's my little sister!

(Ponzi holds Polly back. Grafton whistles, then holds a second photo beside the first. Pascal supplies a third panel, suggesting that Legs is too ample to be contained in just one image. They ogle the full view.)

GRAFTON: "Little"?! I get it. Similar—

POLLY: But not identical.

PASCAL: Supplementary, but not complimentary.

GRAFTON: It's Polly, only . . . more so. You dated her?

PASCAL: A few years and a couple kilos ago. Wait—Blackmail!

GRAFTON: You can't blackmail me! Those files are buried! Wait—what?

POLLY: He was blackmailing her! Legs was so head-over-heels in love, she'd become a fraction of her former self.

GRAFTON: That's one top-heavy fraction.

POLLY: He promised her they'd honeymoon on the Orient Express. And maybe after, get married. Those photos would have ruined Daddy! I came here to buy the negatives.

PASCAL: But he wouldn't sell. So you shot him, then stabbed him for luck. How's that for an order of operations. Ponzi—

POLLY: No, my sister killed him! She did! Or—Oh! You can't prove a thing! Your proof is full of holes!

PASCAL: And so is he.

GRAFTON: She's right. We got nothing. Let's go, Ponzi. Nobody ever solves these rotten acts of twisted—

POLLY: Stop torturing me! Yes! I did it! I shot the worm.
(she produces a cute little cigarette-lighter gun)
Then I stabbed him!
(she produces a cute little cigarette-lighter dagger)
And later came back! To get . . . My lighter! Oh, here it is. *(she takes her lighter from Shifty)*
Yes, yes, I tried to frame her! Legs gets everything! Daddy's trust fund, box seats to the Sox, 800 on her math SATs. I hate her! I could kill her with my bare hands! Oh Blaze. Tell them, I'm good!

PASCAL: Maybe deep down, you are. But only if they're grading on the curve. Ponzi. Take her away. And, carry the three.
(Ponzi exits with Polly, and the "3".)

GRAFTON: Buy you a drink, Pascal? If you can figure a 12% tip.

PASCAL: This could be the beginning of a beautiful retirement.

END OF PLAY.

WANDERING POLES

Brent Englar

ORIGINAL PRODUCTION

Originally produced by Stay Awake! Theatre (Denver, CO) from October 23 to November 1, 2014. Directed by Alicia Wheelock. Featuring Jenna Weinberg (Piho), Bethany Richardson (Thala), and Kent Pringle (Ursu).

PIHO: a wild polar bear; female or male.
THALA: a captive polar bear; female.
URSU: a captive polar bear; male.

TIME:

The not-too-distant future.

PLACE:

A zoo; the polar bear enclosure.

As with costumes, the set should be simple: the only necessary element is a barrier to separate the captive bears from the wild.

Actors should stand on two legs, and their costumes should be simple and non-literal—suggestive rather than representative of polar bears.

Scene 1

(Lights up on THALA and URSU lazing in the shade. Outside their enclosure, the midday sun beats down. Eventually PIHO wanders on, notices the captive bears, and stumbles to a halt)

PIHO: Hey! HEY! Excuse me . . . ?
(PIHO roars, suddenly ferocious. THALA blinks open her eyes; URSU remains asleep)

THALA: Hello . . . ?

PIHO: Are there seals?

THALA: I don't—

PIHO: —Do you have seals in there?

THALA: Whatever for?

PIHO: I'm starving!

THALA: It's too early for feeding.
(THALA yawns and closes her eyes. PIHO roars again and exits. After a moment, URSU opens his eyes)

URSU: What was that?

THALA: I didn't ask. Are we expecting another bear?

URSU: Another—what? Have you heard something?

THALA: Have you?

URSU: There's scarcely room here for us.

> *(URSU closes his eyes. He flops around, unable to fall back asleep. Finally he rises)*

URSU (Cont'd): Damn interruptions.

(He roars several times. THALA sighs and rises)

THALA: What do you want to do?

URSU: Swim! It's hot!

> *(URSU ambles off. THALA peers through the barrier)*

THALA: *(to herself)*Maybe I was dreaming. Maybe we're both dreaming.

> *(She scratches herself vigorously. PIHO re-enters with bloody paws and muzzle)*

THALA (Cont'd): What happened!

PIHO: I found the seals.

THALA: Where?

PIHO: All clumped together in a pit. It was incredible.

THALA: They were good?

PIHO: No.

THALA: They weren't good?

PIHO: I think it was too easy. I think I miss the ice.

THALA: You're so red. You're a mess.

PIHO: So what if I am?

THALA: You'll frighten people.

PIHO: There are humans here?

THALA: I think today's a holiday. Or a shutdown. I lose track. We're usually very popular.

PIHO: What happened to your friend?

THALA: *(turning to look)*
Did something happen?

PIHO: What?

THALA: *(spotting URSU offstage)*
Oh! He's fine.

PIHO: Where did he go, I mean?

THALA: For a swim. Aren't you hot out there?

PIHO: Of course I'm hot.

(peering through the barrier)
That's where you swim?

THALA: Where do you?

PIHO: It'll have to do, I guess.

(PIHO clambers over the barrier and exits to swim. THALA watches, astonished. She grips the barrier tentatively, testing its weight. Finally, with great effort, she hauls herself over the barrier and exits toward the seals.)

(Offstage, URSU roars, followed by PIHO. They tumble onstage—they are both wet, and PIHO is no longer bloody—swiping and wrestling, until PIHO manages to flip URSU onto his back and escape over the barrier. URSU staggers to his feet)

PIHO *(Cont'd)*: What's your problem, oaf?

URSU: Coward! Call me that to my—

PIHO: *(shouting through the barrier)*—OOOOAAAAF-FFF!!!!
(URSU roars and throws himself at the barrier. PIHO laughs. THALA races onstage)

THALA: What's the matter? Ursu!

URSU: Thala!

THALA: *(to PIHO)* You made him angry!

PIHO: I did nothing! The oaf was sleeping, snoring like a walrus—

URSU: —I DO NOT SNORE—

PIHO: —I hopped into the water, and before I could even surface he attacked me.

THALA: Oh Ursu . . .

URSU: Thala, that bear is trouble—stay back! I—
(He blinks, for the first time really seeing her)
How did you get there?

THALA: You can do it, Ursu—just pull yourself over!

PIHO: I really don't think—

URSU: —SHUT UP!
(He studies the barrier, pushes against it, and finally grasps the top)
I pull now?

THALA: Pull!

(URSU pulls himself over the barrier and leaps to the ground. PIHO tenses, ready to fight, but instead URSU whoops and hugs THALA. They laugh together)

THALA (Cont'd): Ursu, you need to apologize.

URSU: For what?

THALA: For fighting with . . .

(to PIHO)

I don't know your name.

PIHO: Piho.

URSU: I've never heard of any bears named Piho.

PIHO: What you've never heard of would fill the—

THALA: —Piho, you need to apologize too.

PIHO: I don't need to do anything. I'm leaving.

THALA: Where?

PIHO: None of your business. Don't tell the humans *anything.*

(PIHO snarls and exits)

URSU: I should teach that bear a lesson.

THALA: Ursu, we're *free!*

URSU: Free?

THALA: Where should we go?

URSU: Let me think—

THALA: —Are you hungry? There's seals! Piho says they're disappointing, but—

URSU: —Don't tell me what Piho says! Don't mention that name!

THALA: But Ursu, if it weren't for Piho, we'd still be on the other side.

(URSU scans the zoo. Finally, he points in the direction opposite PIHO's exit)

URSU: We'll go this way.

THALA: Okay.

(They exit together. Blackout.)

Scene 2

(Lights up on THALA, URSU, and PIHO lying unconscious in the enclosure. A tranquilizer dart protrudes

from each bear. The barrier is noticeably higher than in Scene 1. In the distance, an elephant trumpets. PIHO twitches and finally, groggily, rises)

PIHO: Ow . . .
  (PIHO yanks out the dart, looks around, and suddenly realizes what has happened)
PIHO (Cont'd): No! No no no no no no—
  (shaking the others)
Wake up! WAKE UP! UUUUPP!
  (PIHO yanks the darts out of THALA and URSU. They wince and awaken)
THALA: Piho?
URSU: Where are—
PIHO: —We're caught!
URSU: What?
  (looking around)
We're home.
PIHO: This is not my home!
URSU: Agreed.
PIHO: Don't stand there agreeing, idiot—help me!
  (URSU snarls)
PIHO (Cont'd): Please.
  (URSU bends and allows PIHO to straddle his shoulders. With URSU's help, PIHO manages to grasp the top of the barrier. PIHO then clambers across and drops carefully to the other side)
THALA: Where are you going?
PIHO: The ice.
THALA: Where is that?
PIHO: I'll find it.
  (to URSU)
Thank you.
  (PIHO hurries off)
URSU: Time to swim. It's hot!
  (URSU begins to exit. THALA remains by the barrier)
URSU *(Cont'd)*: What's wrong?
THALA: I want to be free.

URSU: Free to what?

THALA: Free.

URSU: To starve? To be hunted? To end up back here tomorrow with another needle in your neck?

(He crosses to THALA. She embraces him)

URSU *(Cont'd)*: To leave me alone?

THALA: I'm sorry.

(URSU bends, and THALA climbs on his shoulders. They approach the barrier. THALA pulls herself across and drops to the ground)

THALA *(Cont'd)*: Ursu . . .

URSU: Thala, go!

(THALA nods and hurries after PIHO. URSU paces. He roars. Finally he settles beside the barrier and stares into the distance.)

Blackout.

End of play.

CALL ME © 2014 by Michele Markarian. Reprinted by permission of Michele Markarian. For performance rights, contact Michele Markarian (michele.markarian@gmail.com).

CASEY229 © 2014 by Elin Hampton. Reprinted by permission of Elin Hampton. For performance rights, contact Elin Hampton (elhampton@aol.com).

THE CRAFT © 2010 by Andrew Biss. Reprinted by permission of Andrew Biss. For performance rights, contact Andrew Biss (andrewbiss@gmail.com).

CROOKED FORK © 2014 by Jonathan Yukich. Reprinted by permission of Jonathan Yukich. For performance rights, contact Jonathan Yukich (yukich5@gmail.com).

THE DAY TOWER PIZZA STOOD STILL © 2014 by Darrah Cloud. Reprinted by permission of Peregrine Whittlesey. For performance rights, contact Peregrine Whittlesey (pwwagy@aol.com).

DOCTORS AND LAWYERS (1st Edition Rules) © 2014 by David Strauss. Reprinted by permission of David Strauss. For performance rights, contact David Strauss (dstrauss@gmail.com).

DREAM LOVER © 2014 by Michael Weems. Reprinted by permission of Michael Weems. For performance rights, contact Michael Weems (michaeltw721@gmail.com).

DRINKS BEFORE FLIGHT © 2014 by Lisa Kenner Grissom. Reprinted by permission of Lisa Kenner Grissom. For performance rights, contact Lisa Kenner Grissom (lisakenner@gmail.com).

FILM APPRECIATION © 2014 by David Susman. Reprinted by permission of David Susman. For performance rights, contact David Susman (davidsusman10@yahoo.com).

POST MORTEM © 2014 by Cheri Magid. Reprinted by permission of Beth Blickers, Abrams Artists. For performance rights, contact Beth Blickers (beth.blickers@abramsartny.com).

RAGHEAD © 2014 by Tom Coash. Reprinted by permission of Tom Coash. For performance rights, contact Tom Coash (thomascoash@sbcglobal.net).

RESEARCH SUBJECTS or THAT CREEPY GUY TAPING ME IN MY SLEEP © 2014 by Erin Moughon. Reprinted by permission of Erin Moughon. For performance rights, contact Erin Moughon (erin.moughon@gmail.com).

SARAH STEIN SENDS A SELFIE © 2014 by Michael McKeever. Reprinted by permission of Barbara Hogenson. For performance rights, contact Barbara Hogenson (bhogenson@aol.com).

THE SCOTTISH PLAY © 2014 by Theo Reyna. Reprinted by permission of Theo Reyna. For performance rights, contact Theo Reyna (tnreyna@gmail.com).

SMART BRA © 2014 by Sylvia Reed. Reprinted by permission of Sylvia Reed. For performance rights, contact Sylvia Reed (sylviareedw@gmail.com).

SMITTEN © 2011 by Mark Harvey Levine. Reprinted by permission of Mark Harvey Levine. For performance rights, contact Mark Harvey Levine (markle9@hotmail.com).

SUPERNATURAL SEMINAR © 2014 by Jenny Lyn Bader. Reprinted by permission of Jack Tantleff, Paradigm Agency. For performance rights, contact Jack Tantleff (jtantleff@paradigmagency.com).

TEEMING SHORE © 2014 by Nick Gandiello. Reprinted by permission of Alexis Williams, Bret Adams Ltd. For performance

Actors Theatre of Louisville
www.actorstheatre.org
Amy Wegener (awegener@actorstheatre.org)

Acts on the Edge, Santa Monica
mariannesawchuk@hotmail.com

American Globe Theatre Turnip Festival, Gloria Falzer
gfalzer@verizon.net
.

Appetite Theatre Company
Bruschetta: An Evening of Short Plays
www.appetitetheatre.com_

Artist's Exchange, Cranston RI
Rich Morra (rich.morra@artists-exchange.org)

Artistic New Directions
Janice Goldberg - Co Artistic Director - ANDJanice@aol.com
Kristine Niven - Co Artistic Director - KNiven@aol.com
www.ArtisticNewDirections.org

The Arts Center, Carrboro NC
10x10 in the Triangle
Jeri Lynn Schulke, director
theatre@artscenterlive.org
www.artscenterlive.org/performance/opportunities

A-Squared Theatre Workshop
My Asian Mom Festival
Joe Yau (jyauza@hotmail.com)

Association for Theatre in Higher Education New Play Development Workshop
Charlene A. Donaghy
Email address of theatre/contact person: charlene@charleneadonaghy.com
http://www.athe.org

Auburn Players Community Theatre Short Play Festival
Bourke Kemmedy
email: bourkekennedy@gmail.com
The Barn Theatre
www.thebarnplayers.org/tenminute/

Barrington Stage Company
10X10 New Play Festival
Julianne Boyd is the Artistic Director
jboyd@barringtonstageco.org
www.barringtonstageco.org

Belhaven University, Jackson, Mississippi
One Act Festival
Joseph Frost, Department Chair
theatre@belhaven.edu

Black Box Theatre
FIVES New Play Festival
Producer: Nancy Holaday
(719) 330-1798
nancy@blackboxdrama.com

Blue Slipper Theatre, Livingston, Montana
Marc Beaudin, Festival Director
blueslipper10fest@gmail.com
www.blueslipper.com

Boston Theatre Marathon
Boston Playwrights Theatre
www.bostonplaywrights.org
Kate Snodgrass (ksnodgra@bu.edu)
(Plays by New England playwrights only)

Boulder Life Festival, Boulder, Colorado
Dawn Bower, Director of Theatrical Program
dawn@boulderlifefestival.com
www.boulderlifefestival.com

The Box Factory
Judith Sokolowski, President
boxfactory@sbcglobal.net
www.boxfactoryforthearts.org

The Brick Theater's "Tiny Theater Festival"
Michael Gardner, Artistic Director
mgardner@bricktheater.com
www.bricktheater.com

The Brooklyn Generator
Erin Mallon (contact)
email: brooklyngenerator@outlook.com
website: https://www.facebook.com/TheBrooklynGenerator/info

Camino Real Playhouse
www.caminorealplayhouse.org

Chalk Repertory Theatre
Chalk Repertory Theatre Flash Festival
Contact person: Ruth McKee
ruthamckee@aol.com
www.chalkrep.com

Chameleon Theater Circle, Burnsville, MN 55306
www.chameleontheatre.org
jim@chameleontheatre.org

Cherry Picking
cherrypickingnyc@gmail.com

Chicago Indie Boots Festival
www.indieboots.org

City Theatre
www.citytheatre.com
Susan Westfall (susan@citytheatre.com)

City Theatre of Independence
Powerhouse Theatre
Annual Playwrights Festival
Powerhouse Theatre
www.citytheatreofindependence.org

The Collective New York
C10 Play Festival
www.thecollective-ny.org
thecollective9@gmail.com

Colonial Playhouse
www.colonialplayhouse.net
colonialplayhousetheater@40yahoo.com

Company of Angels at the Alexandria
501 S. Spring Street, 3rd Floor
Los Angeles, CA 90013
(213) 489-3703 (main office)
armevan@sbcglobal.net

Core Arts Ensemble
coreartsensemble@gmail.com

Darkhorse Dramatists
www.darkhorsedramatists.com
darkhorsedramatists@gmail.com

Distilled Theatre Co.
submissions.dtc@gmail.com
Driftwood Players
www.driftwoodplayers.com
shortssubmissions@driftwoodplayers.com
tipsproductions@driftwoodplayers.com

Drilling Company
Hamilton Clancy
drillingcompany@aol.com

Driftwood Players
www.driftwoodplayers.com

Durango Arts Center 10-Minute Play Festival
www.durangoarts.org
Theresa Carson
TenMinutePlayDirector@gmail.com

Eden Prairie Players
www.edenprairieplayers.com

Eastbound Theatre 10 minute Festival
Contact Person: Tom Rushen
ZenRipple@yahoo.com

East Haddam Stage Company
Contact person: Kandie Carl
Kandie@ehsco.org

Eden Prairie Players
www.concordspace.com
Reed Schulke (reedschulke@yahoo.com)

Edward Hopper House Nyack, NY

Rachael Solomon
edwardhopper.house@verizon.net
www.edwardhopperhouse.org

Emerging Artists Theatre
Fall EATFest
www.emergingartiststheatre.org

En Avant Playwrights
Ten Lucky Festival
www.enavantplaywrights.yuku.com

Ensemble Theatre of Chattanooga
Short Attention Span Theatre Festival
Contact Person: Garry Posey (Artistic Director)
garryposey@gmail.com
www.ensembletheatreofchattanooga.com

Fell's Point Corner Theatre 10 x 10 Festival
Contact Person: Richard Dean Stover (rick@fpct.org)
Website of theatre: www.fpct.org

Fine Arts Association
Annual One Act Festival-Hot from the Oven Smorgasbord
ahedger@fineartsassociation.org

Firehouse Center for the Arts, Newburyport MA
New Works Festival
Kimm Wilkinson, Director
www.firehouse.org
Limited to New England playwrights

Fire Rose Productions
www.fireroseproductions.com
kazmatura@gmail.com

Flush Ink Productions
Asphalt Jungle Shorts Festival
www.flushink.net/AJS.html

The Fringe of Marin Festival
Contact Person: Annette Lust
email: jeanlust@aol.com

Fury Theatre
katie@furytheare.org
Fusion Theatre Co.
http://www.fusionabq.org
info@fusionabq.org

Future Ten
info@futuretenant.org

Gallery Players
Annual Black Box Festival
info@galleryplayers.com

Gaslight Theatre
www.gaslight-theatre.org
gaslighttheatre@gmail.com
GI60
Steve Ansell
screammedia@yahoo.com

Generic Theatre Co.
www.generictheatre.org
contact@generictheatre.org

The Gift Theater
TEN Festival
Contact: Michael Patrick Thornton
www.thegifttheatre.org

Good Works Theatre Festival
Good Acting Studio
www.goodactingstudio.com

Half Moon Theatre
www.halfmoontheatre.org

Heartland Theatre Company
Themed 10-Minute Play Festival Every Year
Contact Person: Mike Dobbins (Artistic Director)
boxoffice@heartlandtheatre.org
www.heartlandtheatre.org

Hella Fresh Fish
freshfish2submit@gmail.com

Hobo Junction Productions
Hobo Robo Festival
Spenser Davis, Literary Manager
hobojunctionsubmissions@gmail.com
www.hobojunctionproductions.com

The Hovey Players, Waltham MA
Hovey Summer Shorts
www.hoveyplayers.com

Illustrious Theatre Co.
www.illustrioustheatre.org
illustrioustheatre@gmail.com

Image Theatre
Naughty Shorts
jbisantz@comcast.net

Independent Actors Theatre (Columbia, MO)
Short Women's Play Festival
Emily Rollie, Artistic Director
e.rollie@iatheatre.org
www.iatheatre.org

Island Theatre 10-minute Play Festival
www.islandtheatre.org

Kings Theatre
www.kingstheatre.ca
Lake Shore Players
www.lakeshoreplayers.com
Joan Elwell
office@lakeshoreplayers.com

La Petite Morgue (Fresh Blood)
Kellie Powell at Lapetitemorgue@gmail.com
www.lapetitemorgue.blogspot.com

Lebanon Community Theatre Playwriting Contest
www.lct.cc/PlayWriteContest.htm

Lee Street Theatre, Salisbury, NC (themed)
Original 10-Minute Play Festival
Justin Dionne, managing artistic director
info@leestreet.org
www.leestreet.org

Little Fish Theatre Co.
www.litlefishtheatre.org

Live Girls Theatre
submissions@lgtheater.org

Little Fish Theatre
Pick of the Vine Festival
holly@littlefishtheatre.org
www.littlefishtheatre.org

LiveWire Chicago VisionFest
Joel Ewing joel.b.ewing@gmail.com

Lourdes University Drama Society
One Act Play Festival, Sylvania, Ohio
Keith Ramsdell, Drama Society Advisor
dramasociety@lourdes.edu
www.lourdes.edu/dramasociety.aspx

Luna Theater
Contact: Greg Campbell
Email: lunatheater@gmail.com
Website: www.lunatheater.org

Madlab Theatre
Theatre Roulette
Andy Batt (andy@madlab.net)
www.madlab.net/MadLab/Home.html

Magnolia Arts Center, Greenville, NC
info@magnoliaartscenter.com
www.magnoliaartscenter.com

Manhattan Repertory Theatre, New York, NY
Ken Wolf
manhattanrep@yahoo.com
www.manhattanrep.com

McLean Drama Co.
www.mcleandramacompany.org
Rachel Bail (rachbail@yahoo.com)

Miami 1
Acts Festival
Contact: Steven A. Chambers, Literary Manager
schambers@new-theatre.org
Ricky J. Martinez, Artistic Director
rjmartinez@new-theatre.org
www.new-theatre.org

Milburn Stone One Act Festival
www.milburnstone.org

Mildred's Umbrella
Museum of Dysfunction Festival
www.mildredsumbrella.com
info@mildredsumbrella.com

Mill 6 Collaborative

John Edward O'Brien, Artistic Director
mill6theatre@gmail.com

Monkeyman Productions
The Simian Showcase
submissions@monkeymanproductions.com.
www.monkeymanproductions.com

Nantucket Short Play Competition
Jim Patrick
www.nantucketshortplayfestival.com
nantucketshortplay@comcast.net

Napa Valley Players
8 x 10: A Festival of 10 Minute Plays
www.napavalleyplayhouse.org

Newburgh Free Academy
tsandler@necsd.net
New American Theatre
www.newamericantheatre.com
JoeBays44@earthlink.net

New Urban Theatre Laboratory
5 & Dime
Jackie Davis, Artistic Director:
jackie.newurbantheatrelab@gmail.com

New Voices Original Short Play Festival
Kurtis Donnelly (kurtis@gvtheatre.org)

NFA New Play Festival
Newburgh Free Academy
201 Fullerton Ave, Newburgh, NY 12550
Terry Sandler (terrysandle@hotmail.com)

North Park Playwright Festival
New short plays (no more than 15 pages, less is fine)
Submissions via mail to:
North Park Vaudeville and Candy Shoppe
2031 El Cajon Blvd.
San Diego, CA 92104
Attn: Summer Golden, Artistic Director.
www.northparkvaudeville.com

Northport One-Act Play Festival
Jo Ann Katz (joannkatz@gmail.com)
www.northportarts.org

NYC Playwrights
Play of the Month Project
http://nycp.blogspot.com/p/play-of-month.html

Northwest 10 Festival of 10-Minute Plays
Sponsored by Oregon Contemporary Theatre
www.octheatre.org/nw10-festival
Email: NW10Festival@gmail.com

Nylon Fusion
nylonsubmissions@gmail.com
www.nylonfusioncollective.org

Open Tent Theatre Co.
Ourglass 24 Hour Play Festival
opententtheater@gmail.com

Over Our Head Players, Racine WI
www.overourheadplayers.org/oohp15

Pan Theater, Oakland, CA
Anything Can Happen Festival
David Alger, pantheater@comcast.net
http://www.facebook.com/sanfranciscoimprov

Pandora Theatre, Houston, Texas
Vox Feminina
Melissa Mumper, Artistic Director
pandoratheatre@sbcglobal.net

Paw Paw Players One Act Festival
www.ppvp.org/oneacts.htm

Pegasus Theater Company
Tapas Short Plays Festival
www.pegasustheater.com/html/submissions.html
Lois Pearlman lois5@sonic.net

Philadelphia Theatre Company
PTC@Play New Work Festival
Jill Harrison
jillian.harrison@gmail.com
www.philadelphiatheatrecompany.org

PianoFight Productions, L.A.
ShortLivedLA@gmail.com

Piney Fork Press Theater Play Festival
Johnny Culver, submissions@pineyforkpress.com
www.pineyforkpress.com

Playhouse Creatures
Page to Stage
newplays@playhousecreatures.org

Play on Words Productions
playonwordsproductions@gmail.com
Megan Kosmoski, Producing Artist Director

Playmakers Spokane
Hit& Run
Sandra Hosking
playmakersspokane@gmail.com
www.sandrahosking.webs.com

Playwrights' Arena
Flash Theater LA
Jon Lawrence Rivera
jonlawrencerivera@gmail.com
Website: www.playwrightsarena.org

Playwrights' Round Table, Orlando, FL
Summer Shorts
Chuck Dent charlesrdent@hotmail.com
www.theprt.com

Playwrights Studio Theater
5210 W. Wisconsin Ave.
Milwaukee, WI 53208
Attn: Michael Neville, Artistic Dir.

Renaissance Guild
www.therenaissanceguild.org/article/aos-xv
actoneseries@therenaissanceguild.org

Ruckus Theatre
Allison Shoemaker
theruckus@theruckustheater.org
www.ruckustheater.org/home/contact.html

Salem Theatre Co.
Moments of Play
New England playwrights only
mop@salemtheatre.com

Salve Regina University
www.salvetheatreplayfestival.submishmash.com

Santa Cruz Actor's Theatre
Eight Tens at Eight
Wilma Chandler, Artistic Director
ronziob@email.com
http://www.sccat.org

Secret Room Theatre
Contact: Alex Dremann
Email: alexdremann@me.com
Website: www.secretroomtheatre.com

Secret Rose Theatre
www.secretrose.com
info@secretrose.com

Secret Theatre (Midsummer Night Festival), Queens, NY.
Odalis Hernandez, odalis.hernandez@gmail.com
www.secrettheatre.com/
She Speaks, Kitchener, Ontario.
Paddy Gillard-Bentley (paddy@skyedragon.com)
Women playwrights

Shelterbelt Theatre, Omaha, NB
From Shelterbelt with Love
McClain Smouse, associate-artistic@shelterbelt.org
submissions@shelterbelt.org
www.shelterbelt.org

Shepparton Theatre Arts Group
"Ten in 10"
info@stagtheatre.com
www.stagtheatre.com

Short+Sweet
Literary Manager, Pete Malicki
Pete@shortandsweet.org
http://www.shortandsweet.org/shortsweet-theatre/submit-script

Silver Spring Stage, Silver Spring, MD
Jacy D'Aiutolo
oneacts2012.ssstage@gmail.com
www.ssstage.org

Sixth Street Theatre
Snowdance 10-Minute Comedy Festival
Rich Smith
Snowdance318@gmail.com

Six Women Play Festival
www.sixwomenplayfestival.com

Source Festival
jenny@culturaldc.org

Southern Repertory Theatre
Aimee Hayes (literary@southernrep.com)
www.southernrep.com/

Stage Door Productions
Original One-Act Play Festival
www.stagedoorproductions.org

Stage Door Repertory Theatre
www.stagedoorrep.org

Stage Q
www.stageq.com

Stageworks/Hudson
Play by Play Festival
Laura Margolis is the Artistic Director
literary@stageworkshudson.org
www.stageworkshudson.org

Stonington Players
HVPanciera@aol.com

Stratton Summer Shorts
Stratton Players
President: Rachel D'onfro
www.strattonplayers.com
info@strattonplayers.com

Subversive Theatre Collective
Kurt Schneiderman, Artistic Director
www.subversivetheatre.org
info@subversivetheatre.org

Ten Minute Playhouse (Nashville)
Nate Eppler, Curator
newworksnashville@gmail.com
www.tenminuteplayhouse.com

Ten Minute Play Workshop
www.tenminuteplayworkshop.com

Ten Tuckey Festival
doug@thebardstown.com
https://www.theatrelab.org/
Contact: Buzz Mauro buzz@theatrelab.org

Theatre Odyssey, Sarasota, Florida
Tom Aposporos Vice President
www.theatreodyssey.org

Theatre One Productions
theatreoneproductions@yahoo.com
Theatre Out, Santa Ana CA
David Carnevale david@theatreout.com
LGBT plays

Theatre Oxford 10 Minute Play Contest
http://www.theatreoxford.com
Alice Walker

10minuteplays@gmail.com
Theatre Three
www.theatrethree.com
Jeffrey Sanzel
jeffrey@theatrethree.com

Theatre Westminster
ATTN: Terry Dana Jachimiak II
jachimtd@westminster.edu

TouchMe Philly Productions
www.touchmephilly.wordpress.com
touchmephilly@gmail.com

Towne Street Theatre Ten-Minute Play Festival
info@townestreet.org

Underground Railway Theatre
www.undergroundrailwaytheatre.org
Debra Wise, Artistic Director
debra@undergroundrailwaytheatre.org

Unrenovated Play Festival
unrenovatedplayfest@gmail.com

Vivarium Theatre Co.
www.vivariumtheatre.com

Walking Fish Theatre
freshfish2submit@gmail.com

Weathervane Playhouse
8 X 10 Theatrefest
info@weathervaneplayhouse.com

Wide Eyed Productions
www.wideeyedproductions.com
playsubmissions@wideeyedproductions.com

Wild Claw Theatre:
Death Scribe 10 Minute Radio Horror Festival
www.wildclawtheatre.com/index.html
literary@wildclawtheatre.com

Winston-Salem Writers
Annual 10 Minute Play Contest
www.wswriters.org
info@wswriters.org

Write Act
www.writeactrep.org
John Lant (j316tlc@pacbell.net)